PASTORAL CARE IN THE CHURCH

PASTORAL CARE
IN THE
CHURCH

———

THIRD EDITION

REVISED AND EXPANDED

C. W. Brister

HarperSanFrancisco

A Division of HarperCollins*Publishers*

Library of Congress Cataloging-in-Publication Data

Brister, C. W.
   Pastoral care in the church / C. W. Brister. — 3rd ed. rev.
     and expanded.
     p. cm.
   Includes bibliographical references and indexes.
   ISBN 0-06-061065-4 (alk. paper)
   1. Pastoral theology—Baptists. I. Title.
   BV4011.B68 1992
   253—dc20   91-55421
                                                   CIP

92 93 94 95 96 RRD(H) 10 9 8 7 6 5 4 3 2 1

This edition is printed on acid-free paper that meets the American National Standards Institute Z39.48 Standard.

To
members of the congregations with
whom Gloria and I served as pastoral family,
and
to my students through the years
with appreciation and affection

CONTENTS

PREFACE TO
THE THIRD EDITION

The Church must be forever building, and always decaying,
and always being restored.

—T. S. Eliot, *The Rock*

Any aspect of theology—biblical, historical, systematic, moral, or pastoral
—interacts with human experience, reflects a given age and culture,
responds to forces shaping thought, corrects errors, supplies omissions of
previous epochs, and addresses issues in contemporary contexts. That
theologians continue to speak to current movements of history, complex
religious and moral issues, profound changes in human consciousness, and
the nitty-gritty of everyday existence gives us hope. Healthy religion
embraces *all* of life, including the universe itself, yet is intimately personal.
New paradigms and tapestries of ideas emerging in this era sound more like
poetry than theology.

Practitioners of caregiving arts—whether Christian pastors, priests,
rabbis, theological or clinical educators, institutional chaplains, church
staffers, vocational counselors, missionaries, or laypersons attuned to critical human needs—all recognize we are turning significant corners as we
live into the next millennium. Life's realities are becoming "more-so": more
expansive into global ways of thinking; more intercultural; more hideous in
cruel, bizarre acts of inhumanity that human beings may perpetrate upon
one another; more complicated in concerns, risks, and controversies life
brings; more sensitive to traps into which people fall—by chance, circumstance, oppression, or deliberate choice; more hopeful in an age when
instant destruction is possible for a world without wars; more competent in
health care delivery and in the pioneering of lifesaving research and medical treatment modalities; more graceful toward planet Earth; and more
humble in recognizing that salvation does indeed come from God alone,
not from politics, technology, education, or society, as important as each of
these processes may be. Caregivers are challenged to discover what it takes
to practice pastoral ministry in response to this *more-so-ness* of life.

The major goal for this revision of *Pastoral Care in the Church* is to interpret pastoral care for a new generation of theological students and pastors. This edition offers an introductory chapter on the context for advancing faith wisely in a perplexed world. Its language reflects inclusiveness and respects women's experiences, both as providers and receivers of pastoral care. Recent research on key issues is brought into dialogue with themes from the earlier version. Some new clinical materials and commentary have been introduced. The book deals with universal human experiences and offers guidance across national, ethnic, and cultural lines. It casts its net over important areas of concern and suggests guidelines for caregivers who seek to respond with integrity to difficult issues in people's lives.

Christian pastoral care's history embraces a number of traditions, not all of them complementary. *Pastoral Care in the Church* examines ministry functions from both a biblically and clinically based perspective. It articulates a fresh vision of the pastoral action of the whole congregation, with appreciation for the Hebrew Scriptures and New Testament (NT) teachings about mutual priesthood.[1] It recognizes that Christian influences in Western nations have lessened; further, that diverse religious configurations are emerging. At best, this book offers a road map to Christian service providers, policymakers, and caregivers who face confusing demands, risky encounters, emotional drains, endless expectations, sometimes unjust criticism, daily fatigue, even legal opposition in a volatile time.

One of the most serious problems in religious vocation today is the lack of ministry models. This is true for both women and men in professional ministries. Congregations face anxious times as aspiring caregivers grapple with their faith, find their way, and seek to obey their own "heavenly visions" of usefulness to God. In Bernard Malamud's novel *The Natural,* a character says that when we are without heroes we "don't know how far we can go." Guidance is needed as churches seek wisdom and skills for shaping partnership in ministry; learn to share power; manage the effects of ethnicity and gender on traditional symbols; attend families with unique connections and different lifestyles; face unorthodox moral views and cultural practices; survive ethical failures of prominent religious figures; and experience diverse religious traditions, including deep divisions between progressives and conservatives along a theological continuum. The reorganization of American religious pluralism and restructuring of Christian mission and ministry call for a new generation of wise leaders. A new depth of commitment is needed in order to sustain our caring in a conflicted world. I address such issues in the design of this book.

Suggestions from several friends and former students have influenced my thinking. Special thanks go to those individuals who have helped me think about and work through this project: Rodney J. Hunter, Candler School of Theology, Emory University; James Poling, Colgate-Rochester Divinity School; and James N. Lapsley of Princeton Theological Seminary. Larry Kent Graham of the Iliff School of Theology, in Denver, provided an excellent bibliography. Others who have invested in this process of writing include: Nancy Ellett Allison of Monrovia, Liberia; N. Larry Baker, pastor, First Baptist Church, Pineville, Louisiana; Mark A. Brister, my son and pastor, Broadmoor Baptist Church, Shreveport, Louisiana; Nehemiah Davis, pastor, Mount Pisgah Missionary Baptist Church, Fort Worth, Texas; Douglas Dickens, my colleague at Southwestern Seminary; Emma J. Justes, Northern Baptist Theological Seminary, Lombard, Illinois; Steve Lyon, a missionary in Los Teques, Venezuela; and David K. Switzer, of Perkins School of Theology, Southern Methodist University, Dallas, Texas. Karl F. Fickling, my former graduate fellow, assisted with the indexes.

I am the beneficiary of a fine sabbatical leave program and an excellent library at the Southwestern Baptist Theological Seminary, where I have taught more than three decades, and convey gratitude to our administration and trustees for such privileges. Deborah Jones, a transplanted Virginian and cherished secretary, assisted with each phase of manuscript preparation.

A special thanks is due my wife, Gloria, for her encouragement, intuitive wisdom, cautions, challenges, and companionship through the years.

C. W. Brister
Fort Worth, Texas

Notes

1. Abbreviations OT and NT refer to the Old Testament and New Testament. Biblical passages are quoted from the New International Version (NIV) unless otherwise indicated.

INTRODUCTION:
CONTEXT FOR MINISTRY

Randy Stephens, pastor of Broadway Church, visited with a member, Libby Lyles, when he made his rounds at St. Luke's Hospital. Libby's mother, Mrs. Ann Pearl, had experienced a stroke. An only child, Libby maintained a constant vigil each day at her mother's bedside. A neurologist had diagnosed the stroke as a rupture of Mrs. Pearl's left, middle cerebral artery, so massive that all functions of personality were disrupted. She could not speak, but could only make guttural sounds; could not distinguish visual images; was unable to swallow, thus required hydration therapy; and was paralyzed completely on the right side.

A decision had been made by the family's physician to insert a feeding tube surgically into Ann Pearl's stomach in order to administer life-sustaining liquid nourishment. But Libby knew this procedure was in direct violation of the Living Will and Directive to Physicians her mother had signed, with advice of an attorney, the year before. Her mother had said she did not wish to remain "hooked up" with tubes, in a heroic life-prolonging manner, in the event she became helpless in some medical situation.

"Pastor Stephens," Libby asked in desperation, "what is there to do when there's nothing you *can* do?"[1] Her query, marked by hesitancy, hurt, and frustration, involved profound existential, ethical, and religious issues. Clearly, it was more than a rhetorical question. Like so many inquiring laypersons, Libby was searching for a path through an increasingly complex and threatening world.

Randy's dialogue with his grieving, searching parishioner required him to call on all of his professional educational background and experience. As a theological student, he had lived a somewhat sheltered life at the edge of the "real" world. Now, reality was inescapable. He discovered for himself the polarities in Peter Drucker's description of an educated person: "In the [coming] knowledge society, education will have to transmit *virtue* while teaching the skills of effectiveness."[2] The pastor shrank back from seeing himself as a theological helper with *the* answer, but sought to be a friend as Libby lived with the questions. Given the awfulness, mystery, and isolating symptoms of a stroke, Randy wished to represent God, his congregation, and clinical reality well as he shared the experience with this family member.

Though Libby was her pastor's senior by two decades, she sought help from him in order to understand her own predicament. The anxieties and heartaches of a fateful medical prognosis rang through her mind. A team of physicians had said, "There's nothing we can do. Your mother cannot be rehabilitated." In order to minister effectively, Randy had to know more than the mechanics of hospital calling. He needed the substance of a carefully crafted theodicy and basic facts about strokes in order to care well in a situation of acute suffering.[3] He sought to help Libby Lyles make sense out of life and live with herself as the nutrition regimen was discontinued.

In less than three weeks, Ann Pearl died. There was a memorial service in her home state and interment beside the grave of her late husband. Cards and letters came in abundance to the Lyles's home. But the question did not die! The painful agonies persisted. How does the church help its families to face life-and-death matters, like stroke, AIDS, or cancer; or a community to emerge from natural disasters, like devastating earthquakes, floods, or tornadoes; or a split culture, like the two Germanys after World War II, to reunite in spirit as well as in economics and politics? What do people do when there seems little they *can* do? Such questions require a faith response.

The human condition rests ultimately in transcendent hands—the promise of God's abiding presence in circumstances of evil, suffering, injustice, uncertainty, and death (Rom. 8:37-39). Biblical faith in divine providence is the ground of human longing and realistic hoping. The OT speaks more of obedience than of hope; but in the NT the concept of hope prevails. The Apostle Paul made faith and hope coequal aspects of his triad of abiding virtues (1 Cor. 13). The church as community of faith, ideally, is to cradle the vision and nurture the hopes of its members. Given the complexity of mental functioning, "it makes sense to approach hoping and wishing, and hoping and despairing, as zones on a continuum, with most cases a mixture."[4] Pastors like Randy Stephens live in the dialectic with their congregants between hope and despair. Christian friends who wish to minister to strugglers like Libby Lyles, wrestling with the uncontrollable malevolence by which life is tainted, move between belief and unbelief in their search for a more humane order.

Ultimately, the Bible admonishes us to "hope in God," not in wish-fulfillment or in some magical force called *luck* (Job 13:15; Ps. 42:5, 147:11; Isa. 40:31; Rom. 5:4; Heb. 11:1). Some interpreters approach hope with apocalyptic imagery—God will destroy all oppressors and exalt the down-trodden in a great reversal. Others are convinced human beings must search for a meaningful concept of reality through theological imagination, then construct a "concept of God appropriate to contemporary life."[5] I am more comfortable admitting with the Apostle Paul that now we "see through a glass darkly," but at least, we can see the hand of a caring God outstretched to all creation. Biblical faith beckons us to believe in an orderly world and to explore "ways God participates in the suffering of nature and humans."[6] The practice of Christian pastoral care and wise counsel proceeds with awareness of God's love for all creation, abiding hopefulness, and faith in God's eternal care.

In reflecting upon his participation in the life-world of Libby Lyles, Pastor Stephens felt a sustaining ministry of presence was crucial. His verbal care did not alter the circumstances of Mrs. Pearl's stroke and subsequent death; yet, he sought to incarnate Christ's suffering love in *being* with the family. Numerous laypersons also shared the Lyles family's burdens through helpful acts and sympathetic participation in their pain. Such ministries within a Christian community are anchored in Jesus Christ's redemptive suffering for hurting humanity and in mutual accountability of persons sharing ministry in the congregation.

With such profound issues clustering in partnership ministry, questions about pastoral identity and accountability for the practice of Christian caregiving emerge. How does a pastor track through the maze of exhausting tasks and often unrealistic congregational expectations? The first step in thinking about pastoral tasks is developing a sense of identity in ministry. Discover who you are.

I. Identity in Ministry

In the mid-twentieth century, H. Richard Niebuhr wrote that people in the Church-at-large, including theological educators, were not clear about the purpose and meaning of Christian ministry. (Please note that throughout this book I use the term *church* with reference to local congregations, and *Church* to designate the inclusive idea of major traditions in Christendom.) He called ordained clergy the "perplexed profession," then proposed *pastoral director* as a generative metaphor for the conception of ministry emerging at that time. With the care of what Donald Schon has called a "reflective practitioner," Niebuhr held that elements like biblical wisdom, participation in the tradition of the Church, experiences and reflections of ministers themselves, and needs of the time all melded into his concept of pastoral direction of the work of the church.[7] His notion of the congregation proper becoming "the minister" and the pastor directing it in its service has influenced my own thinking; yet his metaphor was never widely recognized.

Numerous guiding images of ministry have emerged through the years: preacher, discipler, wounded healer, guide of the congregation's interpretative process, creator of a faith community, political mystic, professing professional, caregiver, servant leader, and negative images based on feudal, military, and business models. Each of these guiding visions of ministry has claimed attention and generated further research.[8] But cultural fragmentation, loss of prophetic vision, and increasing secularization create further problems in establishing the Church's core purpose, or what Charles V. Gerkin called the "center of gravity" for church and minister alike.

Niebuhr's assessment was an oversimplification of emerging theological diversity and cultural complexity and an understatement of the Church's missiological function in a world that has become a "global village" through telecommunications and the changing character of international relations.[9] New players have appeared on America's religious stage: the young, seeking to envision their places in religion and public life; New Age devotees and special purpose groups outside churches, seeking both nonprofit status and influence akin to denominations of an earlier day; unique racial and ethnic religious traditions, East and West; promoters of civil religion, seeking political alliances; and liberation movements, claiming status for oppressed and marginalized individuals.

With reference to Niebuhr's vision of universal priesthood, Lynn N. Rhodes notes correctly that the Church has only partially achieved the Protestant ideal of the priesthood of all believers. "While affirming the ministry of the whole church, we are still practicing a ministry that is largely seen as carried out by clergy."[10] It is also important to understand the secularization that has occurred in the appointment or calling process of ministers. Influenced by professional sports, government agencies, and corporate practices, many congregations "hire," instead of call, ministers. Like so much else in our disposable society, geared to built-in obsolescence, pastors have often been depersonalized into "services" people use, pay for, and dismiss at will.

The issue of pastoral identity remains open-ended, subject to varied interpretations of calling within diverse contexts of ministry. Randy Stephens, in the pastoral event just recounted, gained his bearings from a sense of divine initiative and assignment to ministry. His authority came both from God and the congregation he served. Some pastoral theologians invest heavily in examining care praxis imaginatively before conceptualizing pastoral identity and interpreting one's action in a faith community.[11] Randy Stephens, working in a church setting and not a specialized clinical pastoral education (CPE) center, focused on more traditional theological exploration and sought wisdom from an OT paradigm to gain his sense of direction in a difficult situation.

II. A Biblical Paradigm

Biblical insights into life and ministry have provided steerage for pastors across the ages. Randy's search led to an examination of Isaiah 6:1–13, an autobiographical narrative by an idealistic young prophet dated the same year as the death of ancient Judah's King Uzziah (740 B.C.). It reports his "call" to a prophetic vocation. Isaiah's justification for delivering a particular message of judgment and restoration to the people of Judah linked his own personal experience of loss and grief with a vision of God's power and glory.

> In the year that King Uzziah died, I saw the Lord seated on a throne, high and exalted, and the train of his robe filled the temple. Above him were seraphs, each with six wings: With two wings they covered their faces, with two they covered their feet, and with two they were flying. And they were calling to one another:
>
> "Holy, holy, holy is the Lord Almighty;
> the whole earth is full of his glory" (Isa. 6:1–3).

Ahaz, grandson of Uzziah, was king of Judah when Isaiah sought to obey his divinely appointed commission. The prophecies that follow his obedience of the divine summons, "Whom shall I send?" picture the prophet's confrontation with earthly rulers during the intrigue of the Syro-Ephraimite war. Uzziah had ruled fifty-two years, 792–740 B.C. Isaiah's security and hopes had been shattered by the great king's death. Paradoxically, like the phoenix of Greek mythology, the prophet was reborn from the ashes of mourning. He went into the temple, perhaps to pray; then came the vision of God's glory. His assignment was to illuminate where and how "God is at work in the world" as Creator of the future, and to intercede before God for the welfare of his people (Isa. 62:1).[12]

Isaiah's experience in ancient Hebrew tradition provides an archetype for identifying factors in ministry formation paralleled in our own day. What functions were performed by the burden of the Word of God commissioned in his life that provide biblical roots for our experience?

First, the divine vision helped Isaiah gain his bearings. His life as a young court preacher was going quite well when trouble came. Like the occasion in an earlier century when a pharaoh came to power "who knew not Joseph," Isaiah lost a great advocate when King Uzziah died. Grief has a way of disorienting persons when familiar landmarks are swept away. One can suffer great loss of native lands, families, careers, and fortunes — as with immigrants in our own day — and be forced to start over with a different culture and language, new standards of success, unfamiliar hazards, even new religious symbols in the midst of a changing mythology and ethos. A person might feel alienated in his or her own country if change comes too quickly or if a prized family member, cherished career, valued health, special cause, or influential friend has been lost.

Offering himself in a relationship defying easy explanation put Randy Stephens at risk with Libby Lyles. It is not easy to thrive on chaotic events that have power to erode the self, despite popular advice to the contrary.[13] Like Isaiah, many caregivers have suffered significant losses or shared pain with others and have struggled to make sense of such experiences. Major transitions often test one's sense of place and personhood, may shatter one's worldview, and prompt one to grow in faith or to fall back in unbelief. In *Beyond the Mirror,* Henri Nouwen tells of his narrow escape from death and revisioning of life's meaning as a result.[14]

Second, one's vision of God precedes service to humanity. When Isaiah saw God in the imagery of a heavenly council, he was impressed with the profane world: "I am a man of unclean lips, and I live among a people of unclean lips . . ." (Isa. 6:5). The people had mocked "the Holy One of Israel" (Isa. 5:19). Now God assigned him the task of calling a sinful nation to account. The content of Isaiah's faith was shaped by his perception of the Holy One — a picture rich with ineffable majesty (Isa. 6:3). After a purification ritual of a live coal touching his mouth, the prophet delivered God's warning and promise to a wayward nation. The true OT prophet identified with the shortcomings of his nation and interceded with the Lord as a vicarious sufferer on behalf of the people.

Isaiah's legacy to ministers in the OT prophetic tradition is that one serves humankind, not from the depths of its depravity or need, neither for human approval nor fear of criticism, but primarily from divine assignment and obedience to a heavenly calling. In biblical story, one is sent forth to advance faith and facilitate change in a preoccupied world. Today's pastoral caregiver is "under orders" to identify with human need and share a redemptive story. In ministry, one is sustained by the very message preached from God and energized by his Spirit to reenter the fray.

Third, once a person has been visited by a vision of the Holy One, the remainder of life is spent in greater mystery. Still, one so challenged need not doubt the grace that claimed him or her in such a memorable experience. For Isaiah, God's commission fused judgment and confrontation with mercy and salvation. God, who is "sovereign Lord," far above all nations and rulers, is also, paradoxically, "suffering servant" (40:15–24; 53:1–12). The prophet proclaimed a Messianic Age would come, akin to the Kingdom of God idea in the NT, marked by peace, restoration, and usefulness in the earth (11:6–9).

The salvation story we have seen in this paradigm of divine commissioning to ministry is a process rather than a conclusion. The gospel seed is planted in hope and watered by the river of God's constant care of the earth. We who live in the Christian era recognize that God's "suffering servant" became incarnate in the life, death, and resurrection of Jesus Christ. The challenge to contemporary ministers appears in Jesus Christ's prediction to his disciples: "And I, when I am lifted up from the earth, will draw all people to myself" (John 12:32 NRSV). God's intent for the Messianic Age is world redemption; thus ministry involves a strong missiological imperative in caring for persons.

Caregivers like Randy Stephens, standing with Libby Lyles at the bedside of her stroke-ravaged mother, hear the question once more: "What is there to do when there's nothing you *can* do?" Authentic biblical faith guides one's pastoral actions, not in the sense of manipulating God's glory, but as *hope bearers* of an eternal kingdom. When one's pastoral practice poses complex ethical questions and involves sharing profound suffering, one humbly lets God be God and offers "the water of life" in the Master's name (Rev. 22:1).[15]

Because biblical faith holds personal and social dimensions in tension, ministers like Randy Stephens are drawn into the public arena as well. He supported Libby Lyles in her desire for faithfulness to her mother's Directive to Physicians and Living Will. Authentic caregivers will contribute to the public debate about euthanasia, the sanctity of life, abortion, AIDS, sexual and substance abuse, violence, human rights, and moral responsibility.[16] They will remind physicians, educators, politicians, artists, policymakers, service providers, and investors in their search for "the good life" that it may be found only in the Kingdom of God. They will point outsiders, whom Ronald Takaki calls "strangers from a distant shore," to a transforming Friendship. True to their own versions of "the heavenly vision," authentic Christian ministers are *hope bearers*—advancing faith in a perplexed world.

When we get beneath the surface of the flotsam and jetsam that washes onto shore from ministry seas, or sinks in dead weight of unimportance or obscurity, Christian leaders have a fundamental theological task to perform. It is the arduous labor of "responding to personal struggles, family conflicts, national calamities, and international tensions," notes Henri Nouwen, "with an articulate faith in God's real presence."[17] Preparation for such sharing cannot send one scurrying for conventional wisdom after calamity strikes. One must provide timely nurture for personal or social crisis and be a resourceful communicator of hope in "the naked public square" of human discourse, deep need, and discontent.[18] John Bunyan's allegorical "Mr. Interpreter" may provide a helpful metaphor as we move toward the future. Providing guidance and hope for life's spiritual pilgrimage is a profoundly theological task.

III. The Pastoral Theological Task

Historically, pastoral theology has been a discipline of the churches for almost 250 years.[19] *Pastoral theology* is that branch of "practical theology" that studies human development in spiritual, moral, and behavioral perspective, reflects upon the church's caring functions in light of the Christian faith, enhances pastoral caregiving tasks, and in the process, contributes to the larger body of Christian knowledge. Theological understanding, sometimes called "the language of faith," emerges from focused consideration of the biblical story of creation and redemption, and of human life before God in a particular community of faith. Christian theology thus includes reflections on all of a religious community's literature, symbols, beliefs, and practices and interacts with ideas from across the human spectrum. *Pastoral* theological reflection distinctively moves from pastoral practice to theology; then from theology back to ministry once more.[20] In this sense, pastoral caregiving, properly understood, advances the course of theological reflection.

Take the case of Libby Lyles's search for answers to a profoundly troublesome family health crisis with Pastor Stephens. Her "What to do . . . ?" tapped into doctrines concerning divine providence and human freedom, will and willing, faith and doubt, prayer and fate, grace and guilt, alienation and community, as well as life and death. Her mother's massive stroke enrolled Libby in the "school of the humble," where there are only complex, not simple, courses. The violence of stroke had struck with full fury, like a hurricane at sea, reminding Libby of her linkage with nature and the rest of humankind. It was quite natural for her to ponder quietly with her pastor these profound musings of the spirit. Her own finitude had been called into question!

The theological and ethical nature of the Lyles family's decisions regarding discontinuation of "heroic measures" to stave off Mrs. Pearl's death is clear. Such help-seeking individuals and families turn to the church because it is there! Talking with one's minister, family, and close Christian friends about such lofty matters is natural. The only other recourse in such entrapments is the medical, and in some instances legal, community. There are many sides to such predicaments, and believing people want a religious perspective early on. Libby Lyles turned to like-minded believers, pastoral and laypersons, for the best wisdom they might bring to the agonizing drama of her mother's dying. Physicians, an attorney, her pastor, and family were her confidants and referral resources. Libby cast herself upon God's wisdom and mercy frequently before the "no life support" medical directive was given.

This whole decision-making process was intensified by technology. Ann Pearl had had three heart pacemakers surgically inserted into her chest cavity over a period of fifteen years.

The cardiologist had diagnosed her mother's irregular heart rhythms years earlier as "vasomotor instability." Now, the electronic device that had been her life-supportive "friend" became her "enemy." Behaviorally incapacitated for life by stroke, neither was she fit for dying. A tiny electronic device helped keep her alive much longer than doctors had predicted. Indeed, the family, as well as medical professionals, recognized that life and death are not only in God's hands but in the skills of persons who sometimes "play God."

Part of the fruitfulness of contemplating all aspects of this family emergency, medical diagnostic probes, therapeutic procedures, ethical quandaries, death, and grief work is the lively connection between pastoral care and the human sciences. The Lyles family's earnest dialogues with five different physicians, over time, was never hung up on theistic questions about God's existence. That was assumed by all parties. (There are few atheists in stroke patients' rooms.) Pastoral and lay participants in Ann Pearl's predicament and the Lyles family's losses theologized about personhood, qualities of being human like the sharing of community, ethical issues in treatment, and transformation beyond death. One does not always begin in pastoral theology with a biblical passage or systematic theological question. One begins phenomenologically with hurt or need, conflict and caregiving, then proceeds with identification of key issues as a "reflective practitioner."

It is appropriate to observe that the other purpose of pastoral theology is at work all the while "contributing to the larger body of Christian knowledge." Such implications may refer directly to one practitioner's particular theological position, noted Princeton's James Lapsley. On the other hand, conclusions "may be for another branch or branches of practical theology, or they may be for issues that permeate many positions and branches of theology."[21] The thoughtful inquirer brings a teachable spirit, family and faith traditions, curiosity and patience in examining pastoral events, and focused discipline to meaningful relationships so that coherent and integrative views may be communicated. Such a theological examination of ministry data would be enriched by pastoral support groups since many ministers serve solo in church staff positions.

In their discussion of *Pastoral Care in Historical Perspective,* Clebsch and Jaekle noted four primary caregiving functions in epochs of Christian history: healing, sustaining, guiding, and reconciling.[22] With this carefully documented typology in mind, we may observe that Pastor Randy Stephens sought to sustain Libby Lyles through prayerful consolation. He also filled a reconciling need for the Lyles family in their feelings of distance from God, confusion with certain service providers, and absence from their belief community because of Mrs. Pearl's extended hospital stay and death. At no time did he try to dissuade the family's dependence upon the heavenly Father's providential care (1 Pet. 1:21). Along with them, he avoided magical thinking (like, "She's going to make it!"), a hope being held out to them by one of the medical team members in the hospital. He was a faithful steward of the mysteries, as Paul described the Word of God, but did not misuse the Bible as a fetish, good luck charm, or whip. Knowing that God created people with capacities for belief and unbelief, he stood in the breach of ambiguity with the family and encouraged hope in the "God who is *there*." Randy Stephens thus served as a faithful interpreter of life's stories—human and divine—in the classic sense of pastoral guidance.

Rather than proposing a reductionistic system for Christian caregiving at the outset, I have introduced the metaphor *hope bearer* to depict numerous aspects of pastoral work. It remains to mention some unique pastoral temptations and tasks before we plunge more deeply into the plan of the book.

IV. Pastoral Temptations and Tasks

Some years ago, Henri Nouwen, a Roman Catholic teacher who sought to integrate spiritual direction and pastoral care, left the academic setting of Harvard to work with the mentally challenged residents of the L 'Arche communities in Toronto. In a serious reflection upon his life and work, in relation to unique temptations experienced by Jesus Christ, Nouwen noted that desires for relevance, popularity, and power are endemic to the vocation of Christian ministry.[23] Only in accepting certain disciplines of servant leadership, he said, such as contemplative prayer, confession and forgiveness, and theological reflection, might a minister withstand potential moral ruin and live most usefully for God.

Earlier, the Quaker educator Richard Foster had explored three key ethical themes crucial to people of faith: issues of money, sexuality, and power. He challenges readers with a call to the disciplined life through a threefold vow of simplicity, fidelity, and service.[24] Like his Catholic counterpart, Nouwen, the Friends University educator is serious about spirituality and sacramental living. Both writers caution church leaders, who care for God's flock, lest they themselves "be disqualified for the prize" (1 Cor. 9:27). In a similar vein, pastor Eugene Peterson calls ministers out of presumption, fatigue, and neglect to basics of the pastoral vocation.[25] He sees the minister as someone who, through prayer, Scripture, and spiritual direction, leads people seeking normative boundaries for life closer to God.

While such temptations are common to humankind, there is a matter of another order that requires attention from those who would shape other peoples' souls. A grievous malady afflicts us. The moral bottom has dropped out of our culture. "Americans have no compelling incentive to postpone gratification," notes historian Christopher Lasch of the University of Rochester, "because they no longer believe in the future."[26] Symptoms appear as selfishness, self-serving ambition, instant sex, or some uncontrollable impulse (to kill, steal, do drugs, or whatever). Many people damage their lives in irreparable ways. It is the young especially who doubt the existence of the future. They have grown up in a world of hurt and conflict, environmental catastrophe, betrayed promises, crime and violence, political corruption, ignored blessing, and forgotten grace. So many of their golden-haloed heroes, to whom they attributed godlike status, have gone bad.[27] They do not sense that things are going to get any better. Their temptation beneath the surface of their cheerfulness, notes Lasch, is not only drug abuse, vandalism, or pointless violence. It is hopelessness, giving up on the project of caring anymore, or, with suicide "machines" available, perhaps ending life itself.

Seminarians and pastors are products of culture as well. Their models, through whom they live vicariously, and upon whom they have placed their hopes, fall from their pedestals like broken idols. Their heroes have feet of clay. In many cases, particularly for women in ministry, there are few mentors. Encouragers are rare. Young ministers grow weary of theological intrigue and denominational warfare. In fact, for many people denominationalism has declined in significance because it no longer seems to matter in the marketplace, or because leadership has changed hands.

Theological and clinical educators, senior ministers of key congregations, denominational executives, and wise lay caregivers have a major nurturing task ahead. We must uphold religious truth and moral idealism in the background of daily living. If only the foreground of ambition and desire driven by popular culture fills life's picture, people lacking trustworthy norms and boundaries want instant "everything." When insistent desires collide with economic realities, social limitations, and fallen icons, people discover that, in fact, they can't "have it all." The cure for this malaise comes not in neat formulas or tight prescriptions, but in telling the truth about ourselves. In time, constructive solutions, in line with biblical ethics and realistic hopes, may be realized.

With a context of pastoral identity, mission, theological accountability, and spiritual discipline in mind, how shall we conceive of pastoral care in the church? Pastoral care has been viewed mistakenly in the past as superficial do-goodism; as a crutch for life's cripples; as God's psychiatry aimed at "peace of mind"; or as a form of faith healing that might save us from suffering, fear, and death. This is the mistaken, theologically incapacitated caring of some who have viewed Christianity as a handy palliative administered by pastoral practitioners to sufferers in crises. Again, pastoral care has been construed as *the pastor's work*, usually through a private conversation with an individual. Such concepts fail to communicate the comprehensive caregiving ideal confirmed in the Scriptures and history of the Church.

Biblically and practically, *Christian pastoral care is the mutual concern of Christians for each other and for those persons in the world for whom Christ died*. Pastoral care aimed at both individual concerns and systemic change views the church itself as minister and pastor as one leading congregants in shared ministry. One's role as leader, communicator, and visionary example is fulfilled within the whole Church's caring mission. God's people care for hurt humanity as they incarnate God's redemptive presence in life, where the real needs are (Lev. 19:33–34; Matt. 25:31–46; John 17:16–26). The

Church thus finds its place in the world by grappling with the ethical dilemmas, dangers, and pressing questions of persons "for Christ's sake." A caring church is true to its calling when it serves as a community of identity, relationship, confession, worship, interpretation, mission, and hope.

Given the importance of this background for the Church and its mission, certain points on the compass are noted here in order to chart properly the course of this discussion and to limit our sphere of investigation. In an effort to communicate with a varied audience, we begin with some intrinsic foundations of pastoral care. Subjects in Part I, such as the pastor's identity, the church's caring task, Christian anthropology, and theological education are introduced, not in order to be discursive, but to be theologically discriminating. The early chapters may lack novelty for specialists and educators, but are included in this book as an essential context for seminarians and a general pastoral audience. Part II traces the contours of Christian caregiving through the pastoral action of the whole congregation. Part III offers clinical wisdom to those who share life's common ventures and crises as Christian caregivers. We turn first to an exploration of foundations.

Notes

1. This and all other reports of pastoral relationships represent actual situations and appear by permission. Names and places have been changed to assure anonymity.

2. Peter F. Drucker, *The New Realities* (San Francisco: Harper & Row, 1989), 245.

3. For a theology of suffering, see Thomas C. Oden, *Pastoral Theology* (San Francisco: Harper & Row, 1983), 223–48. Cf. L. Bregman, "Suffering," in Rodney J. Hunter, gen. ed., *Dictionary of Pastoral Care and Counseling* (Nashville: Abingdon Press, 1990), 1230–32. See John E. Sarno and Martha Sarno, *Stroke: A Guide for Patients and Their Families*, rev. ed. (New York: McGraw-Hill, 1979); and Harry A. Cole, *The Long Way Home: Spiritual Help When Someone You Love Has a Stroke* (Louisville: Westminster/John Knox Press, 1989).

4. Paul W. Pruyser, "Hope and Despair," in Hunter, *Dictionary of Pastoral Care and Counseling*, 532–34.

5. See, for example, Gordon D. Kaufman, *The Theological Imagination: Constructing the Concept of God* (Philadelphia: Westminster Press, 1981), 279; cf. his *Theology for a Nuclear Age* (Philadelphia: Westminster Press, 1985).

6. James W. Fowler, *Weaving the New Creation: Stages of Faith and the Public Church* (San Francisco: HarperCollins, 1991), 58.

7. H. Richard Niebuhr, *The Purpose of the Church and Its Ministry* (New York: Harper & Brothers, 1956), 79 ff. Donald A. Schon, *The Reflective Practitioner: How Professionals Think in Action* (New York: Basic Books, 1983), 184–87.

8. Charles V. Gerkin, *Prophetic Pastoral Practice: A Christian Vision of Life Together* (Nashville: Abingdon Press, 1991), 114–15. Cf. Donald E. Messer, *Contemporary Images of Christian Ministry* (Nashville: Abingdon, Press, 1989); Edward Farley, *Ecclesial Reflection: An Anatomy of Theological Method* (Philadelphia: Fortress Press, 1982); and E. Glenn Hinson, "The Church and Its Ministry," in *Formation for Christian Ministry*, edited by Anne Davis and Wade Rowatt, rev. ed. (Louisville: Review and Expositor, 1988), 15–28.

9. The late media theorist Marshall McLuhan coined the metaphor "global village" in the 1960s. Feminist theology, developed by advocates like Rosemary Ruether, had not refined its critique of patriarchy or revised Christian thought to suit its needs in Niebuhr's day. See her *Sexism and God-Talk: Toward a Feminist Theology* (Boston: Beacon Press, 1983). Cf. Clark H. Pinnock, *Tracking the Maze: Finding Our Way Through Modern Theology from an Evangelical Perspective* (San Francisco: Harper & Row, 1990).

10. Lynn N. Rhodes, *Co-Creating: A Feminist View of Ministry* (Philadelphia: Westminster Press, 1987), 15. Cf. Herschel H. Hobbs, *You Are Chosen: The Priesthood of All Believers* (San Francisco: Harper & Row, 1990).

11. See, for example, John Patton, *From Ministry to Theology: Pastoral Action and Reflection* (Nashville: Abingdon Press, 1990). Because his thinking is germinal, though greatly dependent upon theological methods suggested by Edward Farley and John MacMurray, we shall return to Patton's work in subsequent discussion.

12. Elizabeth Achtemeir, *Preaching from the Old Testament* (Louisville: Westminster/John Knox Press, 1989), 110–13.

13. See Tom Peters, *Thriving on Chaos: Handbook for a Management Revolution* (San Francisco: Harper & Row, 1988).

14. Henri J. M. Nouwen, *Beyond the Mirror: Reflections on Life and Death* (New York: Crossroad, 1990). Cf. *The Wounded Healer: Ministry in Contemporary Society* (Garden City, NY: Doubleday, 1972; Image ed., 1990).

15. See Lawrence E. Holst, "Withholding Nutrition and Hydration: Some Old and New Questions," *The Journal of Pastoral Care* 45, no. 1 (Spring 1991): 3–13.

16. See attorney Richard R. Hammar's *Pastor, Church & Law* (Springfield, MO: Gospel Publishing House, 1983); a *Supplement* was published in 1986. Cf. *Church Law & Tax Report*, published bimonthly by Christian Ministry Resources, Matthews, NC; *Current Thoughts & Trends*, published monthly by the Navigators, Colorado Springs, CO; and *Research Recommendations*, issued weekly by the National Institute of Business Management, Inc., New York, NY.

17. Henri J. M. Nouwen, *In The Name of Jesus: Reflections on Christian Leadership* (New York: Crossroad, 1989), 67. Such a dialogical relationship between particular human situations and the biblical tradition is akin to the "fusion of horizons" process suggested by Hans-Georg Gadamer in *Truth and Method* (New York: Crossroad, 1982), 273.
18. Richard John Neuhaus, *The Naked Public Square: Religion and Democracy in America* (Grand Rapids: Wm. B. Eerdmans, 1984).
19. The late Seward Hiltner credited the first book on pastoral theology to C. T. Seidel, in 1749, in *Preface to Pastoral Theology* (Nashville: Abingdon Press, 1958), 224.
20. T. W. Jennings, Jr., "Pastoral Theological Methodology," in Hunter, *Dictionary of Pastoral Care and Counseling*, 862–64.
21. James Lapsley, "Practical Theology and Pastoral Care: An Essay in Pastoral Theology," in Don S. Browning, ed., *Practical Theology: The Emerging Field in Theology, Church, and World* (San Francisco: Harper & Row, 1983), 170. John Patton illustrates a twelve-session structure and theologizing agenda for ministry groups in specialized settings in *From Ministry to Theology*, 121–22.
22. William A. Clebsch and Charles R. Jaekle, *Pastoral Care in Historical Perspective* (Englewood Cliffs, NJ: Prentice-Hall, 1964), 33–66. Reissued by Jason Aronson in 1983.
23. Nouwen, *In the Name of Jesus*, chapters 1–3 *et passim*.
24. Richard J. Foster, *Money, Sex, and Power: The Challenge of the Disciplined Life* (San Francisco: Harper & Row, 1985).
25. Eugene H. Peterson, *Working the Angles: The Shape of Pastoral Integrity* (Grand Rapids: Wm. B. Eerdmans, 1987). Cf. *Answering God: The Psalms as Tools for Prayer* (HarperCollins, 1991).
26. Christopher Lasch, "Restoring Belief in the Future," *The New York Times*, quoted in *The Dallas Morning News* (January 1, 1990): 23.
27. See Leo S. Braudy, *The Frenzy of Renown: Fame and Its History* (New York: Oxford University Press, 1986).

Suggested Reading

Barna, George. *The Frog in the Kettle: What Christians Need to Know About Life in the Year 2000*. Ventura, CA: Regal Books, 1990. Shows how churches can minister for God in the real world. See also his *User Friendly Churches*, Ventura, CA: Regal Books, 1991.
Chandler, Russell. *Racing Toward 2001: The Forces Shaping America's Religious Future*. Grand Rapids: Zondervan Publishing House, 1992. A respected journalist tells us how to prepare for future ministry.

Patton, John. *From Ministry to Theology: Pastoral Action and Reflection.* Nashville: Abingdon Press, 1990. A theological interpretation of pastoral work in specialized settings by one skilled in the wisdom of clinical pastoral education.

Peterson, Eugene H. *Working the Angles: The Shape of Pastoral Integrity.* Grand Rapids: Wm. B. Eerdmans, 1987. Calls attention to three acts of ministry—prayer, reading the Scriptures, and giving spiritual direction—so basic that they give shape to everything else.

Pinnock, Clark H. *Tracking the Maze: Finding Our Way Through Modern Theology from an Evangelical Perspective.* San Francisco: Harper & Row, 1990. Sees this era as a time of opportunity for Christian leaders to articulate their faith and play a larger role in the transformation of human cultures.

Schultze, Quentin J. *Televangelism and American Culture.* Grand Rapids: Baker Book House, 1991. A communications specialist calls for a more responsible Christian use of television media and critiques popular religion.

Wuthnow, Robert. *The Restructuring of American Religion: Society and Faith Since World War II.* Princeton: Princeton University Press, 1988. A rigorous, scholarly examination of religion in America for persons who would shape a new vision of faith and the political process.

PART I

FOUNDATIONS OF PASTORAL CARE

———

CHAPTER ONE

PASTORAL CARE IN
THEOLOGICAL PERSPECTIVE

The pastor who provides moral leadership, spiritual guidance, and encouragement to a congregation is the most nearly normative concept of the Christian minister in history. From the time Jesus Christ chose certain disciples and "appointed [them] to go and bear fruit," pastoral care has been a universal practice in the life and mission of Christian churches. All persons encompassed in Christ's love were to care for each other, strengthen each other in the faith, and minister to those wounded by life's chaos and hurts for whom he died (John 15:12–17). Such care implies not anxiety, nor what Søren Kierkegaard called "dread" concerning life's tragedies, but self-transcendent concern for others. This generous impulse, which can be accepted or stifled, employs the vocabulary of Christian compassion in all human relationships. It is nothing less than living out the goodness and mercy of God in life situations.

Paradoxically, our human tendency is to view wounded spirits from a safe distance. The natural inclination is to refuse aid to life's wounded and pass by on the other side. This is a day when self-affirmation and self-care have been exalted, when people and nations assist only those who can reciprocate in some measure, and self-denial for the sake of others is ridiculed. Responsible parties have difficulty appreciating, let alone connecting with, the naked needs of irreligious individuals. Prejudice closes doors to understanding, and fear of the "other" dictates a policy of caution, a defensive lifestyle, rather than acceptant attitudes of helpfulness. Preoccupation with one's own agenda seals the eyes of would-be helpers to potential objects of care. A postmodern populace, furthermore, may view caring efforts by churches or pastoral practitioners with suspicion, lack of appreciation, or downright opposition.

It is not easy for contemporary individuals, lulled into indifference by "religion in general," to particularize faith by identifying with another person's need. Yet God's concern for creation manifested in the Incarnation remains irrepressible. The NT contrasts Jesus Christ's sacrificial generosity with our solicitous self-concern (for example, 2 Cor. 8:1-15). Those who serve as instruments of God's hands and channels of divine grace cherish the "other" for his or her own sake and for God's sake. In reality, it is not to ministers that the world's desperate or dispossessed citizens turn, but to God, whom they hope to find through us or in spite of us.

This essay was introduced with the commonplace experience of a Protestant minister who, along with members of a congregation, shared one family's burden until the members were able to resume life's tasks again. I have suggested that such pastoral care is the mutual concern of individuals for each other and for those persons in the world for whom Christ died (cf. Gal. 6:2-10). While ordained ministers have a unique social role and ecclesiastical office in a community, the pastor has no monopoly on the whole church's caring concerns. Rev. Randy Stephens, the Lyles's minister, confessed: "The family of believers of Broadway Church played a more important part in this case than did I." With this distinction between general and representative (ordered) ministry in mind, let us explore some criteria for caring, the helper's true identity, and areas of Christian concern for others.

I. Criteria for the Pastoral Task

In a Sprunt lectureship at the Union Seminary of Richmond, the late Daniel Day Williams said: "The pastoral task, as it comes to every minister and every Christian, is to respond to the wonder of God's care for the soul and to share with others such knowledge as [one] has of God's healing power."[1] There is profound wisdom here in that (1) it is God's healing power that Christians offer to wounded persons; (2) transcendent realities, not human needs alone, motivate and inform acts of ministry; and (3) only persons who have first been blessed in God's hands function as true channels of spiritual power. This sensitive, wise theologian held that a desire to help must be matched by an informed understanding if our caring efforts are to be effective.

A physician whose son had been sentenced to prison for a crime reminds us we deal with deep ambiguity: "Sometimes parents think they are doing the best they know how to do, but their best isn't enough." Clearly, we need no new tinkerers with souls nor clever manipulators of human destinies. Rather, persons with a secular worldview require profound wisdom from those who would communicate with them about God's healing power.

We recognize that pastoral care of shattered folk like the Lyles family is only one of a vast variety of ministerial tasks in contemporary church life. So strategic is nurture at the appropriate time, however, that it deserves to be performed well. Like a skilled surgeon who must employ all garnered wisdom to control a laser in delicate eye surgery or suture the edges of a single wound, the Christian pastor must assume theological and practical responsibility for spiritual work. As a modern minister, one needs to know how to perform multifunctional tasks, why one is ministering, and what it is that one is doing. This presupposes self-understanding, technical skills, and theological wisdom as well. Does it imply that individuals who fail to meet certain conditions of caring are thereby exempt from compassionate living? Not at all! It does suggest, however, that we examine basic criteria for pastoral practice and for critical reflection upon that work, leading to pastoral theology.

1. Motivation in Ministry

From the early church period to the present, *the reconciling and sustaining love of God* has motivated spiritual service in his name (Ps. 67:1–2; John 15:17; 2 Cor. 5:14–20).[2] The Apostle John declared: "We know that we have passed from death to life because we love one another. . . . We know love by this, that he laid down his life for us — and we ought to lay down our lives for one another. How does God's love abide in anyone who has the world's goods and sees a brother or sister in need and yet refuses help? . . . Let us love not in word or speech but in truth and action" (1 John 3:14–18 NRSV). Each Christian gifted as an encourager, not merely those who are ordained, is to participate in the church's mission of reconciliation and spiritual direction. Christ calls the Church to care, and simultaneously beckons persons in the world to respond in faith. While such transactions may be unquantifiable in a scientific sense, the motives of giving and receiving care are operative together.

Why do you visit a hospital patient or parishioner? Is it out of a sense of duty, through force of habit, because the community expects you to visit hospitalized persons, because of private vows or ecclesiastical expectations, or by personal request of the family and friends? Primarily, the pastor and congregation act in response to God's care for human hurt. Members of the Christian community who are sensitive to suffering are available to help when a caring opportunity presents itself. They become instruments of God's grace and mercy for a specific time and purpose (Heb. 4:16).

Christian compassion is the primary generating environment of true pastoral endeavor. Fear of involvement or legal penalty for a mistake cautions against such activities. Preoccupation with urgent pursuits brushes needs aside, operates in order to save one's self, and thereby distances the "other." Attentiveness, which transmutes our human incapacities, tunes our care to the inner tempo of people's spiritual needs. Pastoral events are not pursued as an escape from other demanding ministerial obligations. Neither do we share with family members in order to gain control over dependent personalities or to probe the secrets of their souls. Marie Fortune has warned of sexual misconduct by ministers against parishioners in her case for integrity in intimate pastoral relationships.[3] Constrained by the mysterious attraction of "deep calling to deep," a true minister is open to the eternal dimensions of conversations with care-seekers.

Could we interpret the story of the Good Samaritan (Luke 10:30–37) in the light of our own experience? Life thrusts us, at times, into each of the roles filled by the parable's characters. Do we need the reminder that Christians are not above falling to the spoilers and landing injured on life's highway? A theological student once offered transportation to a hitchhiker late at night. In a matter of moments, the recipient of his generosity leveled a pistol at his head, demanded his wallet and his keys, beat him in the face with the gun, then pushed him from his car and drove away. The would-be "helper" was himself left literally stunned and half-dead on the roadside. Suffering knows no partiality. It invades the privacy of the just and unjust alike. Again, there are specific occasions when, like the priest and the Levite, church people pass life's wounded by. Through insensitivity, prudent caution, unwillingness to listen, prejudice, demands of the marketplace, or preoccupation with private burdens, many religious folk leave life's injured bleeding and alone. There is opportunity occasionally to take initiative as the Samaritan, a generous neighbor, ready to aid those in distress or who have gone astray. Some receptive persons are innkeepers who welcome hurt persons into a place of temporary refuge and healing. The role of Christian physician, school counselor, social worker, and sensitive carer in corporate life parallels that of the ancient innkeeper. Help is sometimes given; at other times received.

Pastoral care arises out of the *push* of the pastoral calling and the *pull* of human need, but it is sustained through spiritual energy. The caring heart—Christian response to humanity's hurt—is a gift in some people. It must be cultivated by others. But, as Christ reminded Simon Peter, such a ministry can be sustained over a lifetime only by mature love (John 21:15–17).

2. Theological Responsibility

A glance at the dialogue in the Introduction indicates that the questions the Lyles family asked their minister after Ann Pearl's stroke were basically theological.

1. What can people do when there's deep need and they don't know what to do about it?
2. How shall we manage moral ambiguity in the use of life-sustaining technology and questions of medical ethics in caring for a seriously ill or incapacitated loved one?
3. Given the finite nature of personhood and reality of death, how shall we view resurrection of the body when New Agers advocate reincarnation of the deceased?
4. How can family members cope with feelings of shame or guilt regarding their responsibilities?
5. When death comes, how can survivors move through grief work to resume relationships and responsibilities?

In pastoral practice, a minister moves from action to reflection—from hospital calling, in Randy Stephens's case, to understanding better the consequences of stroke and a family's involvement in it. Sometimes we are called on to care when there is little to hope for. It is insensitive to hold out hope or lift expectations when death is imminent. A family's illusion of immortality on this planet experiences a great reversal in the delicate balance between life and death. Pastor Stephens shared a time of heightened sensitivity with the Lyles family in the full realization that they faced the prospect of losing Mrs. Pearl.

Integrity in pastoral work presupposes theological and clinical wisdom as well as a passionate heart. Preachers are to understand learning theory, hermeneutics, and communications skills in order to help people participate in worship. Church administrators must be skilled in systemic management, finance, denominational polity, the law, and in moving through chaos in group decision making. And pastors are also theologians when they reflect upon God's ways with creation and upon human existence before God. This is the realm of pastoral theology—discriminating reflection upon caring for persons and families in light of the Christian faith.

Theology presupposes God's self-revelation in making the divine nature known to human beings. Yet divine revelation through the Word of God anticipates consequences in human experience. Each doctrine growing

out of biblical revelation and historic Christian interpretation intersects
with human events. Ministers will discover mistaken views of God's nature
and providence, of what constitutes sin, and of guilt and forgiveness in
their pastoral conversations. Such erroneous ideas may serve as "teachable
moments" for the pastor or parishioner in correcting concepts when profound questions are faced through pastoral encounters. On the other
hand, a church member may amaze the pastor with wisdom about the
church's mission, some aspect of family or community life, or the daily
providence of God. We can learn from our people. Thus Canadian William
Schmidt is right: "Theology, whatever else it means, serves as a gathering-
up of God's story and a reclaiming of how God's story intersects with our
story."[4] Theological reflection must take our experiences with God as ultimate object and subject, alongside human stories, into account.

    To theologize, to frame a theology, is every believer's privilege and obli-
gation. With due respect for persons who have witnessed to their faith in
the past, each individual created in God's image is to articulate contemporary belief within a religious worldview (Rom. 14:12; 1 Pet. 2:9). Biblical
truth does not change, though "the task of theological interpretation of
scripture is profoundly complex."[5] One's understanding of Ultimate Reality and of one's own existence in the universe does change. It is open-
ended. God alone is the absolute truth, rather than statements about God
from religious thinkers. Every Christian minister, therefore, has both a
practical and a theological vocation. One must know whereof one speaks
and possess a "ready answer" for the hope resident in one's heart (1 Pet.
3:15). A corresponding responsibility rests upon each community of believers — the church — to reflect upon its faith, life, and ministry, and to
articulate the content of its faith to those in the world.[6] Meanwhile, God
transcends and judges humankind's partial knowledge and, through the
Holy Spirit, guides believers continually "into all the truth" (John 16:13).

    In doing pastoral theology, some interpreters begin with doctrine and
apply wisdom in pastoral situations. The Anglican cleric Martin Thornton
reflects such a perspective by proposing that "pastoral theology may now be
defined as applied dogmatics."[7] Thus his theological method stands with
the didactic tradition of Continental thought rather than with contemporary clinical pastoral wisdom. Other interpreters begin with people or
events, then extrapolate cognitive data. John Patton's method of theological reflection, for example, does not begin with God. Rather, he advocates
imaginative focusing on "a specific character and need of the world"
through a three-storied process of caring event, symbolic construction, and
theological reflection.[8] His approach follows Edward Farley's method in

Ecclesial Reflection, and is suggestive for pastoral theologians in specialized contexts. Neither of these thinkers resembles precisely my own understanding of pastoral theology—a way of "doing" theology pastorally.

Theological wisdom in pastoral work anticipates creative contemplation of pastoral events, disciplined imagination, *and* profound appreciation for one's faith tradition. Jesus Christ taught that concern for persons both precedes and includes religious tradition and practice (Mark 2:27). Clinical pastoral theology approaches ambiguous situations of human hurt, need, and conflict from a threefold perspective of descriptive, normative, and practical data.[9] *In the method of pastoral work advocated here, ultimate human concerns are illuminated by Christian convictions as well as by the priority of personhood.*

3. A *Method for Theological Reflection*

A theology of pastoral care both fashions and is fashioned by an acceptable methodological orientation. Without a comprehensive method of work, the pastor struggles through assignments ill-equipped, often crushed by demands of the office. Such a minister feels inadequate for the stark needs of complex counseling situations, keeps few pastoral records, and seldom reflects theologically upon his or her professional relationships. Clearly, guidance in the formation of a community of faith and care is at the forefront of pastoral work, while contemplation upon one's ministry follows. By such a holistic process of action and reflection pastoral theology is formed.

The clinical pastoral education movement has addressed itself to the need for responsible methods of pastoral work. Its leaders have contributed greatly to our understanding of pastoral theology. The pioneering research of Anton T. Boisen, principal founder of clinical pastoral education (CPE) in the 1920s, has been a shaping influence in the psychology of religion and pastoral practice. Among those thinkers who took Boisen seriously and used his "first principles" in the formulation of a responsible theology of pastoral care were pioneers like Seward Hiltner, Paul Johnson, Wayne E. Oates, and Carroll A. Wise. The thrust of Seward Hiltner's *Preface to Pastoral Theology* was that pastoral work, properly examined, has valid implications for the Christian faith. His perspectival approach of focusing the shepherding spirit (meaning essentially "caring") upon all the operations of the church and functions of the minister served as a generative influence in mid-twentieth-century pastoral theology. Hiltner demonstrated through case-examination an empirical method by which a systematic pastoral theology—healing, sustaining, and guiding—might be constructed.[10] He rightly called his proposal a "preface," which anticipated further investigation.

More recent American pastoral theology has moved in diverse directions, depending upon one's theological persuasion and the context of one's vocational endeavors. Don S. Browning, Donald Capps, James E. Dittes, Thomas C. Oden, and James N. Poling have each sought, in uniquely different academic settings, to picture the reciprocal relationship between theology and pastoral practice.[11] The Hiltnerian perception of pastoral theology has been more influential in the thought of James N. Lapsley, Charles V. Gerkin, John Patton, and Rodney Hunter. Pastoral theology is still in process of formulation as "a specialized form of religious wisdom about how to live, specialized by its focus on the question of how to care for others."[12] The Society of Pastoral Theology was founded in 1985, and the *Journal of Pastoral Theology* is published annually to encourage research and communicate ideas.

While this book introduces Protestant pastoral care to a new generation of readers, other traditions — Jewish and Catholic — have been reflected in literary sources. Regis A. Duffy, for example, drew upon the historic sacramental mission of the clergy in his post-Vatican II theological model of pastoral care. His proposal is based upon the catechumenate, the lengthy process of candidate initiation rites into the church, that has preceded baptism and guided Christian formation. Persons baptized or healed within the Roman tradition are freed "to do the work of Christ," he wrote.[13] Sacraments, as symbols of Christ's real presence in the church, thus clarify the meaning and direction of human existence.

Having studied and taught in British Commonwealth nations as diverse as England, Kenya, New Zealand, and Australia, I am impressed with the generativity of thinkers and strength of pastoral care movements in other cultures.[14] Pastoral theology is coming to fuller self-consciousness with contributions from many quarters still in future prospect.

How, then, shall we think theologically about pastoral events? Negatively, we should note that (1) while pastoral care may be isolated for specialized study, it should not be isolated from classical theology. We cannot erect a complete doctrinal structure on insights from pastoral practice alone. Again, (2) the Church's mission in the world will not permit a minister or congregation to spend full time with ecclesiastical contemplation, thereby neglecting the Church's larger vision and tasks. Theologizing must parallel Christian service, not replace it. (3) Recounting one's pastoral activities in the narrative form of anecdotes (storytelling alone) should not be construed as rigorous theological pursuit. Reports of pastoral counseling are preserved, not as tales of expeditions into the no-man's-land of child abuse, family dysfunction, grief, psychopathology, or depression, but in order that such narratives may become instruments of learning. Another person's pastoral work is inspected, not out of idle curiosity, but as an avenue to self-awareness and improvement as a minister.

Positively, Christian caring should be guided by theological wisdom which grows out of an inductive process. Note that the first two stages are of a different order than the third.

1. Whatever a caregiver's setting—congregational, clinical, or institutional—*one first describes pastoral events by contemplative exegesis of human stories.* Given the priority of personhood and ambiguous nature of existence, one narrates the essence of any "happening" isolated for special investigation. Critical incidents may arise as the result of historic change, accident, conflict, oppression, hurt, disease, natural disaster, abuse, violence, addictive behavior, or multiple causes. Here, as Patton suggests in his method, creative imagination comes into play.

2. *Our human stories are laid alongside the biblical story for normative guidance in daily living.* Pastoral theology at its best interfaces the *oughtness* of the Scriptures with the *isness* of existence, so that human experience is brought to fullest self-awareness and accountability in intimate engagement with divine Reality. Human dramas in history provide the small stage, metaphorically, for God's divine drama of redemption.

3. *Practical observations of a theological order, describing the substance and process of pastoral work, are then noted.* Such creative reflections provide functional data to guide pastoral actions of the church, and may supply fresh vision for traditional doctrinal exploration and restatement of classical theology.

While pastoral care presupposes Christian theology in its *modus operandi*, it is dependent upon cultural disciplines as well. The depth dimensions of personality, dynamics of religious conversion, significance of symbolism in worship, components of guilt and hostility, and soul care of beleaguered persons caught in the twisted existence of our culture, all require disciplined wisdom of today's ministers.

The method of pastoral work outlined in subsequent chapters employs findings from both the behavioral sciences and the theological disciplines. Biblical anthropology (which has a past, present, and future of its own) engages in dialogue with cultural disciplines that have provided fresh ways of thinking about persons in communities and new modes of working with them. Psychological dimensions of human behavior cannot be overlooked; yet neither are they the center and circumference of existence. Ministers are to view "cultural manifestations with Christian eyes," noted philosopher Emile Cailliet, appreciative of scientific penetration into the depth of reality and fresh information disclosed thereby. He wrote: "It would be a strange thing to deal with culture without ever learning anything from culture. . . . The knowledge of faith is no substitute for that of the specialist in [a] field, or of the [person] of culture in [a] cultural circle."[15]

There is need for exchange of information between theologians and scientists in an atmosphere of mutual respect. Do we need a reminder that the revelation of God in the Scriptures does not invalidate scientific research and fresh understanding? Science, correctly viewed, can become an instrument rather than the enemy of the Christian faith. God's design is that science, like every human discipline, should become a divine service. Scientific findings, while immensely helpful, cannot be absolutized into a new faith, for they are descriptive and proximate, not ultimate and absolute. What is true of theology is also true of science; *all* of humanity's partial wisdom falls under the judgment of God. While science's highest achievements have corrected our misconceptions and enriched our lives, science alone can never sustain existence in its eternal dimensions. This is the realm of faith.

The third aspect of method noted above is crucial to the Christian caregiver's theological task. Through reflection upon caring events and stories, in which one has sought to employ both divine and human resources, practical theological wisdom accrues in pastoral work. Imaginative reflection was illustrated above in the case of stroke and grief work, but is applicable in any pastoral endeavor. Let us be cautioned, however, that while certain aspects of religious experience may be investigated, the process does not yield what William James called empirical or scientific theology. God's providence, grace, love, and justice are not reducible to clinical conditions. While the truth of the Christian faith transcends all human attempts to capture and explain its profound mystery, we are able to construct statements "about God's relation to human experience which lead to strategies of liberating action."[16]

In this connection, it may be helpful to distinguish, as did P. T. Forsyth in *The Person and Place of Jesus Christ*, between "theology which is a *part* of the Word, and the theology which is a *product* of it."[17] This is akin to Paul Tillich's distinction between original and dependent revelation. He wrote: "An original revelation is a revelation which occurs in a constellation that did not exist before. . . . There is continuous revelation in the history of the church, but it is dependent revelation."[18] The Bible as "original revelation" stands as the unique and unrivaled record of God's redeeming activity in history. This is the truth of the Word. Theological wisdom that generates from Christian life and work, under the Holy Spirit's illumination, is a product of the Word. Such "dependent revelation" is the area of continuous inquiry of pastoral theologians and students of religious experience.

With certain criteria for caring and theologizing established, it is necessary to raise and answer two questions, significant for this theological perspective. First, what is the minister's essential theological identity? Second, in the light of biblical theology, what should be some primary concerns of caring congregations? Christian pastoral care needs a normative orientation in the light of diverse views concerning the Church and its ministry in our time.

II. Biblical Motifs of Ministry

We live in a "prose" world of advertising, news stories, office memos, acrostics, logos, statistics, and technological jargon. People living on-the-run do not think customarily in such biblical imagery as metaphor, poetry, prophetic idiom, or parable. Some observers think the imagistic wisdom of Scripture is far removed from contemporary understanding—angels, demons, apocalyptic visions, and shepherd and sheep imagery, for example.[19] Our consumerist society is accustomed to salespersons but not servants; to professional service providers but not shepherds; to highly paid sports, music, and film entertainers, but not to stewards of eternal mysteries.

Small wonder that pastors, missionaries, chaplains, and broad-ranging church and religious agency employees seek a clear, compelling identity. Identifying themselves with marketplace language—bottom-line and competitive-edge thinking—or with the latest space, medical, military, and multimedia scripts, ministers can lose their way. Ask a clergy panel to clarify the shape of pastoral identity. Their responses will reveal a plethora of possible elements in sorting out who we are. Admittedly, members of Christian congregations are not naive, helpless sheep; but neither are they patients, customers, victims, or clients! Modern ministers are not hair-shirted shepherds in bleak desert settings; but neither are they chief executive officers, psychotherapists, or public entertainers.

The Church Growth Movement (CGM) advocates an unsentimental, businesslike approach for ministers desiring to reach outsiders. Religious seekers prefer a church that offers a broad range of self-improvement options in personalities and programming. Growth-driven worship and educational programs are pitched to "shoppers" who pick and choose among churches as if they were boutiques in a suburban shopping mall. CGM watchers test a minister's integrity not by faithfulness to the Gospel, as church planner Lyle Schaller expressed it, but whether "the people keep coming and giving."[20] In contrast, authentic biblical leaders avoided certain syncretistic practices of their day (Heb. 13:7). Meanwhile, sympathetic critics wonder, "Should all congregations mutate into megachurches? How can Christian ministry today reflect the life and work of Jesus Christ as pictured in the Scriptures?"

There is a timelessness and truth of infinite worth in certain biblical motifs that represent initially God's care for all creation. Some of these are fragmentary, illuminating a single aspect of spiritual concern. Other motifs rise like mountain peaks as dominant themes, indicating salient features of the pastoral calling. Amid all the confusing pressures, cultural myths, bewildering doubts, and perplexities that beset the modern minister, some models stand fast and stabilize one's identity and calling.

Underlying such occasional word pictures as *salt, light, vine, branches, bread, fruit,* and *fishing,* which illuminate facets of Christian truth, are three central motifs of ministry in the Scriptures. Variations in interpreting the Bible are so great that no single symbol will suffice for everyone. Yet the bedrock of our faith includes essential pastoral actions: growing disciples, responsible caregiving, and shared ministry. Our pastoral identity is thus formed in relationships with God, in communities of faith, and between congregations and the world. While we shall focus on the tasks, relationships, and responsibilities of professional religious workers, all the people of God are included in these models. None of these aspects of ministry seeks an imperialism over the others. Yet the order in which they are presented has meaning. One who serves (redemptive activity) in the work of the Great Shepherd (representative role) participates in the Christian family as a kinsperson to others and as a descendant of the living God (the caring relationship).

1. The Motif of Servant Discipleship

A contemporary compendium of Bible topics includes seventy-seven Scripture references to *discipleship,* fifty-nine citations of *obedience,* and fifty-seven places where teachings about *servanthood* or *service* appear.[21] A servant, technically, is one who labors for another person, while a disciple is a voluntary follower or learner. Servanthood was common in biblical history and often mentioned in the teachings of Jesus (Matt. 10:24, 18:23–35, 24:45–51, 25:14–46; Mark 13:34–37; Luke 14:17, 20:9–18). Why does following God and loving him with heart, soul, mind, and strength—having no other gods before him—come first in all the commands of Scripture (Exod. 20:1–8, Deut. 6:1–9)? And so closely related in Jesus' repetition of the OT requirements was neighbor-love, linked to proper self-regard (Matt. 22:34–40)? Is it not because the covenant love linking God and all persons who walk truly with him on earth finds its meaning in Christian discipleship and obedient service?

"Come with me . . . " is God's eternal invitation to all individuals who "hunger and thirst for righteousness" on earth (Josh. 23:11; Ps. 18:25–26; Jer. 29:10–14; Matt. 5:6; Luke 14:26–27; John 8:31). Persons who obeyed the Lord in Bible times were called his servants and friends (Exod. 33:11; Jas. 2:23). And followers of the Christ in the days of his flesh were recognized as his disciples (Matt. 19:28–30; Mark 10:28–31; Luke 18:28–30). The clear intent of that close connection between servanthood and discipleship in the Scriptures is to continue God's redemptive activity on the earth.

Let us consider some aspects of this dominant theme of ministry. Patriarchs, prophetesses and prophets, priests, sages, kings and queens were leading OT instruments or representatives of God. Jesus Christ was recognized as God's "Suffering Servant," embodying OT themes and enriching them with new meaning (cf. Matt. 12:18 with Isa. 42:1 ff.; and Luke 22:37 with Isa. 53:12). NT writers noted that the Son of God lived among persons "as one who served" (Luke 22:27). When his followers sought prominent places for themselves, Jesus reminded them of his role as a servant under orders: "The Son of Man did not come to be served, but to serve, and to give his life as a ransom for many" (Matt. 20:28). When the disciples argued about their potential places of honor in Christ's anticipated kingdom, he admonished them to humility and warned them of trials to come (Luke 22:24–30). At the Last Supper, he "wrapped a towel around his waist" and "began to wash his disciples' feet" as an added demonstration of the nature of his office of servanthood (John 13:4–11). Small wonder that the Apostle Paul expressed the Savior's Passion thus: Christ "made himself nothing, taking the very nature of a servant" and "humbled himself and became obedient unto death—even death on a cross" (Phil. 2:7–8).

Paradoxically, the high God became lowly servant through the Incarnation, as Kierkegaard noted in *Training in Christianity* (1850). It is not surprising then that *diakonia,* the Greek word for ministry, was employed by NT writers as "the most favored way of referring inclusively to the church's workers and their work."[22] Each follower of Christ had a task to perform, emboldened by Jesus' assurance: "As the Father has sent me, I am sending you" (John 20:21). When Jesus commissioned the twelve disciples to a ministry of preaching and healing he gave them "authority over unclean spirits" and power to "heal every disease." He reminded them of the costliness of their caring. They were to love him above their own parents and families, to serve at personal risk, to be faithful even if they fell into unfriendly hands, remembering all the while that "a disciple is not above the teacher" but is "to be like the teacher" (Matt. 10:1–39 NRSV). Christ himself became the model upon which their discipleship was patterned; their work was conceived as a continuation of his ministry.

The constituency of the early churches performed "varieties of service" as they were endowed by the Holy Spirit, without thought for the prestige of office. In their earliest development the churches knew "nothing of the distinction between priests and laymen," as Emil Brunner wrote.[23] Theirs was a common priesthood (1 Pet. 2:5,9) in which all were active and in which each sought to serve faithfully as a minister of reconciliation (2 Cor. 5:18; Col. 1:7). The Apostle Paul indicated that the authority granted to certain leaders of the primitive churches arose not out of their superiority but out of their serviceability (1 Cor. 16:15 f.). While *diakonia* came to be used in a particular sense for the office of deacon, John Knox affirmed that "Its original more inclusive sense was never completely lost."[24]

The priesthood of the early believers was not canceled by the appointment of bishops and deacons, as the growth and orderly functioning of the churches made a more formal or institutional ministry necessary (cf. Jas. 5:14; Heb. 13:7, 24; 1–2 Tim.; and Titus). Clear expositions concerning the informal charismatic (or grace-gift) offices may be found in 1 Corinthians 12:27–30, Romans 12:6–8, and Ephesians 4:11–12. The Apostle Paul indicated that God has "appointed in the church" ministries, such as those of teacher, prophet, miracle-worker, healer, helper, and administrator. Clearly, these offices, while informal, were less than the total number of members. The Ephesian passage suggests that the purpose of such divinely appointed helpers was "to prepare God's people for works of service" and to build up "the body of Christ." Those who were "strong" spiritually were admonished "to bear with the failings of the weak" in order to "build up" or strengthen their neighbors (Rom. 15:1–2).

What bearing does this servant discipleship theme have upon contemporary ministries? (1) Pastoral care is to be viewed within the context of the *central redemptive mission* of the church. When we meditate upon Christ's seven last words from the cross, we discover his care is inseparable from salvation: he prays, "forgive them" (Luke 23:34); he offers "paradise" to a criminal (Luke 23:43); he entrusts his mother to a disciple's care (John 19:26); he feels Godforsakenness (Matt. 27:46); he is tormented with thirst while offering living waters of redemption (John 19:28); he finishes his work in humble triumph (John 19:30); and Christ commits himself into the Father's hands (Luke 23:46). That interest in persons which omits their relationship to God may be supportive, even therapeutic, but it is not pastoral care in the fullest Christian sense. (2) The *pastor's basic calling* is linked to Christ's own disciplemaking ministry (John 15:1–17).

Spiritual care may be rendered on a representative level by an ordained minister, but it may also be rendered generally on a personal level by any capable Christian. A pastor serves as a leader-consultant to the congregation, as an example to the learner, as a coach instructing those whose zeal outruns their skill, and as a spiritual director in the life and ministry of the congregation. In a classical sense, "the pastor" may be defined as "a member of the body of Christ who is called by God and the Church," duly examined and ordained representatively to proclaim the Word, administer the ordinances (sacraments in some traditions), and "to guide and nurture the Christian community toward full response to God's self-disclosure."[25] Such a definition clarifies both the instrumental identity and operational activity of the true minister and other Christian helpers.

2. The Motif of Shepherding as Caregiving

In the literature of pastoral theology, entire books have been devoted to the shepherd theme, and pastoral theological systems have been built upon it.[26] The character of God himself has been viewed supremely as that of a shepherd—owning, leading, feeding, disciplining, and protecting his people (Isa. 40:1–11). Shepherd symbolism pervades the imagery of the Holy Scriptures. The psalmist viewed God as the Great Shepherd—restoring the soul of a distraught person, leading care-receivers in goodly paths, protecting them from the Evil One, and supplying nurture for body and spirit in God's eternal goodness (Ps. 23). The origin of the term "shepherding" reflects the agrarian lifestyle of the OT world. Prophets who labored in God's behalf were viewed as undershepherds and were required to be faithful (Ezek. 34:2–10; Jer. 23:1–4; Zech. 13:7–9).

Because of its potential misuse by the power-hungry and breakdown of the analogy, given the universal priesthood of believers, some interpreters advocate using a clearer, more contemporary, figure.[27] They hold that it feeds on two unconscious processes—omnipotent feelings of certain religious leaders and dependency needs of many parishioners. When we recover the biblical perspective, however, we discover that the most familiar figure of Palestine was the shepherd. And sheep were esteemed, not despised, in that ancient economy. They provided a livelihood, milk for diet, wool for clothing, and were the shepherd's friends through the long days and nights on the Judean hills.

The Eastern shepherd was characterized by close involvement and great skill in guiding and protecting the flock. To this day, in developing countries and in nations like New Zealand and Australia where sheep are key elements in the national economies, men, women, and trained children work as shepherds. Persons holding uninformed stereotypes that picture shepherds always as males should travel "down under" and into those corners of the earth called "the developing nations." Women as well as men are involved in the work on Australian sheep stations; girls as well as boys tend flocks in Eastern Africa. Thus the central meaning of the shepherding analogy pictures nurturant, life-enabling, and nonviolent tasks except in threatened emergencies, when the sheep are endangered.[28] George Adam Smith has noted that the shepherd of Judea was at the forefront of Israelite history. This suggests the experience supporting the concept of God as a shepherd and people as God's flock (Ps. 23:1, 79:13, 100:3).

In the NT, the imagery of the shepherd was linked to OT history and prophecy (Gen. 4:2; 13:5; 29:9; 1 Sam. 16:11; Amos 3:12; Isa. 53:6; Jer. 3:15; 50:6). Jesus called himself "the good shepherd" who knew the sheep by name (John 10:11, 14). Of all the self-descriptions he used—light, bread, door, way, vine, truth—the shepherd metaphor was paramount in Jesus' thinking. "When he saw the crowds, he had compassion on them, because they were harassed and helpless, like sheep without a shepherd" (Matt. 9:36). He conceived his mission "to the lost sheep of Israel" as costing him his very life's blood (Matt. 15:24). One sheep that went astray required more time, skill, and devotion than ninety-nine safe on the hillside (Matt. 18:12–14). The parable pictured the significance of one person in the divine economy. The writer of Hebrews, reflecting upon Jesus Christ's life and work, referred to him as "that great shepherd of the sheep" (13:20).

The transcendent value of Christ's sacrificial love resided in the cross, which affirmed the worth of all persons (Heb. 13:20–21). Furthermore, Jesus devoted much time to the preparation of the "little flock," who would continue his work following his death (Luke 12:32). It was Jesus' last command to Peter to feed his lambs and his sheep (John 21: 15–19). Small wonder that Simon Peter exhorted his fellow elders to "be shepherds of God's flock . . . not lording it over those entrusted to you, but being examples to the flock." He assured them that "when the Chief Shepherd appears, you will receive the crown of glory" (1 Pet. 5:2–4). The spirit of the true pastor, then, is not superiority but courageous care and significant involvement in the life of God's people.

Caregivers find anchorage here at two points in biblical thought. (1) Jesus' pastorship speaks to a central concern in contemporary pastoral care and counseling—the proper relationship between taking initiative and availability, between law and gospel, and between confrontation and consolation (Matt. 18:12–14; Luke 15:3–7). Clearly, Christian shepherding both includes and transcends the concept of "tender solicitous care." The NT shepherd-sheep relationship is that of one *forming* and *leading* a Christian community, *nurturing* faith with righteous discipline, *guarding* with loving concern, *sharing* the life of associates, even *sacrificing* life itself if need be for one's people. (2) In scriptural imagery, "sheep" represent prized persons, created in God's image, who are beleaguered and burdened (Matt. 11:28). These were persons from all races and classes of humankind who were "harassed" and "oppressed" (Matt. 9:36–37). They filled the city streets, thronged the marketplaces, and walked the rough pathways of Palestine. Pastors today feel similar pulls of the people upon their own personalities, thus need to share ministry to achieve the church's mission (Exod. 19:5–6; 1 Pet. 2:1–10).

3. The Motif of Shared Ministry

We have considered pastoral identity in relation to God as servant discipleship and to the faith community as caregiving. It remains to say how congregational care touches the world in a systemic context. Ministry's concern is aimed at both personal reconciliation and social righteousness. Jesus Christ's call to care was a universal challenge, "and every believer" was "charged with carrying out that covenant."[29] In addressing his disciples as *friends,* he assured them: "Everything that I learned from my Father I have made known to you" (John 15:15). As Jesus structured this missional relationship with his followers, it was clear that after his death they would be compelled to serve in his stead (John 15:16–27). Beyond the cross/resurrection events lay their shared ministry in the world (John 20:21).

Early church leaders were convinced that Jesus' redemptive ministry would be continued through the church's global mission. The Apostle Paul often expressed the idea of mutual accountability with family imagery. "We are God's children," and "If we are children, then we are heirs—heirs of God and co-heirs with Christ . . . " (Rom. 8:16–17). He linked the idea of divine blessing in heirship with responsibility for others, both in and outside God's family. Even as early Christians had all things in common (Acts

4:22), God's people were to share with dispossessed sojourners in the world (2 Cor. 1:7; 8:11–15; 11:7–8).

Those adopted into God's family had a unique responsibility for one another. They were to "carry each other's burdens, and in this way . . . fulfill the law of Christ" (Gal. 6:2), even as each Christian had his or her own work and had to "carry his [or her] own load" (Gal. 6:5). The spirit of this passage lies at the heart of the mutual pastoral care exercised within the family of God. The individual had his or her own personal load to carry, like a hiker's backpack or a soldier's equipment. But when a brother or sister in Christ was overpowered and immobilized by oppression, temptation, grief, or any distress, the "spiritual ones," those who were mature spiritually and secure emotionally, were to "restore" that individual "gently" (Gal. 6:1).

Pastoral care is the task of the entire church family, wherein an individual's burden is lifted temporarily or shared continuously by the group. Ideally, the faith community bears the burden until the individual is able to assume full responsibility for life once more. Churches offering ministries of compassion are thus doing God's work here on earth.

Ministries in the church apply also to the world, for Incarnation means God seeks entry to every facet of humanity's life. Christians are concerned about human rights, religious freedom, peace in the world, and due process for all in a just social order. Christian care opposes oppression, advocates moral order, and seeks to incorporate Kingdom of God ideals in the political arena. For the Christian community to become "a light to the nations" requires consideration of the Church's historic caring concerns (Isa. 49:6).

III. Caring Concerns

The discussion thus far has introduced criteria for pastoral work and called into dialogue biblical models of ministry. Now we are to analyze four classic functions of caring in the Church. That care which distinguishes a true church of the living God from cults like the New Age movement, occult and esoteric sects, and secular social groups is the profound concern for the total range of human existence that pervades its life. Unlike temporal community institutions, which are concerned with limited aspects of existence — education, health, safety, justice, welfare, and so on — the Christian congregation cherishes persons in the totality of life because an opportunity is given. The church's ministry is personal and social, temporal and eternal, ranging from individual salvation to mutual support, community initiatives, and international justice. Let us examine these concerns.

1. The Ministry of Reconciliation

The Christian ministry of reconciliation is addressed to all individuals everywhere who dwell in spiritual darkness, estranged from God, from the universe, and from the human community. Consider some of the ways in which persons experience lostness in life. Jean-Paul Sartre's *No Exit*, a one-act play in the setting of the hell of religious eschatology, mirrors the horror of human relationships without the saving quality of grace. One man and two women, trapped in the sleepless abode of the damned, ultimately reveal why they were sent to hell. Each stares through lidless eyes at the others' shame in a forced fellowship of disgrace, disgust, and distrust. Expecting the judgment of red-hot pokers and torture chambers, the characters try to justify their past, only to discover that "Hell is — other people!"[30] They must experience each other's shame helplessly for "all time."

From Sartre's perspective, the ultimate sadness remains. The characters crystallize in a fixed, anguished hostility. Is this portrait, drawn by an atheistic, existential philosopher, unlike our human situation apart from divine grace? Against such a dark background, the "beginning of the gospel about Jesus Christ" is good news indeed (Mark 1:1)! The Gospels convey God's action to save humanity from rebellion, estrangement, and the bondage of sin through the reconciler—Jesus Christ. Paradoxically, God used the cross and resurrection to bridge sin's chasm, offering humanity himself again. The first Christians perceived their salvation experience in terms of a new relationship with God (2 Cor. 5:18-20; Eph. 2:16; Col. 1:20; Heb. 2:17). It is inconceivable that Jesus' reconciling ministry could have been accomplished apart from persons. Through this ministry, Christ called the Church into being and commanded his followers to incarnate love in all their relationships.

Pastoral care that is theologically sound must concern itself with the demonic forces and deceitful idolatries of worldly existence. Chaucer's Man of Lawe reminds us that "Sathan, that ever us waiteth to bigyle" is an ancient enemy who still delights to engage creation in mortal combat. Christian pastors must grapple earnestly with the final mysteries and verities of existence in order to exercise pastoral ministry with integrity. The Swiss Protestant pastor and theologian Eduard Thurneysen was correct at this point: "True pastoral care does not rest until it has carried the forgiving Word into these depths in the strength of the Spirit and of prayer and has really . . . brought [persons] again under the healing power of grace."[31] The human self, who experiences spiritual lostness in an immoral society, is reconciled to God, to self, and to others in the Christian community of true believers.

Reconciliation is or should be shared most intensely in family experience. Despite this ideal, however, fathers of every age eat "sour grapes, and the children's teeth are set on edge" (Jer. 31:29–30). Often the family circle fails to be an agent of reconciliation for one or more of its members. Family therapists discover every conceivable kind of anomaly in dealing with clients and selecting favorable therapeutic techniques. Attending to parishioners' spiritual well-being forms the core of a pastor's community building tasks. Frequently, one sees families torn by abuse, chemical dependency, or divorce and survivors living in the aftermath of emotional pain.

The *good news* of the gospel is that a Saving Person makes himself available to individuals' deepest strivings and anxious longings. Some family issues seem ultimate—like wanting a new house, having one's newborn infant look like oneself instead of one's spouse, getting a part-time job, or living in Florida instead of Maine. But they are only proximate wishes. Religion's importance in life involves more than getting things or spending time with church activities. Its true value lies in salvation. From the NT perspective, a person is not fully reconciled with God or "at peace" within until he or she deals with unattended family issues (Matt. 5:23–24; 1 John 2:9–11; 4:19–21). Whatever the grievance, one must "rely on the love God has for us" in seeking harmony with others. While peace within one's family may remain elusive, healthy "love never ends" its search for community (1 Cor. 13:8 NRSV).

If the church implements its ministry as a community of faith for burdened, grieved, disturbed, and shattered folk, its care must be carried from a formal place of worship into the human arena. In this life, where else is one to be reconciled except in family, educational, vocational, recreational, civic, and political relationships? A gospel that will not *work* in life is no gospel at all! While it looks at humanity's potential wholeness from the perspective of salvation, the church must also consider potential wholeness from the perspective of life in a radical Kingdom.

2. The Ministry of Righteous Discipline

Our pastoral ancestors were concerned not only with the outset of the Christian pilgrimage but with helping new believers cultivate a grace-filled relationship with God.[32] Discipleship training presupposes membership in a community of faith, or has church membership as its purpose (Matt. 18:15–35, 28:19–20). The ministry of righteous discipline, or Christian discipleship, involves both teaching new believers to "observe all things" and restoring those who have been drawn away. At the heart of "the Christian adventure," notes Edward Thornton, lies the human desire for God (and for fellowship, I have observed).[33] That heart hunger is the entering wedge in freeing persons from desires that are addictive and potentially destructive. The ancient practice of spiritual direction substitutes prayer—conversation with God—and contemplation of God's Word for anxiety, compulsivity, insecurity, and tragic preoccupation with oneself.

The word *discipline* is derived from the Latin *disciplina*, which means "school" and is rooted, along with the word "discipleship," in the Latin verb *discere*, "to learn." Baptist theologian James Leo Garrett has written that the "motif of responsible discipline in the Christian community has been repeatedly emphasized during Christian history."[34] The practice of spiritual direction has involved meaningful conversation, focused instruction, wise admonition, private confession and remission, public penitential discipline, and in extreme instances banning by the congregation or excommunication by ecclesiastical officials. Banning, while extreme, was viewed by at least some of the Protestant reformers as redemptive in intent, purifying the fellowship and prompting repentance in the offending person. The scriptural intent was to gain a member, not to destroy one.[35] Once censured, if the party truly repented, he or she was restored to the Christian fellowship in a spirit of loving forgiveness.

While the Protestant reformers exposed the Pharisaic legalism of discipline as conceived and administered in medieval Roman Catholicism, they did not abandon its practice or righteous intent. Calvin conceived discipline in the church as the ligaments that connect and unite the members of the body. Luther conceived discipline, in the form of personal conversation, as being joined with the public ministry of "Word and Sacrament" in an effort to extend God's forgiveness of sins to the individual. The very nature of the church as the people of God required the discipline of confession and forgiveness, according to Luther. His pastoral concern was directed toward the individual who had become guilty of sin. Calvin's concern was to preserve the integrity of the Christian community, as well as to lead the individual to repentance.

The practice of classic church discipline went into an eclipse in the centuries subsequent to the Reformation. It has been ambiguously conceived and practiced sporadically by various confessions but has claimed renewed attention in the contemporary Church. There is accumulating evidence of interest in a committed, disciplined church membership in both this country and elsewhere.[36] While specific cases of discipline will be noted in chapter 8, the statement of certain principles is in order here.

Positively and preventively, churches should do more than merely offer new members a brief, formal acceptance into fellowship. Instruction should be provided for all ages of persons in discipleship groups as well as in church school groups. Conducting baptism or offering prayer for new members *one* Sunday, while significant, misses the point of positive instruction in the history, faith, and life of the Church. Believers need guidance in the meaning and direction of their own life story, and in Christian vocation and destiny.[37] Negatively and therapeutically, when a church chooses to censure someone who has selected secularism as a way of life, properly "the church does not exclude [a person]; it simply recognizes that he [or she] is not one of them."[38] Such an individual has already excluded himself or herself from an appropriate Christian style of life. Discipline addresses the major growth challenges of the Christian life. Beyond self-care, it includes basic church history and theology, Christian vocation and occupation, family and community relations, spiritual and moral decisions, and civic, even global, obligations. Discipline's objective is spiritual maturity within the community of faith.

There are a number of perils and problems involved in establishing a disciplined church membership, such as radical individualism, shallow moralism, and judgmentalism. In evangelical Christianity it is the congregation proper, not the pastoral leader alone, which conceives and administers discipline in keeping with its polity or constitution. Although aspects of discipline may be exercised by members of the church for each other (such as prayer or confession), those who instruct and discipline represent the whole congregation, not merely themselves.

3. The Ministry of Mutual Encouragement

There has been a tendency in some discussions of pastoral care to conceive the pastor's job as a crisis ministry, a sort of contingency program for the accident victims of life.[39] From a theological perspective, an emergency response to persons in situational crises is only part of the truth. The Lord's care of all creation, described in the Scriptures, places the church's caring concerns upon a broad base. The full ranges of humankind, both within and beyond the confines of the Christian fold, are included in God's concern.

John T. McNeill, in *A History of the Cure of Souls*, examined certain classic documents of *Seelsorge* (soul care) in the Reformation tradition. He refers to the work of the Strasbourg reformer Martin Bucer (d. 1551), *On the True Care of Souls*, as "the outstanding early Protestant text on the subject" of pastoral care.[40] Bucer's writing reflected a concern for persons in the full range of existence, including the strong, devoted Christian who occasionally needed encouragement and affirmation, as well as prayer support. While the English Puritan pastor Richard Baxter (d. 1691) began his discussion of "oversight" in *The Reformed Pastor* with evangelism, he also summarized duties for building up the converted. His practice in the Kidderminster community included conferences with every family of the parish, eight hundred in all, at least once each year.[41] Baxter's intentional approach, because of the breadth of his concern, skilled ministry, and careful reflection and writing, needs to be restudied by modern ministers.

Mutual encouragement refers to a Christian's loving interest in and concern for what matters much to others. This includes the ministry of friendship, like that of David and Jonathan, which "strengthens one's hand in God." Most of us stand in need of encouragement and affirmation of our worth. Such care includes (1) the sharing of burdens (Gal. 6:1–5); (2) speaking a word in season to one perplexed or distressed (Prov. 15:23); (3) extending hospitality to an alienated individual who feels rejected or estranged in the earth (Rom. 12:13; 1 Tim. 3:2; 1 Pet. 4:9); (4) visiting homebound, ill, and imprisoned persons (Matt. 25:31–46); (5) praying for the victims of life's conflicts (John 17; 1 Cor. 7:13; Jas. 5:16); (6) comforting the bereaved (Rom. 15:4; 2 Cor. 7:13; 1 Thess. 4:18, and so on), even as God comforts those who are cast down; (7) and extending skilled counsel to those who seek guidance about some decision, relationship, vocation, or addiction (Prov. 12:20; Ps. 55:13–14; Prov. 11:14).

While laypersons are supposed to care for one another and for their religious leaders, they will look to ministers as models in the ways of encouragement. The church's supportive ministry must extend beyond the confines of four walls and formal meetings. Just as early Christians viewed daily living as a continuous form of divine worship, so caring is to be incarnated in the home, in educational circles, in healthcare delivery, in government, and in work and play. This looks toward the Christian ideal of life as a "living sacrifice . . . acceptable to God" (Rom. 12:1).

4. The Ministry of Social Concern

Our understanding of the Church's engagement with the social order is rooted in the Hebrew experience of covenant, the OT prophets' call for fidelity to that covenant, the ethical teachings of Jesus, and the apostle Paul's challenge to ambassadorship for Christ (Gen. 13:14–17; 15:1–25; Matt. 5–6; 2 Cor. 5:20). The profound concern felt by God's people for the welfare of others, beginning with individual Christian conversion, proceeds along a continuum of obligation that includes all of public life. Following the lines of Christ's summary in Matthew 25:31–46, which relates divine judgment to Christian social concern, churches have extended their caring ministries in institutional fashion through the ages. Jesus' great interest in the welfare of the widow, the orphan, the outcast, the sick, the poor, the prisoner, and the dispossessed has stimulated this extension of his ministry.

To speak of building up the church or of extending the worldwide mission of the church without due concern for the shape of human bondage and social justice would be a travesty indeed! The majority of the Master's miracles were related directly to relieving a specific person's need: blindness, a handicap, demon possession, chronic physical illness, hunger, and bereavement. Jesus' parables are laced with lessons in how to meet human needs. Widowed persons and fatherless children were some of God's special protégées in both OT and NT times. The jobless, expecting Christ's imminent return and history's denouement, were admonished to return to their tasks by the Apostle Paul (1 Thess. 4:11; 2 Thess. 3:10).

Such teachings mean that fair employment practices and the mutual responsibilities of employers and employees—including wage compensation schedules, and health-child-elder care provisions—are spiritual, not merely secular, concerns. In years to come, churches must look out for the deskilled, elderly, minorities, and underemployed persons needing retraining, and for children of single parents. Already, churches are taking urban gang life—as substitute "families"—seriously by providing supervised evening activities, opportunities for youth group discussions, and negotiating services to ease tensions among existing gangs.

In some respects we have witnessed the atrophy of Christian social ministries and relegation of social concerns to public agencies. A subtle process of secularization occurs as churches shift their responsibilities to community agencies and to professionals who may feel no relationship or accountability to God. Such social neglect and buck-passing will shift in tomorrow's churches, according to researcher George Barna, because successful persons will spend more of their free time engaged in social and political activism. National dilemmas like environmental protection, personal safety, crime prevention, abortion, and drunk driving will be addressed in order to have a safer and healthier world in which to live. While attending to such concerns may appear altruistic, "the underlying motivations will, more often than not, be self-centered."[42] Barna sees Americans having more free time in decades ahead and turning to volunteer and leisure activities for fulfillment and satisfaction in life.

How do we grow our congregations to live out these care concerns? Likely, it will be easier to sponsor small community programs than to erase structures of prejudice. Lethargy and indifference heal slowly. Task forces, rather than private actions alone, may be required to implement caring concerns. Provision for a city's underclass, aging, abused, jobless, and ill-housed citizens will involve both individual and institutional actions. The fact that churches establish schools, hospitals, and benevolent institutions does not cancel their obligation, for example, to provide for legal aid and public safety in their own communities. Peace and justice in the international realm are global, systemic concerns. Accountability for the salvation and welfare of the individual must be matched by concern for justice in the social order and peace among all nations.

Summary

Based upon the timeless witness of the Scriptures and corporate experience of Protestantism, these caring concerns are relevant in every age. Such patterns of ministry suggest guidelines for the church's mission in a secular world. The comprehensiveness and cohesiveness of Christ's ministry challenge the partial and superficial concerns of many congregations.

A minister's first concern is the mission and spiritual well-being of the congregation. Christian pastoral care anticipates inclusive interest in all persons without distinction of race, gender, social class, age, or religious condition. Care for one's neighbor should permeate all levels of life: personal, vocational, family, church, and public relationships. In the church, each aspect of ministry—worship, preaching, evangelism, administration, and education—is to be viewed *pastorally*. Such care is a reflection of God's matchless love and attentiveness to the welfare of his whole creation.

The incarnational caregiving introduced by Jesus Christ challenges and sensitizes each Christian to his or her "neighbor." I have said that pastoral care is Christian response to humanity's need. If we follow this clue, it will be necessary to establish appropriate answers to the right question: "Who is my neighbor?" The nature of persons in pastoral perspective is the theme of the next chapter.

Notes

1. Daniel Day Williams, *The Minister and the Care of Souls* (New York: Harper & Brothers, 1961), 147.
2. John T. McNeill, *A History of the Cure of Souls* (New York: Harper & Brothers, 1951).
3. Marie M. Fortune, *Is Nothing Sacred? When Sex Invades the Pastoral Relationship* (San Francisco: Harper & Row, 1989).

4. William S. Schmidt's review of John Patton's *From Ministry to Theology: Pastoral Action and Reflection* (Nashville: Abingdon Press, 1990), in *The Journal of Pastoral Care* (Winter 1990): 402–06.

5. Walter Brueggemann, *Power, Providence, and Personality: Biblical Insight into Life and Ministry* (Louisville: Westminster/John Knox Press, 1990), 13.

6. See Earl E. Shelp and Ronald H. Sunderland, eds., *The Pastor as Theologian* (New York: Pilgrim Press, 1988). Cf. Herschel H. Hobbs, *You Are Chosen: The Priesthood of All Believers* (San Francisco: Harper & Row, 1990).

7. Martin Thornton, *Pastoral Theology: A Reorientation* (London: S.P.C.K., 1956), 7.

8. Patton, *From Ministry to Theology*, 97, 18.

9. Rodney J. Hunter, "What is Pastoral About Pastoral Theology? Insights From Eight Years Shepherding the *Dictionary of Pastoral Care and Counseling*," *Journal of Pastoral Theology* 1 (Summer 1991): 35–52.

10. In his serious attempt to reformulate pastoral theology, Hiltner affirmed the necessity of roots in the "eternal verities of the faith" (*Preface to Pastoral Theology* [Nashville: Abingdon Press, 1958], 51), yet gave scant attention to these verities in his methodology. Hiltner did not begin with biblical categories. He presupposed them, then bypassed them in an effort to assimilate the contributions of contemporary personality sciences "into a theological context" (7). While he appreciated the traditional branches of theology, Hiltner proposed "another kind of branches of theology, whose focuses are a particular perspective upon operations" (21). He perceived three "operation-centered" branches of theology: communicating, organizing, and shepherding, which are to be developed as cognates to traditional theological categories by "critical and discriminating inquiry" (21).

His proposal "brings the shepherding perspective to bear upon all the operations and functions of the church and the minister, and then draws conclusions of a theological order from reflection on these observations" (20). For clinical wisdom, he examined the pastoral records of Rev. Ichabod Spencer, a Presbyterian minister in Brooklyn in the mid-nineteenth century, and extrapolated theory from them. This admittedly was a narrow empirical base for such extensive conclusions. It should be noted that this approach to theology had historic precedent. Schleiermacher, the nineteenth-century German theologian, held that "the proper study of [pastoral] practice would illuminate theological understanding itself" (46–47, 225). His method was akin to Paul Tillich's correlational theology in that "studying shepherding in the light of theological questions and returning with theological answers, can take full account of psychology" and thus remedy the present bifurcation of theology and psychology (26). Some of his critics might say psychologism overpowered his theology.

In introducing his proposal, Hiltner confessed that the "basic clue to the systematic construction of this author has come from Boisen" (51). Anton T.

Boisen's unique study of "living human documents" in the Elgin, Illinois, State Hospital as a source of theological understanding may be found in *The Exploration of the Inner World* (New York: Harper & Brothers, 1936; new ed. 1952) and *Religion in Crisis and Custom* (New York: Harper & Brothers, 1955).

11. Don S. Browning, *The Moral Context of Pastoral Care* (Philadelphia: Westminster Press, 1976); Donald Capps, *Pastoral Care and Hermeneutics* (Philadelphia: Fortress Press, 1984); Donald Capps and James E. Dittes, eds., *The Hunger of the Heart: Reflections on the Confessions of Augustine* (West Lafayette, IN: Society for the Scientific Study of Religion, 1990, Monograph #8); James E. Dittes, *The Male Predicament: On Being a Man Today* (San Francisco: Harper & Row, 1985); Thomas C. Oden, *Pastoral Theology: Essentials of Ministry* (San Francisco: Harper & Row, 1983); James N. Poling and Donald E. Miller, *Foundations for a Practical Theology of Ministry* (Nashville: Abingdon Press, 1985). Each of these Protestant thinkers is indebted to aspects of the classical pastoral care tradition.

12. Rodney J. Hunter, "A Perspectival Pastoral Theology," *Turning Points in Pastoral Care: The Legacy of Anton Boisen and Seward Hiltner,* Leroy Aden and J. Harold Ellens, eds. (Grand Rapids: Baker Book House, 1990), 77. Hunter served as General Editor of the *Dictionary of Pastoral Care and Counseling* (Nashville: Abingdon Press, 1990). Charles Gerkin drew on hermeneutical theory in his *The Living Human Document* (Nashville: Abingdon Press, 1984). John Patton advanced a theology of pastoral events in *From Ministry to Theology.* Cf. James N. Lapsley, "On Defining Pastoral Theology," *Journal of Pastoral Theology* 1 (Summer 1991): 116–24.

13. Regis A. Duffy, *A Roman Catholic Theology of Pastoral Care* (Philadelphia: Fortress Press, 1983), 91. Cf. Robert L. Katz, *Pastoral Care and the Jewish Tradition* (Philadelphia: Fortress Press, 1983.).

14. For example, S.P.C.K., London, has published *A Dictionary of Pastoral Care,* edited by Alastair V. Campbell, now teaching in New Zealand; and a series of pastoral care titles under the general editorship of Derek Blows. Australian scholars include: Graeme M. Griffin, Ormond College, Melbourne, *Death and the Church: Problems and Possibilities* (Melbourne, Australia: Dove, 1978); and Bruce D. Rumbold, Whitley College, Melbourne, *Helplessness and Hope: Pastoral Care in Terminal Illness* (London: S.C.M., 1986).

15. Emile Cailliet, *The Christian Approach to Culture* (Nashville: Abingdon Press, 1953), Preface, n.p.

16. James Newton Poling, "Hearing the Silenced Voices," in *The Abuse of Power: A Theological Problem* (Nashville: Abingdon Press, 1991).

17. P. T. Forsyth, *The Person and Place of Jesus Christ* (New York: Eaton and Mains, n.d.), 15, emphasis supplied.

18. Tillich, *Systematic Theology,* vol. 1 (Chicago: University of Chicago Press, 1951), 126.

19. Oden cites such opinions from writers as diverse as A. Harnack, 1896; R. Bultmann, 1941; and C. Wise 1951, for example, in *Pastoral Theology*, 51.

20. Kenneth L. Woodward, and others, "A Time to Seek," *Newsweek* (December 17, 1990): 50–56. Cf. George Barna, *User Friendly Churches* (Ventura, CA: Regal Books, 1991).

21. Ken Anderson, *The Contemporary Concordance of Bible Topics* (Wheaton: Victor Books, 1988), 109–10, 267–68, 355–56.

22. John Knox in H. Richard Niebuhr and Daniel D. Williams, eds., *The Ministry in Historical Perspectives* (New York: Harper & Row, 1956), 1; cf. also 1–26.

23. Emil Brunner, *The Misunderstanding of the Church,* translated by Harold Knight (Philadelphia: Westminster Press, 1953), 59–62. See also Eduard Schweizer, *Lordship and Discipleship* (Naperville, IL: Alec R. Allenson, 1960), 20–21.

24. Knox, in *The Ministry in Historical Perspectives,* 1. Prof. Knox insists that the terms "bishop" and "deacon" referred originally to functions and are not to be mistaken for the formal offices that appeared later; cf. 10. He notes correctly that the ministry was both "charismatic" (Spirit-given) and "institutional," in that its intent was the growth and proper functioning of the churches.

25. Oden, *Pastoral Theology,* 50.

26. This is in effect what Seward Hiltner attempted in his *Preface to Pastoral Theology*; cf. footnote 10, above. See also his *The Christian Shepherd: Some Aspects of Pastoral Care* (Nashville: Abingdon Press, 1959); and Charles E. Jefferson, *The Minister as Shepherd* (New York: Thos. Y. Crowell, 1912).

27. Carroll A. Wise, *Pastoral Psychotherapy: Theory and Practice* (New York: Jason Aronson, 1980), 223–24. Cf. W. B. Oglesby, Jr., "Shepherd/Shepherding," in Hunter, *Dictionary of Pastoral Care,* 1990 ed., 1164.

28. By rejecting shepherding in favor of the Good Samaritan paradigm of interconnection between love of God, self, and neighbor, Jeanne Stevenson Moessner misinterpreted the complex interplay of self and other in the biblical motif of shepherding as caregiving. See *Women in Travail & Transition* (Minneapolis: Fortress Press, 1991), pp. 198–212.

29. Hobbs, *You Are Chosen,* 80.

30. Jean-Paul Sartre, *No Exit and The Flies,* translated by Stuart Gilbert (New York: A. A. Knopf, 1947), 61.

31. Eduard Thurneysen, *A Theology of Pastoral Care,* translated by Jack A. Worthington and Thomas Wieser (Richmond: John Knox Press, 1962), 67.

32. See S. L. Greenslade, *Shepherding the Flock: Problems of Pastoral Discipline in the Early Church and the Younger Churches Today* (London: S.C.M. Press, 1967); cf. Paul S. Fiddes, and others, *Bound to Love: The Covenant Bases of Baptist Life and Mission* (London: The Baptist Union, 1985); also, Ernest A. Payne, *The Fellowship of Believers: Baptist Thought and Practice Yesterday and Today,* 2d ed. (London: Carey Kingsgate Press Ltd., 1952).

33. Cf. Edward E. Thornton, *The Christian Adventure* (Nashville: Broadman Press, 1991); and Ralph P. Martin, *The Family and the Fellowship: New Testament Images of the Church* (Exeter: The Paternoster Press, 1979).

34. James Leo Garrett, Jr., *Baptist Church Discipline* (Nashville: Broadman Press, 1962), 9. Cf. Frank Stagg, *New Testament Theology* (Nashville: Broadman Press, 1962), 273–76 for an incisive statement concerning church discipline in the NT literature.

35. Cf. Don Baker, *Beyond Forgiveness: The Healing Touch of Church Discipline* (Portland: Multnomah Press, 1984); John White and Ken Blue, *Healing the Wounded: The Costly Love of Church Discipline* (Leicester: Inter-Varsity Press, 1985); and Nigel G. Wright, *The Radical Kingdom: Restoration in Theory and Practice* (Eastbourne, Sussex: Kingsway Publications, 1986).

36. Michael John Collis, "The Theology and Practice of Church Discipline Amongst Baptists with Particular Reference to . . . the United Kingdom," Unpublished Master's thesis in Pastoral Theology, Heythrop College, University of London (July 1988). Cf. Tilden Edwards, *Living in the Presence: Disciplines for the Spiritual Heart* (San Francisco: Harper & Row, Publishers, 1988); Cheslyn Jones *et al.*, eds., *The Study of Spirituality* (New York: Oxford University Press, 1986); Kenneth Leech, *Soul Friend: The Practice of Christian Spirituality* (Harper & Row, 1977); cf. Gerald G. May, *Will and Spirit: A Contemplative Psychology* (Harper & Row, 1987); Gerald G. May, *The Awakened Heart: Living Beyond Addiction* (Harper San Francisco, 1991).

37. A model of such practical discipline is Ernest E. Mosley, *Basics for New Baptists* (Nashville: Convention Press, 1989); also, see Glenn A. Smith and Henry Webb, *Planning and Conducting New Church Member Training* (Nashville: Convention Press, 1989).

38. Stagg, *New Testament Theology*, 275.

39. Some readers of Wayne E. Oates's *The Christian Pastor*, 3d ed. rev. (Philadelphia: Westminster Press, 1982) adopted uncritically his "crisis ministry" approach in chapter 1. They thereby missed the import of his valuable discussion of various levels of pastoral care in subsequent chapters. See also David K. Switzer, *Pastoral Care Emergencies: Ministering to People in Crisis* (New York: Paulist Press, 1989).

40. John T. McNeill, *A History of the Cure of Souls* (New York: Harper & Row, 1951), 180; cf. 177–81.

41. Richard Baxter, *The Reformed Pastor: A Pattern for Ministry*, edited with a preface by Samuel Palmer (London: J. Buckland, 1766), cf. Part II, "A stated minister's duty with respect to his people." A paperback edition of Baxter's work is available (Portland: Multnomah Press, 1983).

42. George Barna, *The Frog in the Kettle: What Christians Need to Know About Life in the Year 2000* (Ventura, CA: Regal Books, 1990), 89.

Suggested Reading

Clebsch, William A. and Charles R. Jaekle. *Pastoral Care in Historical Perspective.* New York: Jason Aronson, 1983. Pictures the chief functions, varied rituals, and twenty-one exhibits of the history of the pastoral art. A major work.

Holifield, E. Brooks. *A History of Pastoral Care in America.* Nashville: Abingdon Press, 1983. Provides contextual understanding of the minister's chief functions in light of American history and culture.

Hunter, Rodney J., ed. "Commitment" and "Pastoral Theology," in *Dictionary of Pastoral Care and Counseling* (Nashville: Abingdon Press, 1990). Comprehensive discussions of current Protestant and Roman Catholic thought. A valuable resource.

McNeill, John T. *A History of the Cure of Souls.* New York: Harper & Row, 1951. (Chapters 1, 4, 5, 15.) A comprehensive account of the poetic-prophetic history of pastoral care from biblical times to the present.

Oden, Thomas C. *Pastoral Theology: Essentials of Ministry.* San Francisco: Harper & Row, 1983. Cf. Oden, *Becoming a Minister.* New York: Crossroad, 1987. A Methodist theological educator returns to classical roots of pastoral care.

Poling, James Newton. *The Abuse of Power: A Theological Problem.* Nashville: Abingdon Press, 1991. Theological reflection based on ministry experiences with survivors and perpetrators of sexual abuse.

PASTORAL CARE
AND THE NATURE OF PERSONS

One of the greatest challenges of our time is the effort to achieve human community in the unfolding dramas of history. Gaining every resource of understanding that will illuminate personality in relationships—human and divine—means we must deal with issues of the self within history. Despite this compelling theological task, the mentality of the marketplace has come to church in America. Researchers tell us what people seek in religion: "They are looking for a congenial group of individuals who will make them feel accepted." Visionary, growing entrepreneurial congregations that offer multifaceted programs for constituents are called successful megachurches. Plateaued churches and synagogues are viewed as merely "maintenance operations." Such a consumerist mindset affects how congregations view and use members. But there is more to this "user friendly" approach to religion. Televised religious persuaders broadcast, not only Sunday morning, but on selected channels day and night all week. Financial support for such expensive media ministries is sought globally, since many TV preachers appeal to multinational audiences. The rise and fall of religious media icons has spawned disdain for the Church in the minds of many people. Spiritual superstars are perceived by some devotees to be infallible. When a religious idol's shortcomings are discovered not only is a reputation lost but the Church-at-large is tarnished. In a media-driven world, the public is a market. Such pragmatism influences our view of human personality.

One church watcher observed, "This is where we are. The churches have to live where the world is." That is *part* of the truth. Ideally, God's persons are shapers of culture, as well as its products. We are compelled to explore, then *understand*, human expectations about religion. How shall communities of faith conceive themselves and meet their constituents' needs? Such concerns prompt us to focus on personality and how churches may reach persons for God.

I. Expectations and Obligations

Churches, historically, have appreciated the unique I/Thou nature of persons created in the image of God and have attended to individual and family needs. It is easy for the contemporary program-oriented congregation to assume that its organizational machinery is geared to serve humanity. The ultimate sadness is that a person or family can come into the life of a church, get caught up in the swing of things, yet fail to experience the worth of personhood within its institutional structure. Individuals are also subtly depreciated in those religious movements that seek mystical or metaphysical experiences by denying one's essential humanity. Herein lie two extremes in ecclesiology. The former is a quasi-realized eschatology, in which the institutional church exists by and for its own spiritualized objectives. It is conditioned to succeed in what is essentially an accommodation to culture. The latter is evidenced in esoteric, sect-type groups that seek to escape the pull of reality. Groups such as New Age devotees focus on cosmic consciousness and seek to move beyond boundaries of the ordinary self in order to realize the divine presence within. One is fulfilled in mystic unity with all creation and is promised reincarnation through death and rebirth of the soul. Religious adherents at another point on the cultural spectrum seek to transcend temporal existence by worship expressions of denial and escapism.

The testimony of a convict's spurious childhood "religious experience" once stabbed a church's conscience into greater awareness of actual human needs. A layperson had heard about the prisoner and asked him to recount his spiritual pilgrimage to a small church group. The man said that he had joined his parents' church as a lad in dutiful conformity to their expectations. However, his formal identification with the church was not confirmed by personal acceptance from the congregation nor by an inner awareness of God's Spirit. As he grew older, he drifted into indifference and immoral behavior, and was eventually caught and convicted for a criminal act. While awaiting transfer to the state prison, he experienced what he interpreted as a genuine spiritual conversion. His plea for human forgiveness, acceptance, and a chance once he was free from prison evoked both shock and sensitivity from those present. Had regeneration come too late, or would there be a chance to help this man here as well as hereafter?

One of the most significant services rendered to the churches by the social and behavioral sciences has been to restore them to a rightful mind about human worth in God's work. A corollary gift is the reminder of the social, historical nature of the church as a human community of God's people. Jesus once said of religious observance, "The Sabbath was made for humankind, not humankind for the Sabbath" (Mark 2:27 NRSV), implying that the church exists for human good as well as for God's glory. Later, the Apostle Paul reminded the Corinthian Christians that they were essentially a divine-human community. Their gospel treasure was communicated through "earthen vessels," focused on human needs, and dependent upon divine enablement (2 Cor. 4:7).

To admit that the church is a human, social community may be for some believers initially a stone of stumbling. Yet it was not to angels that the Son of God was revealed, but to finite individuals (Matt. 9:13; cf. Luke 15). The ideal is clear. Wherever the Church is gathered it is responsible for natural human needs, such as the need for social interaction, authentic worship, appropriate personal development and conduct, vocational usefulness, and the nurturance of hope in eternal life. Indeed, the spiritual and social needs of individuals are the elements in the life of a congregation without which it may not exist.

The Christian pastor's profound concern is to relate the gospel of Jesus Christ to every need and condition of persons. The discipline that vision requires is hard work. It is unglamorous work. To this end, the effective pastor must know the congregation in its social setting and understand its constituents' concerns. A minister's knowledge of human nature from personal experience may be superficial, and his or her gains from theological study may be ambiguous. While one called to lead and care for a congregation cannot dictate its sociological situation, theological climate, psychological health, and economic well-being, such a leader's work will be influenced by these crucial dimensions of human existence.

Recognizing that culture helps set the agenda for today's church is a key to reaching people and meeting their needs. A minister once contemplated an investigative reporter's reflections of profound changes in United States culture in light of his own experiences.[1] The reporter had set out to discover America, and found not one but two cultures. America One was the traditional nuclear family in the cultural middle—committed to career achievement and social status. Dad is in middle management, secure in a large corporation. Mom handles the car pool, Little League practice, Campfire Girls, and keeps the home fires burning. Parenting tasks are shared, but Mom is the biggest sharer as homemaker. America One, sadly, is a vanishing breed.

America Two was comprised of empty nesters, single parents, remarried and stepfamily structures, cohabiting heterosexual couples, and the single person who has no intention of becoming a parent. Instead of nice houses and groomed lawns in the suburbs, America Two lived in high-rise apartment buildings or a two hundred-unit complex near some expressway. The dual-career family was a growing sector, with professional women exchanging domestic role patterns with busy husbands. Commuter marriages and fast-track schedules required new adaptational strategies for the stresses of dual-career family systems.

The reporter, said the minister, concluded there was a profound clash between cultures of the two Americas. Today's Church finds itself enmeshed in a multicultural ethos — challenged to match its resources to many values, tastes, and needs, including persons in poverty.

Had the reporter looked more intently at cultural changes, including hundreds of thousands of new immigrants each year, an even more complex picture would have emerged. Varieties of religious presence may be detected in folks on the cultural left, right, and middle. One social observer has distinguished nine American lifestyles. Another source interested in church and society proposed a pluralistic theology and ministry style, geared to three, not two, Americas.[2] In such a specialized approach, the church is challenged to diverse theologies — of life as *journey* for members of the cultural left; conventional morality and *popular religion* for members of the cultural right; and offering a *meaningful interpretation* to a confusing existence for members of the cultural middle.

Modern culture sends conflicting signals to the church. On the one hand, it says, "Go away. We've got enough problems without your sectarian doctrine, dogma, and hard answers." On the other hand, it is saying, "Help. We need you desperately to pick up the pieces and give some meaning to our lives."[3] Some ministers throw up their hands in despair of reaching diverse expectations in what often is a congregation of congregations. Many churches seek to meet needs like those noted above with pluralistic programs of worship, caring activities, and outreach in cafeteria fashion. Others are attempting to specialize, tailoring ministries to sub-congregations, hoping to tap into the ambitions, hurts, hopes, and strivings of at least some constituents.

Ministers and concerned congregations must do their demographic homework in order to design ministries that meet the needs of real people where they are. With varieties of human expectation and congregational obligation in mind, we focus on the priority of personhood in providing Christian care.

II. The Primacy of Persons

Leaders charged with the spiritual oversight of congregations will remember that God's steadfast love was revealed because of the significance of persons in the divine economy. God's compassion has always been tailor-made, fashioned in response to fallen humanity's needs. Pastoral care acts upon the basis of this principle of particularity—ministry conforming to the actual condition of a specific person or group. Diagnostic attentiveness to sources, not merely symptoms, of personal and social maladies is the hallmark of true pastoral care. One's view of human selfhood in the social order is the tacit and crucial correlate of this principle.

Personal meanings in pastoral caregiving and counseling are understood against developmental and cultural backgrounds. Behind the perceived world of each care-receiver is the pastor's theological anthropology and assumptions about personality.

1. *The minister is a member of the* laos—*the people of God—and is to relate to other members redemptively.* The people who form the congregation, the church committees, the diaconate, the teachers—these are the people with whom the minister and minister's family share a common life under God. What needs shall worship and preaching address? What changes shall a pastor seek to facilitate, and at what risk in ministry practice? Do church members let the pastor lead? What word of hope shall one speak to those "who hunger and thirst for righteousness?" Moreover, pastoral care implies a reciprocal relationship between pastor and people. They are both subjects and objects of mutual care one for the other, and the common object of God's gracious care. A caregiver's family are Christian adventurers, too, with heart hungers, needs for achievement, doubts, and desires for life-in-community. Part of a congregation's calling is "caring for the caregivers," with adequate economic and emotional support for the church staff.[4]

Occasionally, a religious leader's views will clash with those of some power-hungry individual, governing board members, or church group. Painful estrangements may disrupt their life together. Yet one's lot is cast with the faith community that employs his or her services. While agreement may not be reached on all financial or personnel needs and programs of action, a congregation should support its ministers and sustain volunteers for their tasks. Most people who experience their minister's genuine concern will respond in like manner. Trust builds over time. Ideally, their interpersonal communications are helpful and positive and loving. Occasional differences of opinion, hidden agendas, and unethical power plays are stressors pastors must learn to live with.

2. *To understand human nature and needs is imperative because of the crucial place of the meaning of persons in one's theology and pastoral practice.* One must understand the biblical doctrine of the human (*anthropos*) in relation to the divine reality (*theos*) in order to understand the nature of sin and redemption. Theologian Frank Stagg wrote that in the doctrine of humankind, "one stands at the crossroads [of] theology. The road [one] chooses here determines the balance of [one's] theology."[5] The Bible speaks of God creating human beings in God's own image for fellowship with the Creator and of ordering a way of life for persons which was best for them (Gen. 1:26 f., 2:7 f.). God designed the family for human perpetuity and community and placed man and woman in the world for a responsible existence (Gen. 2:15–24). When those beings rebelled against their ordained existence, they selected a way of life different from God's way and were fully responsible for their decisions.

The ingress of sin and resulting human bondage can be understood only in terms of humankind's rejection of God's companionship and way of life (Gen. 3:1–10). Once Adam and Eve exercised their freedom and made their fatal choice, they experienced shame and were estranged from God and from each other (Gen. 3:11–12). As the man fled God's face and blamed the woman for beguiling him, love degenerated into fear. Adam lost the life he prized and was driven from the garden into the tragic plight of sinful existence. Thus mortals became guilty of sin and were destructively related to their Creator, to themselves, to family members, and to all the created order (Gen. 3–4).

Biblical history is the story of humanity's alienation and of God's free gift of spiritual rebirth through the grace of our Lord Jesus Christ. The Apostle Paul wrote concerning the Jewish-Gentile enmity:

> In Christ Jesus you who once were far away have been brought near. . . . For he himself is our peace, who has made the two one and has destroyed the barrier, the dividing wall of hostility, by abolishing . . . the law with its commandments and regulations. His purpose was to create in himself one new [person] out of the two, thus making peace, . . . to reconcile both of them to God through the cross, by which he put to death their hostility. (Eph. 2:13–16)

Those once "not a people" were thus enabled to become "God's people" by divine mercy (1 Pet. 2:10). Through the Atonement, God made true selfhood possible in that the Son reconciled "to himself all things . . . through his blood, shed on the cross" (Col. 1:20). Christ enables each person to face his or her own sinful history with courage and forgives each person who faces the cross with trust and true repentance. For a person honestly to face the cross is like facing death oneself—the death of the old self. The cross focuses the particular shape of each person's sin, frees the person from bondage in sin, restores the penitent to a rightful mind, and gives one power to become a true child of God (John 1:12). The redeemed self is viewed biblically as both a new being and as a "babe," *becoming* through processes of discipleship and faith development. Even an adult believer in Christ may be unable to assume the risks and responsibilities of volunteer religious service immediately. Those who admire the Christian example of the Apostle Paul tend to overlook the quiet years following his conversion experience, which he spent in Arabia, Damascus, and Tarsus, before joining Barnabas for the first missionary journey (Gal. 1:17–18; Acts 9:30, 11:25–26). Paul was not pressed into immediate service by God's Spirit, but was led into quiet places for meditation, spiritual development, and new resources. A dynamic view of salvation recognizes the individual's responsibility for growth as well as God's transforming companionship on what Australian Athal Gill calls "life on the road."[6]

Christian selfhood develops in terms of one's age, personal history, mental ability, previous addictions, relationship patterns, physical and emotional health, intentional goals, community of faith, and cultural milieu. A new convert's past predicament and continuing needs both require skilled pastoral oversight and group support.[7] It would be preposterous to assume that one who has experienced Christian conversion is thereby safe, in a protective vacuum, isolated from temptations and the vulnerability of human existence. Fortunately, the believer approaches life from a new point of view, reinforced by the resources of God's Holy Spirit. One so committed affirms with the apostle: "By the grace of God I am what I am" (1 Cor. 15:10).

3. One's view of persons is crucial in the sense that *the principles of personality drawn from the Bible and life are not to obscure the object of the church's concern, namely the human self and persons in dynamic relationships.* Psychologist Gordon W. Allport, who contributed so much to religious understanding of personality, noted the tendency of some thinkers to espouse theories rather than to cherish individuals. He warned against any view of personality which is so preoccupied with presuppositions that it loses sight of the person's individuality, his or her "uniqueness of organization."[8] In this respect, many ministers are less wise and have less insight into human nature than they themselves imagine. Manifestly, it is possible

to have a proper theological anthropology and still be ineffective in a Christian ministry to persons.

4. The meaning of persons clamors for consideration because *the individual has become obscured in what social researchers call a "world turned upside down."* Some religious leaders have become accustomed to thinking of persons in cultural subgroups and to communicating with the masses impersonally in computer form and broadcast fashion. A hurt person is easily distorted into a stereotype or a caricature, where he or she is cartooned rather than characterized. An individual in mass society is in great danger of becoming an obscure statistic, lost in the crowd: a family, a social class, a political party, an ethnic minority, a gender group, a potential sales market, a professional organization. Our eyes have become accustomed to "worlds of pain," not individual faces. It takes great effort to see one face in a crowd. It was once observed about a famous American pulpiteer that he loved everyone in general so much that he loved no one in particular. In contrast, our Lord is pictured in the Gospels as moving among persons with a masterful capacity to view them as individuals and not en masse. Jesus "knew what was in persons" and thus knew how to relate appropriately to them (John 2:23 f.). This sensitivity to the underlying situation in the other person is essential in pastoral practice today. Good intentions and pious excuses are poor substitutes for facing the intricate perplexities of human existence.

III. A Pastoral Event: How Do We Help?

A counseling situation in a church setting focuses the matter of human complexity and cautions against mere dabbling in spiritual struggles. An issue arose when a teenage girl, popular with her age group at church and at school, approached the church's youth minister. All that he knew about her before the counseling contact was that she was from a fine Christian home, had one brother, was an outstanding high school student, and was considering a church-related vocation. The young lady, whom I shall call Jill, made an appointment, indicating that she wanted to share something that was bothering her.

Jill arrived in the minister's office for the appointment promptly. After a brief greeting, she related a series of incidents from the previous fall season that had provoked her pained state. After a football game, she and a few girlfriends had entertained the team, their dates, and several others at her home. They danced, cut up, ate refreshments, and were having a good time until some of the boys brought in alcohol. With agitation and some hesitance, Jill related how her pleasant party was spoiled by a few guys who became quite rowdy. She confronted them, requesting that they not bring alcoholic beverages into her home again.

The story became more complicated as news of the affair spread at school the following week. But it deepened in intensity in terms of a symbolic interpretation assigned to Jill's experience on the day after the party. The conversation with her minister reflected her vivid memory and sensitive spirit.

JILL: The next morning after the party, my girlfriend and I were cleaning up the den and I came across a picture that my brother had painted on a small block of tile that had come loose from the ceiling. I just glanced at it and saw that it was a crazy picture of a goofy-looking fellow. I put it back in place in the ceiling. Then I stepped back and took a good look. Oh, it was awful! All at once it changed! It had a horrible-looking face and a look in the eyes that I'll never forget.

MINISTER: What did the face look like?

JILL: Oh! It was horrible! [She began weeping.] It looked like Satan! [She wept softly.] I'm sorry I cried, but I just can't get that face out of my mind.

MINISTER: Did anyone else see the picture?

JILL: Yes, my girlfriend saw it and it looked horrible to her, too. She said it made her feel as if she were going to die. I felt that way, too.

Following this acknowledgment of what to Jill was a painful experience even after several months, the minister asked if her parents knew anything about her feelings.

JILL: Oh, no! They would think I was crazy. I took the picture and turned it over and put in back in the ceiling. It scared me so much. [Pause.] What do you think caused it?

MINISTER: Do you have any idea of why the picture changed and frightened you so?

JILL: No, I just feel that God is trying to punish me in some way, but I don't understand why.

Rather than yielding to her plea for an immediate explanation (which he did not have), the minister assured Jill of God's love, of his desire to understand and to forgive her. "You have trusted God for the answer to many other problems," he said, "and with divine help we will work this one out." He asked for the privilege of thinking about the matter and talking with her again later. After a word of praise for her courage in sharing her burden with someone, they turned in confident prayer to God for acceptance and direction. Over the next few weeks, they talked further of Jill's Christian convictions clashing with her conduct at certain parties, and of the conflicts of conscience this moral turbulence had provoked.

They determined together that the face of Satan that she had seen in the "funny face" was in a sense a distortion in her own soul. She attributed much more to the cartoon figure than she knew. The "Satan face" symbolized her own feeling of unworthiness, of being cut off from her trusting parents, of being punished by God, of even momentarily wanting to die. And in a sense her experience was a dying and rebirth to a new relationship of trust in God and in herself. Following confession of her real guilt and feeling true forgiveness, she affirmed: "I believe with God's help I can forget the whole thing. It is so good to know that God will help me in this matter." In a follow-up contact, the counselee reflected that a load had been lifted from her shoulders and that she was functioning happily in life's activities again.

Following this experience of confession, involving an underlying psychic situation, the minister determined to get some supervised clinical experience in pastoral care. He perceived that there was projection at work in Jill's distorted "Satan face," but he was ill-prepared to grasp implications of the ego defense mechanism involved. He discovered empirically that certain acts have eternal, not merely ephemeral consequences; thus pastors must not brush them aside. Human relationships, even in fugitive moments, embody profound mystery, and our Christian ministry shares the deepest mystery of all—the life of the soul before God. He saw that a vivacious girl in a stereotype was just another "harebrained teenager." But, viewed as a sensitive person before God, Jill had deep feelings about her conduct and needed a caregiver's wise presence in order to realize true forgiveness.

IV. Pastoral Understanding of Persons

The youth minister's work with Jill cautions pastors who rely upon what one person called "sanctified horse sense" or the vagaries of intuition alone to apprehend human complexity. Bonafide helpers pay a price to understand the repertoire of potential coping styles of human behavior. A well-intentioned Christian helper may actually become a stumbling block rather than a wise caregiver to hurting persons. We recall the Apostle Paul's warning to presumptuous Corinthians because of their insensitive relationships with immature individuals. "By your [lack of true] knowledge those weak believers for whom Christ died are destroyed" (1 Cor. 8:11 NRSV). It is at the high risk of costly failure of both God and persons with spiritual needs that the contemporary caregiver remains uninformed about human nature. Ministers have often been guilty of a kind of reductionism in thinking about individuals, using labels such as codependent, neurotic, addicted, paranoid, sociopathic, gay, or compulsive to describe personality in an oversimplified concept. "Personality is far too complex a thing to be trussed up in a conceptual strait jacket."[9] With complexity in mind, there are varied perspectives for approaching personality theory that may be perceived by some pastors as being mutually exclusive.[10] Yet considered judgment indicates that the several approaches, taken together, furnish a more complete picture for helping persons-in-relationship. It should be instructive, then, to examine several sources of wisdom about human nature, behavior, and needs. To be disciplinary, Christian counselors will begin with biblical norms, followed by philosophical, empirical, and pastoral reflection approaches.

1. Biblical Revelation

The Christian minister is urged to define a biblical anthropology before fully exploring various other views of personality. In light of their specialized interests and education, ministers should be disciplinary (theological) prior to becoming interdisciplinary (perspectival) in dealing with persons. Such reasoning about sequence lay behind our focus on the primary of persons in Scripture earlier in this chapter. While that theological statement need not be repeated, one additional emphasis should be made here. *Humanity's true identification resides in the heart of God and was reflected in the face of Jesus Christ.* The Incarnation demonstrated God's concern to make himself known and desire that persons should come to true selfhood through life in the Son (John 1:1–18). Jesus Christ addressed us personally as "a life-giving spirit" (1 Cor. 15:45), one through whom persons may experience their *valuableness* and *acceptance* in the cosmic order. Before God visited with humans through the Son, sinful personality was humanity's only measure of itself. True or essential nature was veiled by distorted, alienated nature. The mystery of the Incarnation whereby the Creator visited planet Earth and identified lovingly with his creation pictures what true humanity should be. Biblical anthropology is thus centered in (though not limited to) Christology.

In Hebrew-Christian thought, personality is essentially a holistic, coping, and relational construct — a way of describing the *self* or *identity*. Amid all the prevalent models and partial views of personality in ancient thought, the biblical writers saw the promise of human wholeness inherent in the essential wholeness of God. At last, "the self was seen in its true light: as not the opposition of body and soul, nor the opposition of the natural and supernatural, but as the creature of the Creator, alienated by sin but capable of reconciliation."[11] In Christ, human forgiveness was not merely promised but accomplished. A true believer becomes a new creation by accepting divine love as the focal center of a new identity.

Since an individual's true identification resides in the heart of God and was made effective in the work of Jesus Christ, how is a Christian existence possible in this modern world? After all, that is the relevant question! The theological perspective reminds us that *oughtness* precedes *isness*; that God has a design for us unlike that of the world's fashion. We have been designed "after the mode of heaven" with guidance for life's relationships and "grace to help in time of need" (Heb. 4:16). Humanity's plight is to be perceived not as some pessimistic existentialists and optimistic humanists claim, but in the full light of God's design for creation and God's gracious action in our behalf. Realism envisions not only the urgency of a care-seeker's search for meaning or longing for self-improvement, but also sees the Light shining resolutely in the darkness (John 1:5). With this special kind of hope inherent in the helping process, a Christian minister enables people to perceive the difference faith makes in their lives.[12] Church becomes the caring place where people can learn values, rethink religion in light of eternity, and rear their children among believing friends.

2. Philosophical Reflection

Pastoral understanding of persons is rooted not only in doctrinal thought but in epistemological exercises which have been long in the making. Poets, philosophers, dramatists, political and economic theorists, and some scientists have slowly evolved a speculative anthropology through the centuries. The late Reinhold Niebuhr suggested that all modern views of human nature are adaptations and varying compounds of primarily two distinctive models of self: the biblical view and that of classical antiquity.[13] The latter view belongs to the speculative sphere of knowledge and has influenced concepts of personality even to the present day.

Speculative anthropology has generally developed in the context of a worldview wherein reason and enlightened self-interest have served as a substitute religion. Socrates urged his fellow Athenians toward one pursuit: "Know thyself!" Beginning with Platonic, Aristotelian, and Stoic conceptions, the classic view of life might be called *transcendental*. The ancient

Greeks viewed humans as a hierarchy of matter, body, mind, and spirit, in an ascending order of values. They held wisdom to be life's supreme value and concurred generally that the wise person would be virtuous. Matters of personal identity, growth, and education for life in the social order were most significant for Plato, Aristotle, Spinoza, Leibniz, Kant, Hegel, and William James in this century. Human perfectibility was approached through gaining wisdom in an immense journey over time. Yet the Greeks lived in a relativistic universe and experienced a growing sense of tragedy when it became apparent there was no straight path to human self-fulfillment. The classic view of existence was pervaded by pessimism, primarily because of the brevity of life, the Greeks' cyclical concept of history, and doubts about human perfectibility and immortality.

Transcendental speculations have afforded a meeting ground for educators and artists; poets and playwrights; for theoreticians like Pythagoras; metaphysical theists such as J. E. Boodin and Alfred N. Whitehead; ethical idealists such as R. A. Tsanoff and W. M. Urban; and philosophers such as Ernst Cassirer, Henri Bergson, and John Dewey. The romanticism and liberal optimism of the nineteenth and early twentieth centuries had their antecedents in speculative anthropology. These earlier reflections have given impetus to modern studies of the age—character levels of personality development that are quite significant for pastoral understanding of persons.

Numerous *naturalistic* personality theories arose during the Enlightenment among philosophers and researchers who examined existence as natural phenomena. Rather than seeing a being as a person created in God's image, observers like Hobbes, Darwin, Nietzsche, and Bertrand Russell viewed personality as a phenomenon of the natural order. Religion was treated by such thinkers as symbolic storytelling and a search for meaning by myth-making creatures. Like a train casting a shadow as it speeds along the rails, life was observed in most cultures to cast a religious shadow, which these theorists viewed as an epiphenomenon. The stimulus-response theories of John B. Watson (*The Ways of Behaviorism*) and the case for determinism by B. F. Skinner of Harvard (*Beyond Freedom and Dignity*) are of this naturalistic order.

Existentialist Jean-Paul Sartre coined the best-known catchphrase of one stream of modern philosophy: *existence before essence*. Sartre reversed the essential self of biblical creation and proposed that *existence* refers to the "human reality" of experience. Existence is what is—not what should be or might be. Most speculative personality theorists had only partial views of the self. Personality was conceived by abstractions like reason, will, instinct, feeling, body, mind, and soul. Human nature was bifurcated into essence and substance; reduced to a chain of ideas, a mass of protoplasm, a creature of values, a mechanistic stimulus-response organism, unrelated to a Supreme person.

The chief contribution of mid-nineteenth-century existentialist Søren Kierkegaard toward a proper understanding of selfhood was his insistence that the individual person be viewed wholly. He wrote: "The self is the conscious synthesis of infinitude and finitude . . . whose task is to become itself, a task which can be performed only by means of a relationship to God."[14] He viewed selfhood paradoxically in terms of its possibility and necessity. Becoming a self was "eternity's demand" upon humanity, said Kierkegaard, who viewed personality in eternal dimensions. For him, the individual was both an existential and a teleological being—forced to venture in life, subjected to anxiety and dread, yet directed toward an ultimate destiny.

While the Christian minister cannot just write off all speculative thinking about the self, neither can one uncritically weave its many threads into the tapestry of one's thought. An example of careful pastoral theological analysis of the search for a Christian self in premodern times is Augustine's confessions reexamined in *The Hunger of the Heart*.[15] It is a major study of human bondage and new life in God with relevance for contemporary pastoral practice. Christian anthropology is rooted in biblical faith, yet remains in polarity with this residual body of observation about human selfhood.

3. Empirical Investigation

A whole new arc of light illuminates pastoral understanding of persons as a direct outgrowth of investigations of concrete phenomena of people's makeup and behavior. In the present century, more fully developed scientific criteria have been applied to the study of nature and humanity than ever before. The central passion of scientific personality research is descriptive objectivity. A behavioral observer or social learning theorist, for example, examines observable data of the self-in-operation and excludes herself or himself from participation in human value systems. As a scientist, the researcher is obligated to obtain reliable information inductively on the basis of objective data-examination. An example would be to determine whether depression is related to factors such as age, chemical changes, gender, life stressors, unsatisfactory working conditions or job loss, childhood sex abuse, or alcohol abuse. Generalizations might then be made based on the use of personality inventories, physical examination, self-reports, and what is observable. It is necessary to appreciate the perspective of such empirical observers if we are to profit from their research, or indeed if we are to conduct true research ourselves.

Some personality scientists insist upon dealing with human behavior in abstraction from any relationship to God. They fail to consider intangibles such as a person's search for meaning, the operation of divine love, or the aspiration of faith. Such observers cannot do more than present partial knowledge of the essential realities of human nature. The late Harvard psychologist Gordon Allport held correctly that there is a "mysterious primacy" in religion that "demands our participation rather than proof or verification."[16] Psychology can neither verify nor disprove religion's claims to truth. It can, however, examine religion's diverse expressions and interpret the course of human religious development to its ultimate frontiers of growth.

Depth psychologists have made certain findings available about the rich dimensions of personality, which are indispensable for the wise caregiver's synoptic understanding of personality. Influenced by the pioneering research efforts of the Viennese psychoanalyst Sigmund Freud, modern investigators have looked into intrapsychic conflicts, childhood memories, anxieties, symptom formation, and resistance to change at unconscious levels of existence. Freud, a Jew by birth, wrote much about religion and its influence in the lives of his patients but erred in making his materialistic personality theory into a metaphysical system. His research claims have not gone uncriticized. According to Frank Sulloway, a professor of science history at Massachusetts Institute of Technology, Freud made exaggerated claims of cures, drew conclusions with little evidence, and generally ignored basic principles of scientific research.[17]

Christian pastors have not escaped the pervasive influence of psychoanalytic observations. Freud's contemporary Carl Jung succeeded in linking humankind's religious strivings to a collective unconscious through a theory of cultural archetypes.[18] These theorists and their successors traced a person's neuroses directly to unconscious, unassimilated experiences of childhood and offered therapy for such conditions. Many of their reductionistic observations became deterministic for therapists. Thus psychoanalysis is not just a view of psychical operations, anxieties, and frustrations; it is a philosophy of life and a method of healing as well. Once a person's repressed psychic conflicts were brought to the surface in a therapeutic relationship with an analyst, Freud observed that the patient "recovered." He or she might be viewed as "getting worse" by family and friends, however, for Freud's goal was freedom from unconscious conflicts imposed upon the *id* by the *superego*. Psychoanalysis, accordingly, is a backward look into one's developmental history, rather than an examination of present conscious concerns or an orientation toward life ahead. Its goal, akin to that of religious faith, is increased ego-strength.

Later twentieth-century theorists sought to correct Freud's limited model of dynamic mechanical determinism. Harry Stack Sullivan, Erich Fromm, Alfred Adler, Erik Erikson, and others conducted extensive studies in self dynamisms, interpersonal relations, and creative mastery of drives, as well as in psychic conflicts. These therapists have sought to enable their patients to gain insight into anxiety and stress, and to achieve freedom in relationships in the process of *becoming*.[19] Humanistic and existential views of personality by thinkers like Abraham Maslow, Carl Rogers, Rollo May, and Viktor Frankl arose partly in opposition to the teachings of psychoanalysis and the determinism of behavioristic-learning theories. Researchers in family process, family system theory, and dynamic family therapy have forged far beyond Freud's formulations.[20] They hold family wellness as a goal and are foremost in treatment modalities that view the family system rather then a designated patient as the unit of therapeutic endeavors.

Psychology's services to Christian caregivers are being increasingly recognized, investigated, and verified. Personality scientists have developed varied instruments for data measurement and testing, and for exploring the development, neuroses, and growth of personality. Influential gains have been made in genetics, personality theory, education, studies of crime and delinquency, work with trainable (mentally challenged) youth, addictive behaviors, substance and family abuse, pharmacologic therapy, and the rehabilitation of former psychiatric patients. Studies are being conducted in areas of mutual interest to theology and psychology, such as: faith development, value formation, gender issues, vocational concerns, parenting, guilt and forgiveness, prejudice, spirituality, aging, and grief work.[21] Christian ministers will be wise to observe these distinctions and varied resources when referring to theories of personality.

While clear distinctions exist between theology and psychology at abstract, theoretical levels, the two disciplines converge on the applied level of their mutual concern — life before God and in the human community. Interaction between members of the helping professions in rendering service to those who need it is essential. Some theologians, like Karl Barth, have urged caution in this regard. Others, however, sense the usefulness of learning about human nature from empirical inquiry. Barth's contemporary, Emil Brunner, supported empirical studies and said there is a psychology, a knowledge of facts about persons, which the Christian must weave into a whole picture of personality if that picture is to be true. In addition, psychology of religion exists as an autonomous discipline within theology and deserves careful study by ministers.[22]

With the contributions from empirical research in mind, what factors of human development profoundly influence pastoral relationships?

1. *Persons tend to relive early, primary group (family) experiences in all later relationships.* Personality scientists have demonstrated that behavior patterns are learned much like habits, though often unconsciously. Each person is motivated by unique feelings and drives, which are expressed in life's developing stages. This complicates the pastor's task of communication and ministry, for a helper is usually unaware of a person's self-system and dynamic behavior patterns in the past. While the family analogy of pastor, priest, or rabbi and people is appropriate in the church, some persons distort this connection and relate to ministers according to their secret ambitions or unresolved conflicts. For example, a minister may become the object of one person's affection, of another's dependency, and of another's aggression. Rather than react defensively—meeting one's own needs—the pastor should seek to understand why the person behaves as he or she does. Along with seeking a creative, realistic relationship with such persons, ministers should encourage the transference of their feelings to God, the ultimate caregiver.

2. *We have been encouraged to understand that all behavior is purposeful when viewed in depth dimensions.* This was demonstrated on one occasion when a child crawled under a church pew and would not come out with a mother's coaxing. When the child failed to respond to her soft words, the pastor saw the mother pull him forcefully from under the pew and scold him. As things turned out, it was promotion Sunday, and the child did not want to go into a new church school department. The four-year-old youngster, accustomed to being in one preschool-type group, feared a new situation. His belligerence was a facade for basic insecurity. Had the mother prepared him in advance for the anticipated transfer, it might have prevented his acted-out anxiety over the unfamiliar.

The episode reminds us that pastoral ministry must be tuned to the inner tempo of people's lives. Those in special need may manifest attitudes that are difficult for Christian workers to accept. Their actions may be contrary to the teachings of the Scriptures. As the helper recalls his or her own spiritual autobiography, such a person will "speak the truth in love" and relate as redemptively as possible to persons with varying religious attitudes and behaviors.

3. *Ministers should relate to persons according to identifiable clues in their relationship rather than through the use of prefabricated responses or pre-set techniques.* This takes into account the personal resources and limitations of both pastor and parishioner. We all have our "blind spots." A person may

not recognize the deepest reasons for his or her feelings of being driven by ambition to achieve or control some situation, of needing approval, of being tempted to sin, of feeling hostile toward or insecure with certain individuals. One pastoral technique will not work on all individuals. It is first necessary to assess factors underlying a person's behavior, then to intervene and respond appropriately. The depressed person, for instance, may appear in the community as a potential suicide or as a problem drinker. One's alcohol abuse may be a "way to be found out" during a dark night of the soul before taking some desperate action. Behavior may be a call for help, not a reason for rejection. The sexually abused youth, for example, may be deceptive at home and a troublemaker at school or church. The right question may be, "What lies behind his or her seductive behavior toward others?" not, "How shall that person be punished?" The girl who feels rejected at home or school may act out her resentment by a premarital pregnancy, though she may not love the baby's father at all. Merton P. Strommen's study, *Five Cries of Youth*, reflects what young people are saying about themselves.[23]

After hearing a broken-hearted girl's story of an out-of-wedlock pregnancy, a forced marriage, and an early divorce, a minister replied, "I am experiencing you now, Mildred, as someone who is starved for real love." She sat, weeping and nodding her head silently. She felt understood! Years before, her father had been placed in a mental hospital and her life had lacked male identification and support. Her sexual experiences and brief marriage relationship had failed to satisfy her deep craving for human intimacy. A Christian minister, exemplifying God's love and forgiveness, will seek to meet such a single parent's affiliative needs as a true pastor. At least some of her social needs can be met in a congregational self-improvement group with peers her age and in the church's child-care program. Where Mildred has known only rejection, shame, and betrayal, a Christian caregiver can help her to *realize* self-understanding, acceptance, and trust, so that she may learn to live again. Such a ministry "does not delight in wrong doing but rejoices in the truth" (1 Cor. 13:6 NRSV).

This reminds us that the pastor's concern will not lie in flippant emotional actions or temporary changes in counselees induced by religion used as a superficial aid or palliative. Christian faith is not "rubbed on" wounded spirits; it must be experienced to be authentic. Significant change in *character*, produced by the gracious love of God and growth of persons in community, is the pastor's primary concern. Alterations in *conduct* will accompany, rather than produce, character change. Knowing such aspects of human selfhood, the authentic minister will be able to work with troubled persons and surround them in the church with people who care.

4. Pastoral Interpretation

Concerned with responsible scriptural exegesis by Christian pastors, Eugene H. Peterson relates an incident from Herman Melville's novel *White Jacket* that serves as a paradigm for learning from pastoral counseling.[24] In Melville's story, a sailor complains of stomach pains to the ship's surgeon, Dr. Cuticle, who is pleased to treat an exotic case for a change. He diagnoses appendicitis and presses several shipmates into nursing service. The deckhand is placed on the operating table and prepared for surgery. Using the event like a teacher in a medical school amphitheater, Dr. Cuticle uses his scalpel with precision and carves open the man's abdomen. He points to the diseased appendix, removes it, and makes the proper ties to the intestine. He is so absorbed in his procedure, and in explaining the process to the sailor attendants, that he fails to notice their concern. By the time the patient has been sewn up, he has been a long time dead on the table. Dr. Cuticle, preoccupied with his technique, had not noticed. The sailors, shy in their subservience, had failed to say anything.

Interpreting pastoral conversations is surgical work. First, there must be attentiveness to what Anton Boisen called "the living human document." One listens in early interviews for events and life experiences with which a person grapples. The caregiver must cut through layers of history, culture, gender, race, age, family process, language, and custom in order to lay bare the essential story. The language of life experience should be "interpreted" in much the same way as a biblical text. One's provisional speculations must be "bracketed" so there can be a disciplined *seeing*, according to Patton. The competent counselor uses appropriate therapeutic techniques, but is careful to link the person's or family's needs to resources of the Christian tradition.[25] This process is akin to pastoral theologizing introduced in the foregoing chapter.

Reflection upon one's ministry—using contemplative exegesis of discrete life events, conflicts, frustrations, and the counselee's spiritual resources—enriches pastoral understanding and informs one's pastoral practice. In the past, too many ministers have experienced intense relationships with persons, succeeded with some and failed with others, without noting carefully what was happening. Periodic review of pastoral relationships will yield clues to human nature and supplement the pastor's understanding of one's Christian calling.

The verbatim report, with narration of meaningful events one remembers and shares with significant others, encourages student ministers to reflect upon the substance and style of their conversations. The student reconstructs the significant verbal and emotional content of his or her contact with a person or family and is asked to interpret what occurred between them and what course of action will be pursued in the future. Pastoral reflection upon care events and stories, in the light of the Christian faith, enables one to bring out of one's "storeroom new treasures as well as old" (Matt. 13:52). Let us return to the counseling situation with Jill, the teenage girl mentioned earlier, and state certain practical observations in the light of these criteria.

1. *A person under stress uses as a "minister" a Christian who is available, who is understanding, and who can be trusted.* Such a ministering person may or may not be *the pastor* per se. Jill's willingness to trust and decision to entrust the deepest secrets of her soul to her youth minister has significance for pastors. After all, entering into the initial experience of salvation is a matter of basic trust, of committing oneself to God in faith for life. When a person comes to the pastor or to a fellow Christian in a motive of trust, the minister will do nothing to injure that confidence and will seek to point the person's quest beyond herself or himself to God.

2. *Note how shame for one's attitude or actions brings the matter of one's identity sharply into focus.* Helen Merrell Lynd's *On Shame and the Search of Identity* illuminates this concept. Jill's approach to her minister was in part a quest for an answer to the basic question of her existence: "Who am I?" Her confession was an affirmation of her own Christian identity.

3. *Closely related to identity is the effect of guilt on one's sense of community.* What Jill perceived as sinful behavior cut her off from some of her peers, whose friendship she cherished; from her parents, who might think that she was "crazy" for feeling as she did; and from God, whom she felt she had offended. Her face-to-face meeting with a caring minister was a desire to meet once again with God, to know God's companionship, and to share community with God's people.

4. *Confession to God through a priestly person and the assurance of God's eternal and gracious forgiveness lifts the load of guilt that one has carried in secret.* After several burdened months of pretense, Jill "came clean" with herself and with God, dropped her defensive mask, and found that God had indeed in Christ already accepted her. Each step she took in the direction of restoration strengthened her purpose to know, do, and love the will of God afresh. Sharing reopened the door to Christian community.

5. *God is demonstrated as being active in the heart of things, in fact, in every area of life.* Meaningful life, according to the late Karl Menninger's *Love Against Hate,* involves satisfactory experiencing of five ingredients: faith, hope, love, work, and play. It was in a leisure-time experience that Jill

mismanaged things, along with the others, and felt God's frown. Play was made enjoyable again after her decision to live up to her Christian ideals for herself. In developed nations, where discretionary time and economic resources are available, there is need for a careful examination of options in order to achieve appropriate, healthy leisure activity and self-care.

6. *We should note, too, that the grace of God was made available to Jill and to her counselor by the Holy Spirit.* While the youth minister felt some anxiety because he did not have all the answers, he certainly felt himself to be dependent upon God's Spirit. Jill was strengthened despite her minister's human limitations. In their encounters and the intervals between conversations, the Holy Spirit served as their mutual counselor. God ultimately bore the burden of the relationship, through what we recognize as providence and grace. It is unnecessary to extrapolate further upon the theological dimensions of this one pastoral experience. The importance of imaginative, prayerful reflection upon one's pastoral practice has been adequately demonstrated. Such action and interpretation form the growing edge of pastoral theology from age to age.

Summary

The Christian caregiver investigates these various perspectives for viewing persons, not as a specialist but as a general practitioner. Investigations in each area of wisdom about human selfhood help us "recover our heritage, and to recover from it," notes Patton. One's goal, beyond any theory, is that Christ be formed in individuals as the true "hope of glory" (Col. 1:27). While the minister's technical knowledge is limited, he or she understands that other professionals also have their limits. After all, it is not to the latest theories that one is devoted, but to God and to persons. In that devotion, a caregiver seeks every possible level of knowledge, human and divine, about the life of the soul.

Notes

1. William L. Self, "Caught Between 2 Worlds," *The Atlanta Journal/Constitution* (June 3, 1990): G1–2.
2. Arnold Mitchell, *The Nine American Lifestyles* (New York: Warner Books, 1983); David A. Roozen, *et al.*, *Varieties of Religious Presence* (New York: Pilgrim Press, 1984); Tex Sample, *U.S. Lifestyles and Mainline Churches* (Louisville: Westminster/John Knox Press, 1990).

3. Self, "Caught Between 2 Worlds," G2. See Eugene H. Peterson, *Working the Angles: The Shape of Pastoral Integrity* (Grand Rapids: Wm. B. Eerdmans, 1987), 16–18, for an interpretation of the Church's expectations of people whom it ordains to be its pastors.

4. C. W. Brister, *Caring for the Caregivers: How to Help Ministers and Missionaries* (Nashville: Broadman Press, 1985). Cf. Robert T. Lutz and Bruce T. Taylor, eds., *Surviving in Ministry: Navigating the Pitfalls, Experiencing the Renewals* (Mahwah, NJ: Paulist Press, 1990).

5. Frank Stagg, *New Testament Theology* (Nashville: Broadman Press, 1962), 31.

6. Athol Gill, *Life on the Road* (Homebush West, NSW 2140, Australia: Anzea Publishers, 1989).

7. See LeRoy Aden and David G. Benner, eds., *Counseling and the Human Predicament: A Study of Sin, Guilt, and Forgiveness* (Grand Rapids: Baker Book House, 1989).

8. Gordon W. Allport, *Becoming; Basic Considerations for a Psychology of Personality* (New Haven: Yale University Press, 1955), 21.

9. Allport, *Becoming*, vii.

10. Cf. Les Beach, "Personality Theory (Varieties, Traditions, and Issues)"; K. A. Holstein, "Personality Development . . ."; W. E. Oates, "Personality Types and Pastoral Care"; and E. M. Pattison, "Personality Disorders," in Rodney J. Hunter, gen. ed., *Dictionary of Pastoral Care and Counseling* (Nashville: Abingdon Press, 1990), 899–910.

11. Wayne E. Oates, *Christ and Selfhood* (New York: Association Press, 1961), 213.

12. See James W. Fowler, *Becoming Adult, Becoming Christian* (San Francisco: Harper & Row, 1984; also, *Faith Development and Pastoral Care* (Philadelphia: Fortress Press, 1987).

13. For a trenchant analysis of the classical view of the self in contrast to the Christian view, see Reinhold Niebuhr, *The Nature and Destiny of Man*, vol. 1 (New York: Charles Scribner's Sons, 1949), 5–12. Cf. James L. Christian, *Philosophy: An Introduction to the Art of Wondering*, 4th ed. (New York: Holt, Rinehart, and Winston, 1986), 353–428, 507–604.

14. Søren Kierkegaard, *Fear and Trembling and the Sickness Unto Death*, translated by Walter Lowrie (Garden City, NY: Doubleday, 1954), 162.

15. Donald Capps and James E. Dittes, eds., *The Hunger of the Heart: Reflections on the Confessions of Augustine* (West Lafayette, IN: Society for the Scientific Study of Religion, 1990).

16. Gordon W. Allport, *The Person in Psychology* (Boston: Beacon Press, 1968), 146.

17. See the Modern Library edition of *The Basic Writings of Sigmund Freud*, translated and edited by A. A. Brill (New York: Random House, 1938). Cf. Freud's *The Future of an Illusion, Moses and Monotheism*, and *Totem and*

Taboo. Also, "Freud was a Fraud, History Scholar Says," *Fort Worth Star-Telegram* (February 18, 1991, afternoon edition): A-5.

18. Carl G. Jung's views may be found in *Modern Man in Search of a Soul,* translated by W. S. Dell and C. F. Baynes (London: Paul, Trench, Trubner & Co., 1933); and in two volumes of the *Bollingen Series XX: Collected Works,* vol. 7, *Two Essays on Analytical Psychology,* translated by R. F. C. Hull (New York: Pantheon Books, 1953), and vol. 11, *Psychology and Religion: West and East,* translated by R. F. C. Hull (New York: Pantheon Books, 1958).

19. See C. S. Hall and G. Lindzey, *Theories of Personality,* 3d ed. (New York: John Wiley & Sons, 1978).

20. See Abraham Maslow, *Toward a Psychology of Being* (New York: D. Van Nostrand, 1968); Rollo May, *The Discovery of Being: Writings in Existential Psychology* (New York: W. W. Norton, 1983); Carl Rogers, *On Becoming a Person* (Boston: Houghton Mifflin, 1961); also see W. Robert Beavers, *Psychotherapy and Growth: A Family Systems Perspective* (New York: Brunner/Mazel, 1977); *Successful Marriage: A Family Systems Approach to Couples Therapy* (New York: W. W. Norton, 1985); also, with Robert B. Hampson, *Successful Families: Assessment and Intervention,* (New York: W. W. Norton, 1990); Murray Bowen, *Family Therapy in Clinical Practice* (New York: Jason Aronson, 1978); Gerald D. Erickson and Terrence P. Hogan, eds., *Family Therapy: An Introduction to Theory and Technique,* 2d ed. (Monterey, CA: Brooks/Cole, 1981); and Alan S. Gurman and David P. Kniskern, eds. *Handbook of Family Therapy* (New York: Brunner/Mazel, 1981).

21. See, for example, the pioneering studies by Harriet G. Lerner, of the Menninger Foundation, *Women in Therapy* (San Francisco: Harper & Row, 1989); and *The Dance of Intimacy: A Woman's Guide to Courageous Acts of Change in Key Relationships* (San Francisco: Harper & Row, 1990, Perennial Library edition).

22. See Margaret Gorman, ed., *Psychology and Religion: A Reader* (Mahweh, NJ: Paulist Press, 1985); Cf. James Fowler, *Stages of Faith* (San Francisco: Harper & Row, 1981); Bernard Spilka, *et al., The Psychology of Religion: An Empirical Approach* (Englewood Cliffs, NJ: Prentice-Hall, 1985); Ann and Barry Ulanov, *Religion and the Unconscious* (Westminster Press, 1975).

23. Merton P. Strommen, *Five Cries of Youth,* rev. ed. (San Francisco: Harper & Row, 1988)

24. Herman Melville, *White Jacket* (Evanston, IL: Northwestern University Press, 1970), related in Peterson, *Working the Angles,* 74.

25. Charles V. Gerkin, in *The Living Human Document* (Nashville: Abingdon Press, 1984), 124–60, uses his experiences with "Susan Clark" to illustrate his method of pastoral interpretation. He contrasts psychoanalytic, hermeneutical, and theological perspectives in counseling ministry. In John Patton's "show and tell for adults" interpretative method, pastoral events may "talk back" to ministry and theology only at the conclusion of a lengthy

process. See John Patton, *From Ministry to Theology: Pastoral Action and Reflection* (Nashville: Abingdon Press, 1990), 121–22.

Suggested Reading

Aden, LeRoy, *et. al.*, eds. *Christian Perspectives on Human Development.* Grand Rapids: Baker Book House, 1991. Sets forth diverse views that together picture life-cycle theories in Christian perspective.

Browning, Don S. *Religious Thought and the Modern Psychologies.* Philadelphia: Fortress Press, 1987. Subtitled "A critical conversation in the theology of culture," Browning shows how modern psychologies may become quasi-religious ethical systems. A major critical analysis.

Fowler, James W. *Weaving the New Creation: Stages of Faith and the Public Church.* San Francisco: HarperCollins, 1991; also, *Stages of Faith: The Psychology of Human Development and the Quest for Meaning.* San Francisco: Harper & Row, 1981. Relates findings on faith development to the public ministry of the Church. Fowler applies six stages of faith development to pastoral care in *Faith Development and Pastoral Care.* Philadelphia: Fortress Press, 1987.

Hall, C. S. and Lindzey, G. *Theories of Personality,* 3d ed. New York: John Wiley & Sons, 1978. A detailed overview of personality theory and guide to original sources. Puts technical studies into perspective.

Levinson, Daniel J., *et al. The Seasons of a Man's Life.* New York: Alfred A. Knopf, 1978. Longitudinal studies of the hidden patterns that shape American male personality. Demonstrates how human beings change throughout their lifetimes. Cf. Carol Gilligan. *In a Different Voice: Psychological Theory and Women's Development.* Cambridge: Harvard University Press, 1982. A scholarly study of gender uniqueness and feminine behavior.

Oates, Wayne E. *Behind the Masks.* Philadelphia: Westminster Press, 1987. A psychological study of personality disorders in religious behavior. Important implications for ministry. Also, see *Temptation: A Biblical and Psychological Approach.* Lousville: Westminster/John Knox Press, 1991.

Parks, Sharon. *The Critical Years: The Young Adult Search for a Faith to Live By.* San Francisco: Harper & Row, 1986. Encourages persons working with student populations to help them grow from conventional to owned faith.

—

CHAPTER THREE

PREPARATION FOR PASTORAL CARE

Experience with the real world of vocational ministry is usually an eloquent, often painful, teacher. A young minister and his wife once related to a former seminary teacher their disillusionment about working with people in the church. Joe and Betty Wells visited their seminary following two years of service in a small church on the West Coast. While in school, the couple had done field education with an inner-city congregation. Once away, however, they felt ill-equipped to cope with the varied pressures of life in a western mill town. The lumbermen did not live up to their hopes and dreams of a committed, modern congregation. In turn, they were too sophisticated for their unpolished, blue-collared parishioners.

The people often asked Joe Wells what he did during the week. Some suggested that he should do manual labor alongside them at the mill—"something with his hands." Meeting in an inadequate building, living on less salary than they had anticipated, and facing opposition to their suggestions for improving the church, the Wellses tired and finally resigned. "Why didn't somebody tell us these things?" Joe implored. And Betty wondered anxiously, "Will people feel that Joe is a failure?" The teacher sought to reassure them; the chief problem was their own feeling of having failed.

The young couple had called it quits and moved two thousand miles back to their home state. Clearly, they did not wish to leave the ministry. They were not doubting God's call; rather, they were perplexed about themselves. They hurt. How had they escaped certain issues in school which they came to dread out in the church? Joe Wells sought answers to questions about *who* a minister is in modern life, how a pastor's *authority* differs from that of any other church member, and who a minister's *pastor* might be in future crises far from a seminary campus. The couple had become very lonely in two years. They felt cut off from other ministers, from their people, even from God. Additional seminary instruction was not what Betty and Joe needed, but recovery from excruciating pains of failure, a clearer definition of God's calling, and competence in dealing with people. The Wellses decided that Joe would spend a year in clinical pastoral education and, together, they would decide what they wanted in life before returning to a pastorate.

Such experiences or worse — even forced termination — might be multiplied many times.[1] Ministers return to theological campuses, take a "leave of absence" from a religious vocation, or go to centers for continuing education, more teachable after difficult church experiences. Often, a clergy divorce or family crisis accompanies career shakeups. One graduate expressed a common feeling in this way: "I knew a whole lot more when I finished seminary than I know now after five years in the pastorate." Only commitment to God will sustain one "in season and out of season," whether times are favorable or unfavorable (2 Tim. 4:2).

The present discussion is a response to some persistent concerns of ministers.

1. How is a minister to resolve the tension between the pull of one's own humanity and one's pastoral calling?
2. Given the pick-and-choose orientation of religious consumerism, with conflicting expectations about clergy, what clear vision guides pastoral vocation and gives one enduring hope?
3. With what spiritual grounding may a modern minister face the emotional, ecclesiastical, economic, and ethical hazards of one's high calling?
4. What preparation is essential for doing ministry that is indigenous to different lifestyles in our global culture?

We shall consider some threats to contemporary caregivers and some learning problems and educational possibilities for an effective ministry in an age of challenge and risk.

I. The Ministry and Contemporary Threats

Melody, an alert and caring pastor's spouse, experienced the ambiguity of deep and heated differences between two leading church members when visiting an adult church school group one Sunday. It brought home feelings of powerlessness to her and sensitized her to her husband's daily struggles. Melody's parents were visiting from another city, so she escorted them to an intergenerational class for a Bible lesson. The teacher's preliminary remarks about current events and prayer needs struck fire with a layperson, who expressed opposing views. These churchgoers sought something to enrich their lives; instead, they were caught in verbal crossfire. The profound diversity of opinions expressed reminded them of how easily miscommunication occurs in our high-tech world of religio-cultural persuasions, gender loyalties, ethnic orientations, transnational economies, environmental issues, energy concerns, denominational controversies, new political pluralisms, and a shifting knowledge base. Indeed, the prospect of working in a religious vocation today requires almost superhuman wisdom, endurance, and skill.

A group of church judicatory representatives was once asked by a theological school official, "What do we need to be teaching seminarians that is essential to their survival and effectiveness out in the field?"

A number of skills, like healthy communication and stress management, were mentioned. Then one representative observed: "A person becoming a minister needs to know how to love people." He implied the need for such qualities as *respect* for persons regardless of gender, age, race, health, or social position; *fidelity* in knowing a church's history, strengths, traditions, and unique challenges; *social skills* in greeting new members and families and being appropriately assertive in leadership; *patience* in dealing with different opinions or difficult persons and in receiving criticism (even accepting rejection); *wisdom* in negotiating compromises in committee and board meetings; and *courage* in pursuing goals and following guidelines once a congregation has charted its objectives and directions.

Social skills are essential regardless of the cultural situation and geographic location of one's ministry. Curriculum design skills are ongoing needs in helping constituents solve complex human problems. The caring congregation becomes a resource center for persons with concerns for self-esteem, grief resolution, marriage therapy, coping with family violence and sexual abuse, divorce recovery, and career change adjustments. Above all, one needs heart. As Paul D. Hanson of Harvard Divinity School put it, theological schools are obligated to provide resources "so our students can go out with hope."[2]

It was needs like these raised in the consciousness of Joe and Betty Wells and Melody, above, that they sought to name. With such life skills in mind, today's pastor or priest is confronted with some major threats, challenges, and opportunities in ministry.

1. The Threat of Ambiguous Identity

The threat of ambiguous identity demands an answer to the problem of who the minister actually is in modern life. Viewed from a functional perspective, the images of who a minister is and what he or she does appear labyrinthine in their intricacy. Is one a preacher, counselor, administrator, theologian, teacher, representative churchperson, or simply lost in the maze of passageways of a "perplexed profession"? Answers form a smorgasbord as ministers seek direction in what has been called "a quest for an integrated ministry."

Such a quest for clarity in church-related vocation was experienced by Bill Forrester, a thirty-year-old minister. He had volunteered for mission appointment, was deferred by denominational personnel evaluators, and referred to Edward Thornton for counseling.[3] They contracted for ten sessions; then, after six months, he returned for three additional conferences. Though he was married and a parent himself, Bill had failed to achieved individuation (or, in Murray Bowen's terms, "differentation of the self") from his parents. In an effort to avoid the stresses of leadership and risks of congregational disapproval, he had shifted all church administrative responsibilities to his wife.

Thornton's approach was to focus initially on Bill's motivation for and resistance to counseling. In time, Bill assimilated reasons for his avoidance of ministry tasks and elusive shadowy aspects of his personality. Months later he said, "I guess you could say that *I am possessed of a new purpose for being in the ministry.*" Thornton observed changes in Bill's sense of *selfhood* that directly affected his ministry *style*. In being "possessed" for the work of ministry, God was experienced internally rather than as an external, distant Voice. His "call" had come in the late teens; his "possession of a new purpose" in ministry came in mid-life. Bill now enjoyed Bible study. Freer of approval needs, he distanced himself emotionally from his parents, helped his church design a program to meet its own unique circumstances, related openly with the church's power structure, and freed his wife to be herself rather than working as church secretary.

When a person is *possessed* for ministry, observed Thornton, one is freed from role conflicts (Shall I do *this* or *that* today?), and risks integrity in interpersonal relationships. When one's *identity-as-self* is integrated, the aim of one's ministry may be clarified. I have called this center of gravity in ministry the *hope bearer* in the community of faith and *interpreter* of divine/human existence.

In a similar vein, though with a more focused hermeneutical passion, Charles V. Gerkin viewed the pastor as "guide of the interpretive process of the people of God."[4] Because certain of his ideas parallel my own, we shall return to his notion as the discussion progresses.

Thomas Oden's effort at clarification of clergy identity is both a critique and an appeal. Protestant and Catholic pastoral counseling is guilty of "an accommodationist theology," notes Oden, "that has seduced it into a ... disavowal of historic Christianity, its sacraments, doctrine, ordination, and self-giving service."[5] He criticizes modern pastoral writers for truncating classical texts of pastoral care, and appeals for recovery of a lost identity within the classical tradition. Both Gerkin and Oden have important words for us, but neither of them goes far enough in my judgment. Oden quite properly calls ministers to their heritage; yet he fails to move beyond ancient voices into contemporary contexts. Gerkin, on the other hand, proposes a schematic of narrative theology and hermeneutical theory that belabors method and complicates pastoral vision.[6] The elaborate procedure he proposes for generating pastoral theology is not to be dismissed, but must be tempered with the demanding realities of actual pastoral practice.

Tunnel visionists who tell the minister how to be a skilled preacher or a church growth specialist, for example, often elevate a person's anxiety by adding another function to an overburdened self-concept. The more one reads in the ministerial specialties, the more inept one feels and the more threatened one becomes.[7] In an effort to ease this anxiety and to avoid a merely functional approach, the present discussion views the minister's task as a whole from a pastoral perspective.

The biblical foundation for the caregiver's Gospel is a treasured given. Its redemptive message forms the ongoing missional drama for all the world's beleaguered players (Matt. 28:19–20). The biblical word is *hope* for salvation and the ultimate meaningfulness of human existence. Without this divine assignment and enablement, pastoral work is forlorn—a wasteland. As *hope bearers* in life's mysteries, tragedies, sins, struggles, and triumphs, ministers become interpreters of faith and moral vision. John Bunyan's "Interpreter" in *Pilgrim's Progress* is a timeless metaphor for persons who call others to faith through the practice of ministry today.

2. The Threat of Lost Authority

From the time of Christ, people have asked by what authority the ministry has been performed (Mark 1:22, 27). Disciples like Peter and John testified what had happened, what they had seen and heard as eyewitnesses of Christ's majesty (Acts 4:31). This was the authority of an authentic witness. The Apostle Paul conceived himself to be ministering "in Christ's stead," with an imputed visionary authority (2 Cor. 5:20). Various kinds of authority have been activated at different periods of the church's history: biblical, social, personal, and institutional. Joe and Betty Wells, the pastoral couple from Oregon, felt victimized by a shift of authority in their church to the lay congregation, away from the pastor. They were not prepared for the egalitarian, informal atmosphere of doing "God's business" in the Free Church tradition. Rather than seeking to enhance his influence by cultivating personal relationships, Joe withdrew socially, became bitter, and resigned his pastorate.

Today's churches have witnessed much ambiguity about the authority of the Christian minister. In a context of general education and specialized authorities in many fields of knowledge, people do not give as much weight to the words of ministers as in the past. Consequently, some ministers have sought substitutes for true authority, such as charm or charisma, political connections, prestige through visible success, pietism, and authoritarianism, which "lords it" over people but does not minister to them. This is not to imply that all hierarchical pastoral authorities lack integrity and authenticity. It should warn those, however, who would deify themselves (cf. Acts 10:25-26; 1 Cor. 1:12-17). People who ascribe authority to someone because of special office, knowledge, or skill may also deauthorize such a pastor. Any minister can join the casualty list of castaways who have lost their reason for being.

Some young ministers imagine that when they are older they will be accorded authority by old and young alike. Others, who lack professional training, feel that when certain ministerial techniques are mastered or academic degrees are earned, then their ministry will be genuine. To base one's authority on age or any other social norm, such as gender or ecclesial appointment, is illusory indeed! Some depend upon prayer and piety, hoping that their lives will be infused with power and that people will be moved by the sheer force of their words. Still others use ecclesiastical officials and connections for personal status and church promotions.

Many ministers find their authority in the "thus saith the Lord" of the Bible. It should be remembered that any biblical passage is available to every person of the community, not merely to ministers! Also, how an interpreter uses the Scriptures is influenced by one's own religious experience, by practices in one's particular denomination, and by various interpretations made through the centuries. Biblical authority is inextricably connected with such factors as the Holy Spirit's illumination, interpretation by one's religious community, the limits of reason, and the power of conscience (John 16:13). When the minister consults commentaries, expositors, and trusted friends and discovers contrary interpretations, where shall he or she turn? "What the situation calls for is a deeper and more active faith in God. . . . God alone is the ultimate source of authority."[8] Pastor and Christian community alike live under divine authority and grace. To claim authority as a "teacher sent from God" does not guarantee that one's guidance will be heeded in a day of freedom of conscience. If a minister cannot claim special power and privilege above any other Christian, wherein does one's authority of office lie? Acknowledging God's ultimate authority, the minister offers to parishioners not simply a set of authoritative spiritual facts, but oneself in a relationship that embodies both the spirit and intent of the Christian gospel. The minister's authority, humanly speaking, is vested in the parishioner's perception of the pastor's integrity, specialized wisdom as a credentialed religious professional, and in the unique relationship they share.[9] One is accepted as a Christian minister to the extent that one perceives humanity's spiritual plight and, as a religious guide, makes God known in the particularity of some life situation (Rom. 10:14–15). Christian history illuminates the guidance model of those who shared understanding, courage, and wisdom with persons facing ordinary problems of living.[10] The authentic minister, who can put others in touch with the living God, has authority both *in* and *beyond* himself or herself.

3. The Threat of Professional Competence

Possessing a ready answer for the hope resident in one's heart presses the Lord's servant to the limit as he or she moves like a weaver's shuttle through the tangled threads of people's lives. The Word of God must be related to persons in their situation in life. Yet the face of a parish is a thousand faces. It is not an easy thing to speak words that keep men and women on their feet when there is little ground to stand on. The religious guide's task and dilemma are very great.

Moreover, a minister to students, a military or industrial chaplain, or a missionary has to become a specialist with new breeds of beings, learn new languages, and master new cultures if he or she is to function redemptively. Responsible laypersons who spend their lives in the marketplace, among persons who may reject organized religion, find that they must become "all things to all people" in an effort to win some. Again, there are varieties of unbelief embedded in the secularism and scientism of modern life with which caregivers must be prepared to deal. Karl Heim suggests that if "Christianity is not to allow itself to be relegated to the ghetto," then "upholders of the Christian faith" must call secularists and scientists into serious dialogue.[11] Was Jesus merely employing the language of paradox when he proposed that ministers be as "wise as serpents" and as "innocent as doves" (Matt. 10:16)? From a human point of view, there is something of the quality of an impossible possibility about trying to become "all things to all people."

There is yet another side to this complex matter of competence. Some ordained persons dread what they conceive as an inevitable by-product of professional competence: that is, growing cold and indifferent in a dull professionalism. Ministers, like others in the helping professions, can become perfunctorily repetitious, even calloused, in their pastoral work — visiting the sick, counseling the perplexed, and burying the dead. Some pastors are ground down by life's abrasive pressures. Such weariness in well-doing cannot be charged to professional training and competence, however! It is possible for any minister to be overcome in the monotony of daily routine, to succumb to the depressing drain upon one's own physical and emotional resources. For such a person, life is no longer a mission but a drudgery.

In his book of plays *The Devil and the Good Lord,* Jean-Paul Sartre imagines a scene in the town of Worms, Germany, at the time of the Peasant's Revolt and the Lutheran Reformation. A poor woman pursues a tired priest, Heinrich, who tries to elude her. When he discovers that she wants information and not food, he pauses to hear her question. The sequence reads:

WOMAN: I want you to explain why the child died.
HEINRICH: What child?
WOMAN: My child. Don't you remember? You buried him yesterday. He was three years old, and he died of hunger.
HEINRICH: I am tired, my sister, and I didn't recognize you. To me, all you women seem alike, with the same face, the same eyes. . . .

He tries to explain to the grief-stricken, starving woman that "nothing on earth occurs without the will of God."

"I don't understand," she replies. The weary priest limps along with the pathetic figure at his side as he admits that he does not understand either. But, almost desperately, he admonishes: "We must believe — believe — believe!"[12] We see ourselves speechless in the presence of such deep hurt. Yet even when there is little to *say* or *do,* ministers must still attend to faith-care needs of their people.

The true spiritual guide realizes that life is never transformed from quantitative existence into qualitative experience by itself. As a catalyst accelerates a chemical reaction, so the skilled minister in the midst of persons induces changed lives, by the power of the Holy Spirit. Yet, like the catalyst, a caregiver is vulnerable, subject to change, and needs renewal in the process of pastoral work. "Who," one ponders occasionally, "is equal to such a task?" (2 Cor. 2:16). Even with the finest preparation, the minister knows that, ultimately, one's sufficiency "is from God" (2 Cor. 3:5).

4. The Threat of Human Existence

With a sense of pastoral identity more clearly understood, recognizing God's ultimate authority, and gaining professional competence, the minister is still threatened by the fact of his or her own humanity. A person in holy orders is a member of the human race and must face the problem of evil and experience the mystery of suffering in his or her finite existence. Each member of the minister's family is subject to the temptations, stresses, and hurts that are common to humankind. Yet some clergy cherish denial more than personal change. A Christian counseling center once received a "request" referral from county juvenile officials — a Protestant minister's son who had been arrested for auto theft. As things turned out, the youth complied with the legal authority's request for counseling despite his father's protest! His parents resented their son's arrest and preferred denial to substantial change in family patterns.

The minister is linked to what Arthur O. Lovejoy once called "the great chain of being." Like other humans, ordained men and women require inner renewal in a perishing universe (2 Cor. 4:16). The pastor labors in the faith that healing is available for human woe and divine grace is present in time of need. Yet this is not a blind faith requiring that all problems have final solutions. At least, from our viewpoint they do not! I recall a conversation with a Christian layman who had suffered long from an incurable neurological condition. "It may take death to cure me," he admitted cryptically one day in his hospital room.

Sometimes the minister's allegiance to God is the last nail that holds life together. A sensitive German preacher during World War I pondered this riddle of human existence in a sermon, "Concerning the Hidden and Revealed God." He had visited the wounded in a military hospital in 1916, and recalled the contacts with those brave soldiers who had fallen under enemy fire. "My thoughts went out to those who still stood outside in the peril of battle," he said, those for whom "the rays of the sun cast no light." God seemed hidden temporarily in the chaotic smoke of the conflict. Yet, he concluded, when "the contradictions of life threaten to break our hearts, we will still give thanks in humility and reverence that nothing has been spared us. . . . Never before have we been so permitted to gaze into the depths of God!"[13]

These poignant testimonies from literature and life have let us inside the minister's skin. These two—a layman and a preacher—confessed what ultimately every religious guide must learn. God instructs the heart, not merely with facts and propositions but by pains and contradictions. Such experiences explain why some ministers are threatened by the intimacy of pastoral care. Their clay feet are exposed; they become vulnerable and are subject to human limits. Intimate contact places one's own personality at stake. A pastor once burst into tears in the presence of a colleague and his wife whose lives had been temporarily crushed. Their sorrow over a child's rebelliousness reminded him of failed relationships in his own family. True pastors should rest their defenses and identify with needs when they walk through the shadows with their people.

Why should the priest or pastor deny personal creatureliness and dread to reveal one's own clay feet? After all, giving oneself to others is central in the Incarnation! That is what Christianity is all about—God risking himself to bring new life to all creation. Robert Frost once surmised:

> But God's own descent
> Into flesh was meant
> As a demonstration
> That the supreme merit
> Lay in risking spirit
> In substantiation.[14]

When one is tempted to shrink back from life's risks and relationships, the pastor should recall that Jesus Christ "emptied himself" and took "the nature of a servant" in order to bring about human redemption (Phil. 2:7).

5. The Threat of a Lost Heritage

Certain ministers who have been involved deeply in the behavioral sciences and in the practice of pastoral counseling have tended to become isolated from theological moorings. This loss of direction and process of specialization has occurred despite warnings against developing a "priesthood within a priesthood." Since the tendency of some leaders in the counseling field has been to minimize theology and ethics in favor of psychology, a departure from the pastor's classic heritage was inevitable. The chief metaphor for human maladies became *illness*, and interventions took the form of *psychotherapy*. In the process, much biblical imagery was lost.

If we begin with the premise that a minister's basic calling is to reach people and provide spiritual guidance to them, then pastors are moral agents and educators, not merely healers. Persons facing conflicting moral

claims in the private or public realm and, particularly, those who have violated their value systems, often turn to the church for direction.[15] We
recall from the Introduction that Libby Lyles consulted an attorney, her
pastor, and five physicians about the continuation of technological life supports for her mother. Other calls for pastoral care are more common:
adolescents, like Jill, bombarded with pressures about sexual conduct; parents torn between obligations to their children and their occupations; persons seeking recovery from family violence, drugs, or sexual abuse;
decisions about abortion and the right to life; and complex social and political issues in the public realm.

"The illness metaphor tends to mitigate the sense of accountability that
persons have for their conditions," notes ethicist James Gustafson, since illness is usually "something that happens to a person, not something they
caused ... for which they are morally accountable."[16] The challenge for
modern pastors is not to lay aside responsibility by providing casual explanations or dismissing concerns. Rather, one must be prepared to enter the
deep, often murky, waters of human confusion, confession of failure, and
desire for moral counsel with "accounting for hope" as a faithful guide
(1 Pet. 3:15 NRSV).

Accordingly, a look at these threats and obligations leads into a consideration of education for a pastoral ministry.

II. Education for a Pastoral Ministry

The serious theological student enters a professional community of learning desiring to address issues like: one's own personhood, life-cycle events
and family development, vocation under God, and pursuit of truth and ultimate matters of human existence and responsibility. A minister-in-training
is not a learner as far as the foregoing threats are concerned. Their shadows
have in some way been cast across the lines of one's existence. Yet the novice pastoral practitioner is not defeated by them. During preparation, the
student usually shapes a workable rationale as to motives for entering the
ministry. This task is tackled when the professions are under attack, and
some critics argue that ministry is not a profession. Others disagree about
the Church's purpose and clergy's place in public life.[17] The task of personal assessment and establishing a framework for Christian service, within
God's vision, is a complicated process. Meanwhile, the special shape one's
own particular ministry will take is formed—the pastorate, missions,
chaplaincy, denominational service, teaching, and so forth—subject to
reinterpretation in years ahead.

A seminarian's personal and professional learning tasks proceed in dialogue with new insights, occasional defeats, and determined pursuit. The student's identity formation is influenced by biblical paradigms, mentor models,
cultural images, current history, and personal participation in the life of
Christian congregations. The student's self-concept generally parallels an
emerging perception of the *raison d'être* of the Church. One's path points
to an increasingly complex and threatening world. Thus theological education involves more than learning skills alone or about one's religious heritage.
The theologue must fashion a consistent self-concept, develop character and
ego-strength, and acquire a disciplined style of life that will sustain his or her
ministry anywhere through a lifetime. Conversely, *even as the seminarian
receives, he or she must learn to give up some things.*

Facilitating the student's concerns for competence and character
becomes a prime requisite of theological schools. The seminary's imperative task is to create a comprehensive and mutually edifying environment
of theoretical and practical studies. The design of its curriculum, chapel
services, contacts among students and faculty, guest lecturers, and clinical
and field education experiences—all should enhance one's ministry for
God. And as with biblical Job's comforters, there are many to advise us
about that task.

Stanley Hauerwas and William H. Willimon have attempted a critical
assessment of contemporary culture and Christian ministry in *Resident
Aliens,* and have suggested an experienced-based curriculum for theological schools focused on preaching and worship. These authors scorn the
idea of ministry being one of the "helping professions," particularly if our
ultimate goal becomes performing "services" or providing "fellowship" for
church members. They believe such "sentimentality ... is the most
detrimental corruption of the church today. ... We are *not* called to help
people," they emphatically say. "We are called to follow Jesus, in whose service we learn who we are and how we are to help and be helped."[18] They
hope to turn theological education away from an emphasis on helping people per se toward a revitalized identity as "God's colony" in an alien world.

Typical of current self-studies of religious life in the United States,
sponsored by the Lilly Endowment, are Robert Wuthnow's words: "We find
ourselves faced with new realities that are sometimes difficult to understand or appreciate."[19] His examination of the restructuring of American
religion points to new religious identities, deep divisions among liberals and
conservatives, and new issues of faith and life. With such changes and
needs in mind, what elements should characterize education for the
demanding tasks of ministry in our dynamic world?

1. Learning as Quest and Commitment

A student minister carries his or her religious, cultural, and emotional background, as well as physical and intellectual equipment, to the theological school campus. If one is married, as many seminarians are today, there are added economic pressures and child-rearing concerns. One's vocation as a student must be shared and stretched to include the obligations of family member, provider, church member, and responsible citizen. These givens, along with one's goals, health, prejudices, study habits, and capacity for critical inquiry and creative thinking, color one's teachability.

The typical student is characteristically *atypical*. Some are pietists; others are activists; still others are bookish. Some have a sense of humor, are flexible and sociable; others are severely serious, rigid, and isolated. Some are radiantly winsome and outgoing; others seem preoccupied and withdrawn. Some are progressive; others are not. The common denominator for the majority of students is their *spirit of concerned quest and devoted commitment.* Within three or so years, the student's original intent to obey God usually becomes clarified, refined, and informed. The student has been challenged to look at himself or herself and at the Christian faith, and to lay the groundwork for an emerging life work. The seminarian has been stimulated to see a shockingly real world approximately as it is and to relate to persons redemptively in their situations in life.

In the course of this theological pilgrimage, the prospective minister is subjected to a rigorous "shaking of the foundations." This is not due to a deliberate attempt on the faculty's part to shatter and confound the novice. Far from it! Generally, one's struggle of soul is prompted by personal stirrings of heart and mind, the desire to be a real person, and ambition to learn and serve. Most seminarians are thrown back upon the ultimate resources of their existence as they tread the deep waters of theological disciplines. These years of mind-stretching and soul-searching have divine and human dimensions. Humanly speaking, sympathetic faculty members, fellow students, churchpersons, and family members are all involved directly or indirectly in the student's quest. Yet the student needs a *referent* beyond herself or himself for the ordering of life. God is this referent.

Through diligent study and service the seminarian learns the merit of working together with God. To gain Paul's perspective is a great blessing: "I worked harder than all of them—yet not I, but the grace of God that was with me" (1 Cor. 15:10). The ministry is God's work before it is humanity's work! Learning to rely upon the strength and guidance of God's Spirit is more than an intellectual proposition. Faith must become the vocabulary of the minister's existence. All of one's intellectual pursuits, service tasks, leisure activities, and human relationships must be undergirded by a dynamic relationship with God. Moreover, neither diligent study nor devoted contemplation is an end in itself. Both point beyond themselves to a life of obedient service. This counterbalancing process of quest and commitment is both preventive and therapeutic, challenging all human idolatries of the academic community. Herein lies true spirituality. God takes human aspirations, flaws, and breakings of the heart and hallows them for divine purposes. The person "thoroughly equipped for every good work" will love the Lord with heart and soul, mind and strength, while serving as an instrument of God's grace (2 Tim. 3:17).

2. Learning to Communicate in Depth

The minister's most compelling idea of vocation may be stated simply: proclaiming Jesus Christ as Redeemer and living this truth out in shared ministry. To proclaim Christ's vulnerability to us and salvation for all creation involves incarnating his love as an indispensable virtue. The people of God find their true vocation beneath the cross and, after baptism, go through the "servants' entrance" to the world. In obedience, they recognize the gospel's priority in the church's life. The gracious *koinonia* is thus the bearer of God's good news, both in proclamation and in personal relationships. *The pastoral perspective of ministry cherishes proclamation as central and precious and challenges believers to communication in depth.* Preaching and teaching employ public address as their primary mode of communication. Technical training is provided for seminarians in an effort to perfect their sermonic style and delivery. It is not easy, however, to determine the core interests and needs of a particular congregation. They are constantly changing. Haddon Robinson cautions wisdom in using the phrase *for example.* "Those two words promise to connect an abstract truth to the human condition."[20] A basic purpose of preaching is applying biblical truth personally—to ourselves, and to our congregations. Along with pulpit work, the pastor's primary mode of address is the *relationship language* of the interpersonal encounter.

Distinguishing public speech and personal dialogue appears artificial and unnecessary or arbitrary and unreasonable. Yet a minister is constantly aware of this distinction in pastoral work. Ministers should be capable of both *proclamation* in the celebration of worship and *dialogue* in the conversation of pastoral administration and counseling. Depth communication is essential in the pastoral perspective of worship, evangelism, education, and administration. The pastor is as much a "steward of the mysteries of God" when meeting with official boards, conducting a funeral service, or making a pastoral call as when preaching on Sunday!

Pastoral communication occurs at multiple levels, verbally and nonverbally. Research reveals that nonverbal communication precedes and supports spoken language.[21] Ministers encounter persons with unique cultural backgrounds, specialized religious biases, and with emotionalized relational language. A minister is experienced nonverbally by others through his or her age and gender; spirit of kindness or brusqueness; unique mannerisms; body language of gestures, facial features, attentiveness, and general bearing; and, above all, through his or her character and conduct. Pastors and parishioners are made known to each other through their lifestyles of flexibility or rigidity, security or anxiety, generosity or extractiveness, humor or severity, ego-strength or weakness, integrity or duplicity, and humility or pride. The pastor tells about God and oneself through the touch of a hand, tone of one's voice, fairness in decisions, participation in worship, work, and play; resolution of differences when conflict comes; and through attentiveness to those in crises.

The writer once asked a member of a noted church in New York to contrast her pastor with his distinguished predecessor. "Dr. B.," she said on the spur of the moment, "never seems to be certain that he is accomplishing anything, whereas Dr. A. was always so courageous, so strong, and sure." This congregant experienced security with her former pastor's words *and* ways; she sensed weakness in her new minister's uncertainty. This does not imply that the church is a hospital observation ward in which pastors and people check out each other's pathology. Obviously, however, God has endowed us with complex communicative equipment—antennae of the soul—with which we listen, respond to, and experience each other. Such two-way experiencing of the "other" is respectful and responsive or it is not true communication.

How a person feels about herself or himself determines, to a great degree, their effectiveness in communicating care. For a generation thoughtful readers have profited from the creative reflections of Presbyterian minister Frederick Buechner. In *Telling Secrets* he reveals why it has been easier all these years to live privately as a writer in Vermont than on the firing line as pastor of some large, key congregation.[22] Buechner shares his darkest childhood secret—his father's alcohol abuse and suicide—and articulates the healing and freedom found in the revelation. One who has given the world widely acclaimed "peculiar treasures" has opened his heart so that we may *know* him. True communication is thus sculpted from the soul.

"Telling the truth" is not enough however. Incarnational caregiving goes beyond cognition to loving apprehension through depth communication. Parents desire fellowship when they talk heart-to-heart with a son or daughter. Authentic spiritual renewal occurs within the arena formed by talk, gesture, and attentiveness among Christians. Each church member, therefore, must shoulder responsibility for avoiding what the Apostle termed "trickery, craftiness, or deceit" and for "speaking the truth in love" (Eph. 4:15).

Communications theorist Harry A. DeWire has noted that true communication occurs in a loving faith community.

> Suppose . . . that people are drawn together on the basis of love. Rather than being guarded, our language is free. We do not need to press for our integrity, for we know it is accepted by the other simply because he (or she) is Christian. We do not need to protect ourselves from the threats of another because we know that the other is looking upon us in terms of love. In this kind of relationship, it seems almost certain that the consequences will be in an entirely different form of communication. . . . Though we do not need new equipment to accomplish the change, the processes by which the equipment is set into motion and the dynamics at work in them certainly will be changed.[23]

Viewed thus, pastoral care addresses persons *within* the preoccupations, lonely crises, brokenness, and isolation of human existence. *Listening* is crucial in such a process. Some pastors do most of the talking, make the major decisions, and thereby create a conforming church. Being sensitive to and in "the pains of childbirth" for Christian maturity in persons, however, requires careful attentiveness (Gal. 4:19). Work rhythms require the practicing pastor to speak and to listen—a dynamic, not a static endeavor! Listening in counseling, with perceptive feedback, is an engaging gesture, a beckoning to begin, an invitation to disclosure, an avenue to hope beyond despair, and a claim to religious affirmation. To "be quick to listen" to a person requires the helper's interest in that individual for his or her own sake, as well as for the sake of God's Kingdom (Jas. 1:19).

Consequently, pastoral care is accomplished in a dynamic communications field, where persons sense and respond to the "other." Seminarians are to master such skills as how to:

1. Initiate genuine conversation,
2. Understand by participant listening,
3. Invite the other person to speak by true respect, and
4. Demonstrate concern in a me-first, preoccupied world.

Caring communicators need goodwill to permit others to be themselves and courage to maintain their own integrity. Our words have our lives in them. The significance assigned to a minister's words is largely determined by one's manner of life. Thus theological education is concerned with both the student minister's *being* — true Christian selfhood — and with his or her *behavior*. Adeptness in depth communication is a learned skill, not a charismatic gift. Clinical pastoral education, one of the most significant developments in ministerial training of this century, is directed precisely toward this objective.

3. Learning from Clinical Experience

Medical educators have long recognized the value of teaching clinically by (1) treating patients in the presence of students, (2) performing surgery in an observation theater, and (3) requiring students to practice clinically under faculty supervision. The crucial test from the clinician's perspective is the doctor-patient encounter in the hospital sickroom. The student's performance in making hospital "rounds" is the essential correlate of reciting principles from medical textbooks. In like manner, theological educators have developed clinical teaching methods of reflecting on ministry events which contribute significantly to pastoral practice and prophetic imagination.

Clinical pastoral experience implies a face-to-face ministry to hurting persons by practitioners under skilled supervision.[24] A "clinic" may be a general or psychiatric hospital, a church, a prison, a military base, a university chaplain's office, or a counseling or social service center affiliated with a theological school for teaching purposes. Such institutional connections are generally based on informal agreements. A teaching program in a hospital, for example, is conducted cooperatively with a chaplain supervisor in the department of pastoral care. Through records of pastoral conversations, role plays, videotape recordings, feedback in peer groups, and individual evaluation with clinical supervisors, students learn from demonstrations and reflection on the actual practice of ministry.

Clinical pastoral education (CPE) has been developed as an integral part of theological education since its inception in the mid-1920s. Beginning with the pioneering work of Anton T. Boisen, the mental hospital chaplain who examined struggles of "living human documents" as a source of theological understanding, CPE has developed steadily since the Association for Clinical Pastoral Education was formed in 1967.[25] While relationships between seminary personnel and clinical teachers have sometimes been strained, because of misunderstood objectives and/or a lack of administrative ties and clear communication, clinical centers render a valuable service in theological education. CPE has become a resource for the study of pastoral theology and practical ministry for hundreds of seminarians in many nations each year.

In essence, clinical pastoral experience embodies (1) opportunities for students to minister to persons facing crises or stressful experiences in many kinds of contexts; (2) to form relationships with helping professionals in related fields of medicine, nursing, education, social work, and the like; (3) to share peer interactions and feedback with fellow students; and (4) to reflect theologically on their pastoral work with people, all under competent theological supervision. While clinical pastoral supervisors are usually employed by treatment/teaching type institutions, they often function as adjunct faculty members of theological schools. In some instances, joint employment and salary considerations are arranged by a seminary and a clinical facility. These clinical teachers are required to have a standard theological degree, significant pastoral experience, advanced clinical training, ecclesiastical endorsement, and certification from a national chaplaincy certifying organization.

Some have mistakenly viewed the supervised practice of ministry as an inexpensive form of student psychotherapy. The interplay of forces in the parallel processes of ministry-supervision-therapy have long been recognized.[26] Yet psychiatric treatment for the student is neither CPE's primary design nor its major intention. *The student's personal-professional growth remains a central concern since the self is the instrument of ministry.* Thus a supervisee might be referred for professional counseling if it were needed. While integration of theological studies and pastoral practice is at the forefront of clinical experience, the theoretical content of such programs is also significant. When clinicians isolate themselves from a classic theological heritage, they are subject to superficiality and cynicism. Theological education without pastoral experience, on the other hand, is subject to pedantry and lack of awareness of life's deepest spiritual needs.

Notes from a clinical supervisor's evaluative report to a theological school dean indicate some of the concerns, struggles, and growth of a student engaged in clinical ministry during an academic semester:

> Stan's beginning interviews revealed a concern in watching for relevant signals in the patient. He revealed a rather flat affect [emotional feeling tone] and did not show too much creativity in making conversation with the patient. Later in the term he began to develop an ability to reveal his concern.

Stan is tenacious and sticks with his goal very closely. One seminar session he demonstrated persistence in trying to get specific answers for counseling. He first saw counseling as a set of scientific principles which had to be mastered and which would automatically produce results. During the latter half of the course he came to see more clearly the meaning of relationships and the art of pointing caring events toward a therapeutic and helpful goal.

The student's final evaluation reflects real insight into preparation for and reflection upon practice of ministry with patients and their families.

The clinical teacher's role in relation to students is not to foster an unhealthy dependence upon oneself, nor to wean the student from his or her theological heritage. Clinical experience and growth processes for the student represent a time of profound self-examination, vulnerability to learning issues, letting go of painful emotions and counterproductive behaviors, and developing more effective relationship patterns. Gender and authority issues often surface. Poor pastoral vision is improved with helpful clinical lenses. Like much pastoral work, clinical education is a time for afflicting the comfortable and comforting the afflicted—a pain/gain process. The supervisor's goal is to motivate each student to match cognitive ways of learning with creative imagination and empathic understanding in a working alliance for ministry.

Despite their learning contract, a clinical educator may experience stubborn resistance to personal development or professional growth, or both, in a student. Rather than leading to failure, defensiveness or resistance may provide occasions for new learning. The following excerpt from a supervisor's report reflects this resistance-growth rhythm:

> Jennifer Cox was very defensive at first when her interviews were used in the group discussion. She was careful not to risk anything before the seminar that would cause criticism or possible rejection. Jennifer soon moved through this anxious phase, which was displayed in many ways. Her fear of rejection by the group would make her hesitant about presenting ideas or material. She defended pastoral interviews with explanations, which served as buffers.
>
> Jennifer showed a lot of naiveté in calling on patients and their families. She tended to classify them in two categories and assumed that all people in these spiritual camps were alike. In time, she developed some ability to perceive differences clinically.
>
> The mid-term evaluation involved Jennifer's ability to perceive clinical differences and diagnostic distinctions. . . . I feel that she responded well to the course and grew considerably throughout the semester.

Learning from clinical pastoral experience involves theological reflection and skill development. Students get an insider's view of the structure, systemic nature, and functioning of pastoral practice in a specialized setting. They also gain new insight into theological concepts, themselves, and their interpersonal relationships. Individuals so trained are subject to the illusion of thinking they know more than they actually do. Involvement with patients, families, physicians, God, and supervisors can *distort* as well as *correct* a student's vision. One may become bloated with pride as a result of an educational advantage over non-clinically prepared ministers. Clinical preparation for ministry may be counted effective if it opens new channels of divine grace for human need.

Educators will not read more, or less, into clinical pastoral education than reality permits.[27] The perceptive, healthy student usually experiences significant gains as he or she becomes more authentically a participant in the educational process. Resourcefulness and security, consolidated from theological classroom and pastoral clinic, should make one's Christian service more effective throughout a lifetime. Some theological schools require one semester or summer quarter of clinical education for the divinity degree, regardless of the student's vocational goals. Clearly, it benefits those who enter missions or teaching as well as those who prefer chaplaincy or the pastorate of a church.

Supervisory skills learned in CPE may be passed on to laypersons involved in ministry as well. New frontiers in pastoral education for all theological students will require the exploration and development of additional clinical resources. As far as possible, such resources should be developed in conjunction with theological schools for correlation with curriculums and administrative purposes. Much that transpires in parish ministry cannot be taught in seminary; it must be learned in the "school of hard knocks."[28] Thus one must become a lifelong inquirer through continuing education.

4. Continuing Education of Ministers

Leading God's people in the church is an unending exercise. As far as a pastor sees ahead on the church calendar there are worship programs, seasonal events, religious emphases, weddings, and a wide range of special, lay-focused ministries. Parishioners become ill, face surgeries, endure loss and grief, so pastoral care emergencies never stop. Responsibilities for church growth, fiscal integrity, and community involvement are *constants.* Thus, the need and climate for continuing education is *there!* Programs of continuing education for ministers have become noted for their helpfulness as renewal events, review of current religious issues, and for encouraging interchange among participants. A few days away from one's demanding sermon preparation schedule, phone calls, committee meetings, and conversations with every conceivable kind of person can be spiritually refreshing and may prevent burnout.

Theological schools can anticipate some future experiences for prospective ministers. Yet most seminarians have not borne full ministerial responsibilities: the loneliness of leadership, the sting of criticism, the joy of seasons like Holy Week, the accountability of the prophet's chamber. Students seldom ask some of the frustrating questions that occur to pastors several years after graduation. Paralleling this limitation of education for a pastoral ministry is the lack of adequate feedback from graduates to theological educators. How is a person five years away from campus to tell a former theological dean how to strengthen the curriculum? Many schools are inviting groups of selected ministers to return briefly to their campuses, in order to test the effectiveness of their previous training and to continue their education.[29]

Numerous projects of continuing education for ministers are under way; some experimentally, others well advanced.[30] The concept of continuing education includes, yet transcends, traditional lectureships or pastors' conferences, some of which are little more than an alumni relations medium. Administrative, faculty, housing, and financial considerations are involved in developing centers for continuing education. When such provisions are made, select groups of ministers are invited to a theological school or university campus during the year for brief periods of seminars, discussions, and library study.

Continuing education was conceived (1) to stimulate religious leaders and churches to be more effective in their ministries; (2) to explore actual needs of ministers in varied settings; (3) to note trends of current theological study; (4) to encourage stimulating interchange of ideas in workshop settings; and (5) to explore avenues for continuing research and more effective ministry endeavor. Ministers in such settings share with and learn from one another. Practicing professionals become their former professors' teachers.

While such programs are structured and content-centered, they are intentionally informal and person-centered as well. Since continuing education programs are designed primarily for parish ministers, they are usually brief events. Specialized groups, such as Christian laypersons, campus religious directors, military and institutional chaplains, religious journalists, college teachers of religion, church staff members, and denominational executives, may be incorporated into a school's continuing education program. In light of stimulating developments in continuing education for ministry, institutional trustee boards should explore avenues for maximum use of available resources in adult education.

If the minister is the growing kind, he or she will not wait for a formal invitation to continue learning. One accepts spiritual disciplines; subscribes to a variety of journals; purchases and reads books and commentaries; enriches notions of life from drama, music, poetry, the arts, and entertainment; travels widely; and keeps abreast of the changing world on one's own. Again, through quiet hours of devotional reading, prayer, and sermon preparation, the pastor searches regularly for divine rekindling of compassion for broken, pained, and sometimes troublesome persons. A lifetime learner reflects upon family and professional relationships, and upon the successes and failures of an entire ministry, in order to achieve his or her dream.

Summary

Preparation for pastoral care, while reminding one of hidden reefs to be avoided, should magnify personal qualities which one is to incarnate in life—strength of character, spiritual wisdom, self-understanding, family harmony, awareness of persons, and flexible use of time and resources. Such qualities represent ideals that are more *pursuits* of one's potential than *achievements* of one's goals. It is hoped that the religious leader will live as a principled person, not merely a technician, as his or her ministry unfolds under the grace of God.

Fortunately, the good minister of Jesus Christ does not stand or serve alone. While he or she experiences certain threats, pursues learning, works and prays for the kingdom of God, and anticipates Christ's *parousia* at the end of the Age, a faithful minister is supported by human friendship and the fellowship of God. This sense of a shared ministry should mean for the minister what Jonathan's friendship was to David. It should "strengthen one's hand in God." The concept of shared ministry by the entire congregation has received fresh emphasis but is actually a biblical concept. As we turn from principles to the process of pastoral care, the idea of a ministering church will be magnified.

Notes

1. Myra Marshall with Dan McGee and Jennifer B. Owen, *Beyond Termination* (Nashville: Broadman Press, 1990).

2. In Paul Wilkes, "The Hands That Would Shape Our Souls," *The Atlantic* (December 1990): 70.
3. Edward E. Thornton, *Theology and Pastoral Counseling* (Englewood Cliffs, NJ: Prentice-Hall, 1964), 102–11.
4. Charles V. Gerkin, *Widening the Horizons: Pastoral Responses to a Fragmented Society* (Philadelphia: Westminster Press, 1986), 98–127.
5. Thomas C. Oden, *Care of Souls in the Classic Tradition* (Philadelphia: Fortress Press, 1984), 41. Cf. *Pastoral Theology: Essentials of Ministry* (San Francisco: Harper & Row, 1983); and *Becoming a Minister* (New York: Crossroad, 1987).
6. Gerkin, *Widening the Horizons*, 26–75 et passim. Cf. his *Prophetic Pastoral Practice* (Nashville: Abingdon Press, 1991), 67–115.
7. See Earl E. Shelp and Ronald H. Sunderland, eds., *The Pastor as Theologian* (New York: Pilgrim Press, 1988), and other role-based essays in the series.
8. Leonard Hodgson, *et al.*, "God and the Bible," in *On the Authority of the Bible* (London: S.P.C.K., 1960), 67.
9. Jackson W. Carroll, *As One with Authority: Reflective Leadership in Ministry* (Louisville: Westminster/John Knox Press, 1991).
10. John T. McNeill, *A History of the Cure of Souls* (New York: Harper & Brothers, 1951), 67–87.
11. Karl Heim, *Christian Faith and Natural Science* (New York: Harper & Row, 1953; Torchbook series, 1957), 5.
12. Jean-Paul Sartre, *The Devil and the Good Lord* (New York: Vintage Books, 1962), 10.
13. Rudolf Bultmann, *Existence and Faith,* translated by Schubert M. Ogden (New York: Meridian Books, 1960), 24, 29–30.
14. Robert Frost, in the Frontispiece of *In the Clearing* (New York: Holt, Rinehart & Winston, 1962), 7. Used by permission.
15. See Charles V. Gerkin's discussion of "presence" in *Prophetic Pastoral Practice* (Nashville: Abingdon Press, 1991), 113-15; and Gaylord Noyce, *The Minister as Moral Counselor* (Nashville: Abingdon Press, 1989).
16. James M. Gustafson, "The Minister as Moral Counselor," unpublished paper (Pittsburgh, PA: June 20, 1982). Reprinted in LeRoy Aden and Harold Ellens, eds., *The Church and Pastoral Care* (Grand Rapids: Baker Book House, 1988), 93–102.
17. See, for example, Peter Jarvis, "The Ministry: Occupation, Profession or Status?" *The Expository Times* 86, no. 9 (June 1975): 264–67; Thomas M. Gannon, S.J., "Priest/Minister: Profession or Non-Profession?" *Review of Religious Research* 12, no. 2 (Winter 1971); C. W. Brister and others, *Beginning Your Ministry* (Nashville: Abingdon Press, 1981); also, Paul Wilkes, "The Hands That Would Shape Our Souls," *The Atlantic* (December 1990): 59–88.
18. Stanley Hauerwas and William H. Willimon, *Resident Aliens: A Provocative Christian Assessment of Culture and Ministry for People Who Know That Something is Wrong* (Nashville: Abington Press, 1989), 117-27.

19. Robert Wuthnow, *The Restructuring of American Religion* (Princeton: Princeton University Press, 1988), 5. Cf. William R. Hutchinson, ed., *Between the Times: The Travail of the Protestant Establishment in America, 1900–1960* (New York: Cambridge University Press, 1989); also, Wade Clark Roof and William McKinney, *American Mainline Religion: Its Changing Shape and Future* (New Brunswick, NJ: Rutgers University Press, 1987). A serious examination of Evangelical theological education is underway, chaired by Richard Mouw, the provost of Fuller Theological Seminary, sponsored by the Lilly Endowment's Religion Division.

20. Haddon Robinson, "Bringing Yourself into the Pulpit," in *Mastering Contemporary Preaching* (Portland, OR: Multnomah Press, 1989), 139.

21. See Jurgen Ruesch and Weldon Kees, *Nonverbal Communication* (Berkeley, CA: University of California Press, 1956).

22. Frederick Buechner, *Telling Secrets* (San Francisco: HarperCollins, 1990).

23. Harry A. DeWire, *The Christian as Communicator* (Philadelphia: Westminster Press, 1961), 124–25.

24. See David A. Steere, ed., *The Supervision of Pastoral Care* (Louisville: Westminster/John Knox Press, 1989).

25. For a comprehensive history and critique of clinical education see Edward E. Thornton, *Professional Education for Ministry: A History of Clinical Pastoral Education* (Nashville: Abingdon Press, 1970). *The Journal of Pastoral Care* is published quarterly by a consortium of professional caregiving organizations through the business office, Association for Clinical Pastoral Education, 1549 Clairmont Road, Suite 103, Decatur, GA 30033.

26. Margery Doehrman, "Parallel Processes in Supervision and Psychotherapy," *Bulletin of the Menninger Clinic* 40, no.1 (1976): 4–17.

27. Theological educators will be interested in Alexa Smith's report of "Student Response to Clinical Pastoral Education" in Steere, *The Supervision of Pastoral Care*, 129–45.

28. See Disciples of Christ minister Robert Cueni's, *What Ministers Can't Learn in Seminary: A Survival Manual for the Parish Ministry* (Nashville: Abingdon Press, 1988).

29. See "Continuing Education: A Means for Making Dreams Come True," in C. W. Brister, James L. Cooper, and J. David Fite, *Beginning Your Ministry* (Nashville: Abingdon Press, 1981), 104–25.

30. In addition to denominational workshops and theological school programs, resources of numerous agencies are available. For example: (1) Leadership Network, headquartered in Tyler, Texas; (2) Institute for Advanced Pastoral Studies, in Detroit, MI; (3) The Alban Institute, Mount St. Alban, Washington, D.C.; (4) centers accredited by the Association for Clinical Pastoral Education and the American Association of Pastoral Counselors; (5) and programs sponsored through *Leadership*, a publication of Christianity Today; spiritual retreat centers, and the American Management Association.

Suggested Reading

Aden, Leroy and J. Harold Ellens, eds. *Turning Points in Pastoral Care: The Legacy of Anton Boisen and Seward Hiltner*. Grand Rapids: Baker Book House, 1990. Fourteen pastoral theologians assess the Boisen/Hiltner legacy and provide the field a mid-course correction.

Brister, C. W. *Caring for the Caregivers: How to Help Ministers and Missionaries*. Nashville: Broadman Press, 1985. Helps laypersons look beyond the veil of privacy into the everydayness, struggles, and aspirations of persons in professional religious occupations.

Ford, LeRoy. *A Curriculum Design Manual for Theological Education: A Learning Outcomes Focus*. Nashville: Broadman Press, 1991. College and seminary educators will benefit from this comprehensive guide to performance-based learning. Shows how different teaching techniques work in the classroom.

Messer, Donald E. *Contemporary Images of Christian Ministry*. Nashville: Abingdon Press, 1989. While aware of traditional concepts of priest, pastor, and prophet, Messer offers fresh metaphors to illuminate identity in ministry: wounded healer, servant leader, political mystic, practical theologian, and enslaved liberator, with implications for pastoral practice.

Roof, Wade Clark and William McKinney. *American Mainline Religion: Its Changing Shape and Future*. New Brunswick, NJ: Rutgers University Press, 1987. Explores the religious mainstream's shifting currents, weakening denominational identities, and striking changes in church leadership, including increasing roles and power of women.

Salter, Darius. *What Really Matters in Ministry: Profiling Pastoral Success in Flourishing Churches*. Grand Rapids: Baker Book House, 1990. Salter surveyed pastors in growing churches in an attempt to determine the secrets of their effectiveness. His biblical definitions of success provide guidance for ministers desiring to honor Christ in their calling.

Schnase, Robert. *Testing and Reclaiming Your Call to Ministry*. Nashville: Abingdon Press, 1991. Examines ministry at three critical stages—transition from seminary to congregation, the first few years, and mid-life—and helps ministers envision the essentials of their Christian calling.

Steere, David A., ed. *The Supervision of Pastoral Care*. Louisville: Westminster/John Knox Press, 1989. Fifteen pastoral supervisors point students to varied aspects of the supervised practice of ministry.

Wuthnow, Robert. *The Struggle for America's Soul: Evangelicals, Liberals, and Secularism*. Grand Rapids: William B. Eerdmans, 1989. Examines the rise of new polarizations of liberals and conservatives that cut across denominational lines.

PART II

THE SHAPE OF THE CHURCH'S MINISTRY

CHAPTER FOUR

THE PASTORAL ACTION
OF THE CHURCH

We have now investigated a theological framework and method for pastoral care. Some attention has also been given to the nature of persons, based on the insights of theology and psychology, and certain implications of this synoptic wisdom have been noted for Christian caregivers. Educational opportunities were clarified for those who wish to become more skilled in pastoral ministry. The minister's own selfhood and relationships were viewed as valuable resources for getting things done. To go a step beyond this we need to clarify the shape of the church's ministry, including the respective tasks of the pastor and the people.

The servant motif of ministry was established in our thinking in chapter 1 as the Bible's most characteristic way of viewing the people of God. The Church, like her Lord, is to be in the world as one who serves. Every Christian is involved in the Church's pastoral ministry, as either the channel or the object of its concern. The consuming goal of such concern is that "Christ be formed" in persons as they choose to "conform to [his] image" (Gal. 4:19; Rom. 8:29). A ministering style of life is pictured, for example, in Christ's metaphor of the vine and the branches (John 15:5) and is implied by the Pauline "in Christ" concept. To this end, Christians of every age are summoned to contribute their strength and spiritual gifts "for building up the body of Christ, until all of us come to the unity of the faith and . . . to maturity, to the measure of the full stature of Christ" (Eph. 4:12b–13 NRSV). A ministering congregation experiences mutuality in caring; there is a reciprocal rhythm of receiving and giving under the Holy Spirit's guidance.

People in the Church conceive their relationships and responsibilities from varying perspectives. Some prefer an individualistic religion of the inner way, rationalizing: "Am I my brother's keeper?" Such private individuals offer no strategy for real-life problems and avoid involvement in the institutional church's life. A broad segment of the population practices religion as a pious habit, but faith fails to influence their daily lives in the social order. Bliss Carmen captured the portrait of those who merely log hours at church in order to remain respectable.

> They're praising God on Sunday
> They'll be all right on Monday
> It's just a little habit they've acquired.

A third stratum of the religious community represents a more involved pattern, that of *interconnection* with God and the world. Such persons are convinced that the Christian fellowship has no life in itself. It lives only as it shares the eternal life of God in the celebration of worship and in the common life.

I. The Idea of a Ministering Church

The Christian *koinonia,* by its very nature, implies a shared ministry by the pastor and one's people. When the church is gathered for worship, the pastor is the chief minister. Yet when God's people are scattered (dispersed) in the world, each layperson is to *be* the church where he or she lives and works. There one finds that, while religion is everybody's business, God is often left on the edges of human existence. Only when a personal emergency arises or some public catastrophe, like war, threatens do some persons sense God in the heart of things. Vast multitudes view God as a cosmic lifeguard to rescue them from troubled waters. While pastoral care is not merely a first-aid, rescue operation, sensitive Christians are to listen for the cry of help. Frequently, it is in such a teachable moment that the Christian caregiver becomes a priest to another.

Being available with a transformational ministry to citizens of a secular society, where one lives and labors, is *being the Church* in the world. An oil executive once recounted a critical incident involving a member of his office staff. A secretary who thought that she had achieved the victory of an unprejudiced heart returned to the office one afternoon in tears. He listened as her angry words spilled out.

> I was in line, getting a sandwich and things for lunch at Sam's, when this African-American woman came up to me. She had passed five or six in the line, then shoved me out of the way, saying that she was running late and hoped I didn't mind. Oh! Honestly, I thought I had my past feelings about "blacks" whipped until today. Now I don't know.

I don't mind being with people of different ethnic origins than myself . . . but . . . it makes me mad when anyone, white or black, pushes me around. That woman had her nerve!

They talked a while about the need for patience and understanding during a time of resurgent prejudice in the nation's history. He reminded her of "the good old boys" in America who abuse Vietnamese fishermen or block credentialing of immigrant professional persons, then encouraged her to try to understand strangers immigrating from many lands. Thus a Christian layman challenged the racism of an associate who had linked a woman's abusive behavior with her own prejudice.

A generation ago, Carlyle Marney examined prejudices that remain in all our lives under the guise of their usefulness, rightness, or inevitability.[1] He analyzed four major forms or structures of prejudice: Materialism—Prejudgment of Reality; Provincialism—Prejudgment of Community; Institutionalism—Prejudgment of Value; and Individualism—Prejudgment of Personality. He indicated ways of mitigating prejudice in culture through a Christian understanding of the problem and by recovery of the value of human personality. With prophetic force, Marney exposed prejudice for its denial of community, distortion of reality, perversion of value, and misuse of power. His emphases are needed in our own day.

Certain obligations emerge from the church's responsibility for a shared ministry, despite the hesitation of some persons to communicate their concern. *First, ministers who have prepared themselves for a pastoral ministry are obligated to educate their people for their mutual tasks.* Many key concepts about human nature, for example, and about counseling apply generally to all religious counselors. *Second, today's agents of reconciliation must shape their service to people where they are.* It is easier to stay within the sanctity of the walls of an established fellowship than to reach out to those who are hostile toward the Church. Churchpersons who sit in a snug office, waiting for the troubled world to call, may convey indifference and unavailability when help is needed. The compassionate Samaritan ministered to a neighbor as he traveled on the open road (Luke 10:25–37). That implies risk and availability in talking with persons or groups about really important things.

Authentic pastoral care is possible only when a church establishes contact with those who suffer the anguish, deprivations, and temptations of existence in a hostile world. Some adventuresome ministers have established new kinds of ecclesiastical command posts near the front lines of life's conflicts.[2] While we all may not elect to leave the historic established churches for nontraditional faith communities, we can learn exciting ways to care from such imaginative persons. Charles Gerkin illustrates a "centrifugal model" of caring tasks in dislocated places, far "from the sanctuaried center of Christian community," in *Prophetic Pastoral Practice*.[3] More often it is the discipline of a new alertness and availability that God's people need, not a new location. The church's service is shaped to the dimensions of its concern, not merely to the givens of geography. What then is the manner of shared ministry in the church?

1. *The Church as a Redemptive Society*

Jesus Christ created the Church to be a redemptive society *in society*, not isolated from the world but devoted to service in the world (John 17:15-25). Before his ascension into Heaven, Christ prayed that his followers would maintain their personal loyalty to him *and* take up missionary tasks in the world. Christ continues his ministry in and through his chosen instrument, the Church, for which he died, which he both loves and empowers for service, and of which he remains the head (Eph. 4:15, 5:25; Acts 1:5).

T. W. Manson was profoundly correct in *The Church's Ministry*, when he noted that each congregation has a dual role to perform in the world — *evangelistic* in relation to those outside and *pastoral* in relation to those within. Church leaders should not try to separate these tasks, for they are two aspects of a single life. Citizens in the pagan world of the first century watched love at work in the life of the Christian community and were won by what they saw and felt. In our day, it is not enough that strife-torn persons simply hear about a gospel of peace; they must actually experience the gospel making peace in life.[4] The Holy Spirit turns persons to righteousness through the power of compassionate living, as well as by impassioned preaching. Wise churchpersons recognize that evangelism occurs as God uses whatever we do as a means to bring people to him in Jesus Christ.[5] While churches and their agencies cannot go back to the literal *shape* of the first-century ministry, they can develop continuities with the dynamic *spirit* of Christ and the apostles. Only as Christ establishes its ministry and serves through its members is the Church conducting a truly redemptive ministry.

How effective is this ideal in the life of contemporary churches? Seeking to attract a pick-and-choose, secularized constituency, a megachurch may become a one-stop shopping mall complex "that offers an array of affinity groups where individuals can satisfy their need for intimacy yet identify with a large, successful enterprise."[6] A church can easily become dedicated to perpetuating itself or the American way of life rather than continuing the ministry of Christ. A congregation that lives for its own sake alone has ceased to be a true church!

There is a story in the Southwest, probably apocryphal, of a church that discovered oil on its property. Immediately, the congregants formed a closed corporation, refused new members, and privately shared their royalties from oil sales. One may imagine a church under the shadow of an oil derrick rather than of the cross. That *would* reshape its outlook upon the world. To resist secularity, crises of faith, and *loss of direction* churches must anchor renewal in Scripture and the tradition of a believing, worshiping community.

Are churches actually functioning as "salt and light" in the real world? Katarina Schuth, a Ph.D. in cultural geography and director of planning at a Jesuit institution in Cambridge, Massachusetts, surveyed Catholic seminaries in the United States and reported findings on the state of the Church's ministry. Schuth found "intractable problems" in talking to hundreds of Catholic educators and students. Despite pockets of pessimism, she found *reason for hope* from persons "discouraged by the small number of first-rate candidates applying for ordination, from administrators who are concerned about [low] enrollment and finances, from faculty who fear loss of academic freedom and feel overburdened by the multiple expectations attached to their positions, and by students who are uncertain of their role and identity as ministers in an unpredictable future."[7] Her hopefulness centers in evidences that a remnant dedicated to Christ's ministry is alive and growing, despite many challenges.

It was the remnant concept in Scripture, and the sociological fact that only a remnant of responsible members survive in the Church of England, that led Martin Thornton to formulate a "remnant-type" pastoral theology for Anglo-Catholic communions. Thornton argues that just as Christ ministered to the whole world without moving more than a few miles from his home and by concentrating on twelve persons, so priests can coach their parishioners in prayer and by this vicarious action lead new believers into Christ's body. "The only positive method of attaining conversions is epitomized in the worshipping Remnant," says Thornton, "that forgets all about trying to convert."[8] Discipline, through "ascetical rule" or prayer coaching, is viewed as the priest's essential task. Thornton's passion for discipline is akin in some respects to Thurneysen's doctrine of pastoral care, which was influenced considerably by Continental pietism.

Thornton's "reorientation" lacks the theological relevance of the Reformation principle of the universal priesthood of believers. While retaining a profound sense of the meaning of the pastoral office, Luther, Calvin, Zwingli, and Bucer felt that every Christian should be a minister of the Word of God by virtue of his or her faith. Involvement in society, living out one's vocation as a Christian, was expected and, therefore, commendable. Wilhelm Pauck wrote of the reformers' intentions for ministry in the time of the Protestant Reformation: "[Every believer] must express his faith in loving social action and thereby communicate it to others. All Christians are such ministers; they cannot but bring about a new kind of society—the fellowship of believers."[9] A "remnant-type" pastoral theology tends to be inverted and exclusivistic and is too clerical a concept to be applied rigidly in caring churches. Were such asceticism to be practiced, the pastoral work of the church would fall into the hands of the *few* rather than the *many*. This seems to me to miss the basic New Testament intent of the corporate responsibility of God's people for each other and the world.

Here is the New Testament pattern of thinking: "All that is said of the ministry in the New Testament is said not of individuals, nor of some apostolic college . . . but of the whole body, whatever the differentiation of function within it."[10] The idea of a ministering church, asserting the vocational identity of every Christian as a servant and defining patterns of participation in pastoral care, is both rooted in Scripture and relevant in the contemporary situation.

2. The Interrelatedness of Ministry

The idea of the priesthood of the *whole church* is clear in the New Testament, was enunciated by the Protestant reformers, and is to be understood in *corporate* rather than individualistic terms today. In its practical expressions, the corporate priesthood of pastors and parishioners consists in their interrelatedness of ministry. While this is not the occasion for tracing all the branches of ministry, springing from the high priesthood of Christ through the centuries (Heb. 5–8), some things may be said.

1. The term "pastor" *(poimen)* in the New Testament originally implied a function performed and later was applied to an *office* held in church life. It means "to tend or feed as a shepherd."[11] Pastoral ministries were performed in the early churches by two groups: (a) those many spontaneous general ministers who received the charismatic (grace) gifts of the Spirit (1 Cor. 12:12–28; Eph. 4:7–12; Rom. 12:5–8); and (b) those *few appointed* as local ministers, elders or bishops, and deacons by the apostles (Acts 20:28; Phil. 1:1; Heb. 13:7, 17, 24; 1 Tim. 3:8–13, 5:17). Pastoral functions, such as healing, supporting, and teaching, were performed by many unofficial ministers. As churches developed, elders *(presbuteroi)* or bishops *(episkopoi)* were appointed to exercise pastoral oversight over congregations. Deacons *(diakonoi)* were ordained as their associates in such tasks as oversight,

personal and family ministries, conducting worship, and administering the rites of baptism and the Lord's Supper.

2. A practical strategy, which I shall term the *principle of adaptive ministry,* is evident in NT church life. Each group of believers adapted its witness to its environment (today we call this localization or contextualizing), without major distinctions being made between pastors and people. All of the early Christians stood on common ground, shared an imperiled existence, and were called *(kletos)* to serve in the world as the people of God. Theirs was a theology of the catacombs, as well as of the housetops. Before laying hands on a person in ordination, early congregations were to "test the spirits to see whether they are of God: for many false prophets have gone out into the world" (1 John 4:1-4). Churches must still avoid the "spirit of the antichrist" and move wisely in the ordination of their ministers.

The interrelatedness of ministry recognizes the pastoral services performed by ministers in denominational and interchurch offices, beyond the bounds of a local church. Service and institutional chaplains, missionaries, denominational executives, religious directors on university campuses, and seminary professors all fulfill pastoral functions in discharging their responsibilities. Though functionally unique, no distinction of intrinsic value should be made between these offices and that of a senior pastor. They, too, have been called to a ministry of witnessing and caring, as "workers together with God."

Carrying this principle further, the churches do not exist in isolation; they strengthen each other. "Partisans of the parish are inclined to romanticize its possibilities. We shall have to keep in mind the plenitude of things the local congregation can *not* do."[12] Denominations can serve a real purpose in focusing support, channeling ministry in institutions, sending missionaries, creating literature, and offering a structure for churches in their varied services. Despite the trendiness of adherents who switch denominational allegiance to gain fellowship with kindred spirits in a community, God's work here on earth is systemic. Globalization requires cooperation among Christians.

Churches today are wise to follow the spirit and strategy of the New Testament regarding their ministers, rather than certain ecclesiastical developments that are subject to misunderstanding. While recognizing the biblical principle of the priesthood of all believers, the appointment and work of a formal ministry is clear in the New Testament. There is no limit on the number of ministers and deacons which one church may ask to lead its ministry in a community. The early churches frequently had a multiple ministry. Moreover, there should be opportunities provided for concerned laypersons to share intercessory prayer ministries and perform *pastoral* functions in their daily living.

3. *The Layperson's Calling to Care*

The spiritual renewal of the church's laity is actually a reemphasis of an ancient biblical truth.[13] Nowhere does the Bible advocate that a Christian pastor has a monopoly on the church's ministry. The preacher-teacher's role is to "equip the saints" for their own task of ministering — in family life, in daily work, in the church, and in the world (Eph. 4:11–12). Hendrik Kraemer's A *Theology of the Laity* emphasized that "the Church *is* Ministry," and that the services of clergy and laity "are both aspects of the same *diakonia*, each in their proper sphere and calling."[14] The worlds of the professional minister and the responsible layperson intersect at the point of who they really are — the people of God! Their ministry actions are on a continuum, with pastors having a greater responsibility to enhance their calling by reflecting on it and learning from it.

While this book seeks primarily to illuminate the caregiving work of the pastor, we remain aware of "passport skills" required by compassionate laypersons for ministries in all the worlds of their living. Some churches observe perfunctorily a Laity Day, permitting one or a few persons to share in a worship service. The church thereby recognizes the tasks members have performed and challenges men and women to renewed zeal. Their work, in many cases, is restricted to fiscal management, Christian education, upkeep of church properties, committee tasks amounting to "leg work" for the pastor, food preparation for special events, choral work, and church-oriented offices or tasks. Some men and women are more devoted to policy-making in positions of power than to personal service. Others are preoccupied with sponsoring a pet program rather than sharing warmly in the church as a caring community of faith. Many members, however, do participate in ministries of compassion and show Christian love in the relationships of daily life.

Studies by sociologist Wade Clark Roof and others have identified some distinguishing features of the baby boom generation that have direct bearing on laity-shared congregational ministries. Between 1945 and 1965, about 75 million newborns were added to America's population. Meeting their needs now as adults has caused churches to take notice and revamp ministries with a marketplace mentality. Baby boomers reveal two key traits: desires for personal freedom and individual fulfillment.[15] Reared by television and generally well-educated, this young to middle-aged generation is returning to churches and synagogues in record numbers with the same independent tastes that marked their nonconformity in adolescence.

In general, the boomers are seen as "consumers" shopping around for something specific from a church, regardless of its denominational label. They are — by general agreement of those who study them — not only picky, but highly pragmatic. More than 40 million of them now attending church look for two things in particular: religious education for their children and some kind of spiritual guidance for themselves. Congregations that are attentive to "young-adult themes" and that take childrens' needs seriously are growing.

One such congregation is All Saints Episcopal Church in Pasadena, California, where less than a third of its three thousand members were born Episcopalians. Ninety-eight percent of the communicants attended college, and more than half have additional education beyond a bachelor's degree. Its location between a twelve-story hotel and the Moorish-style city hall in downtown Pasadena is not the main reason for its magnetism. Rather, All Saints views itself as a "peace and justice church" and offers at least twenty "ministries of compassion," including an AIDS Service Center.[16] Their services range from a children's communion to opportunities for lay-led services. Many such faith communities offer support groups for recovering alcoholics, the divorced, codependents, internationals learning English as second language, and victims of sex abuse, crime, and war.

Some congregations see a unique opportunity to equip Christian workers for effective ministry in underdeveloped nations and economically depressed areas. In a spirit akin to Peace Corps endeavors, sharp, sensitive laypersons are encouraged to give attention to spiritual concerns of nationals during overseas vacations, during travels for multinational corporations, during trips to international conventions, and the like. "Whether one works in the inner-city of Kansas City, Dallas, Denver or Los Angeles, or among the folk who live in the plastic bag 'shelters' in Mathare Valley in Nairobi, Kenya," noted missiologist Edgar Elliston at Fuller Seminary, "the ministry takes the church worker across cultural barriers."[17] Congregations are encouraged to prepare volunteers for cross-cultural caregiving by studying a broad range of disciplines, including cultural anthropology, economics, linguistics, sociology, and missiology. They draw resource persons as facilitators from backgrounds in denominational missions and service with relief agencies, such as World Vision International.

Numerous talented, committed laypersons are making themselves available for such time-limited ministries. Some, like a mid-forties attorney I learned about, "have it all"; yet they yearn for spiritual significance through specific acts of ministry. The note sounded here is one of deep gratitude for the laity's interest and commitment to both witnessing and caring aspects of the Christian life. What have to be ironed out are authority and power issues between ordained careerists in ministry and lay volunteers, moving into what may have seemed "preachers' territory." Let us examine some patterns of participation in pastoral care.

II. Patterns of Participation in Pastoral Care

Lest I be perceived as proposing *the* "right approach" to lay-pastor church organization, there is no *one path* to shared ministry. Whatever one's denomination, getting a clear understanding of the congregation and the way they prefer to do ministry is basic. A senior pastor, familiar with his seminary's focus on forming relationships with people in small churches, confided to his former seminary professor. "I don't have the time or energy to do *that*. With a large employed staff and thousands of parishioners, I've shifted to a synergistic leader style. I need skills in working with power-hungry executives and in organizing large groups. Sure, we have people who care, but most of them want to 'get a job done.' They are task-oriented, not person-centered. My people want church growth above all else." Other pastors discover apathetic and indifferent church members where institutional maintenance is "the name of the game."

It could go the other way; one hopes that it often does, as caring occasions come near at hand. For example, "the church in your house" is more than a phrase for many parents and children (Philemon 2). A family becomes a foster home for two orphaned girls. A Christian lawyer spends an evening answering the questions of some youths who are considering the legal profession as a career. A hospital administrator admits a charity patient—a child of an ethnic family—to his institution's full services and excellent staff. A homosexual employee of an industrial company confers with a Christian sales executive in order to seek career guidance. This particular sales official, in turn, confers with his minister about a plan of redemptive action for a person of homosexual orientation who desires appropriate behavior and expresses strong religious values.

When defining patterns of participation in pastoral care, the place to begin is not with some idyllic religious movement or a specialized clinical setting, but with the local church and one's own community. Retreats and institutes render a service in self-discovery and spiritual renewal; yet they must point beyond themselves to ministry by God's people in the real world. The local congregation is strategically poised to serve today "because it is already existing. Whether it plays its role or not . . . the parish is a fact. It is, by right, if not a reality, that tiny cell of Christianity, of the Incarnation. . . . Every community has its own."[18] Each community of faith is concerned with the ultimate dimensions of life—its hopes and fears, its joys and sorrows, its achievements and failures. Its ministry is to be directed to the universal needs of the human heart.

1. Levels of Participation in Church Life

An untrained eye might view the members of a given congregation as an undifferentiated group at the base of a church organizational pyramid diagram. Names of the paid staff, the diaconate, and members of official boards and committees would appear at the top. Participation in church life is more than a hierarchy of titles and offices, however. Pastors frequently misjudge the motives of their most faithful members, as well as the inaction of marginal members. Those who have a spatial concept of the church as a *place* and a limited concept of ministry as *getting things done* for the pastor tend to overlook the caring dimensions of daily life.

A typology of levels of participation in church life constructed by sociologist J. H. Fichter is of interest here: (1) *dormant*—indifferent members, new arrivals, invalids, those with formal ties only; (2) *marginal*—adherents, the withdrawn, the sinful, the rejected, occasional helpers; (3) *modal*—the dependable members of the church, most frequently present and participating; and (4) *nuclear*—a central core of Christians who form the nucleus of a warm, caring fellowship.[19] They are also devoted to facing problems of great magnitude in the world—crime, poverty, racism, family disruption, depletion of resources, and war. Like NT Barnabas, they are encouragers and evangelists.

When we examine the motives of active laypersons, it appears that a number of drives inspire their work for the Lord. Some persons need the pastor's approval and will try to do everything he or she asks of them. Beneath this compliance may lie a guilt dynamism, prompted by some failure or missed blessing. Such a "pastor-pleaser" hopes that generous self-sacrifice will win acceptance or favor. Latent hostility often characterizes this lifestyle, along with an inability to receive help from others or to trust God's gracious care. Others are what therapist Harriet Lerner describes as *over-functioners*, often firstborn or only children, whose characteristic style of managing anxiety and negotiating relationships is control.[20] To understand people who appear "always together" or "totally reliable," Lerner characterizes them as: (1) knowing what's best for themselves and others; (2) moving quickly to advise, fix, rescue, and take over when stress hits;

(3) unable to permit other persons to struggle with their own problems; and (4) avoiding the appearance of weakness. Over-functioners make rather powerful, sometimes difficult, congregants.

Some helpers need to be needed; however, they manifest this as a desire to serve where and when necessary. A certain amount of satisfaction comes in fulfilling one's inner urge toward creativity ("to amount to something"), particularly when this is related to God, either out of a great love or a great fear. People who need approval usually work without too much external pushing, because of an inner drive to please God in all things. Finally, rewards have their place in a person's investment in church activity. There is a matter of family approval, community status (some choose a "prestige church" because it commands general admiration), and the eschatological consideration of one's ultimate destiny after death. Empirical findings on this subject are almost nonexistent, indicating the need for social science research into motivations of the laity in church life. Pastoral understanding, not judgment, of people lies behind interest in their motives.

We cannot compartmentalize life, surmising that what is done in the church building is spiritual and what is done in the world outside is secular. For example, parents are called upon to practice faithcare in their own household, as citizens of the community, and as employees of a business firm or other institution. This multifaceted assignment is particularly difficult for single parents. An executive who tyrannizes office personnel is not merely a severe boss; he or she is a person who needs to grow. A politician who teaches a Bible class on Sunday and favors special legislative groups on Monday for a "price" is a false prophet. The work of God refuses to be isolated from the world, despite the tendency of some in this direction. While pastors are obligated to enlist congregants in formal church offices, they should understand that healing, sustaining, guiding, and reconciling tasks will also be performed where Christians live and work day by day.

2. The Responsibility of the Christian Pastor

The pastor's task is initiating, organizing, motivating, and primarily encouraging people in ministry. Ideally, the good shepherd knows the sheep and is known by them (Acts 20:28; 1 Pet. 5:2). Actually, a minister may know and care for only a fraction of the members of a large congregation. When one metropolitan minister was interviewed concerning pastoral relations, he lamented the fact that he did not even know hundreds of parishioners. Another urban pastor admitted: "While my people do not *love* me, at least they do *respect* me."

A psychiatrist lecturing at a theological school claimed that he could love only five patients as a caseload at any one time, along with his university teaching assignment. The psychiatrist deplored large churches but offered no alternatives to them. While the minister cannot limit a congregation's size to achieve intimacy, and is in fact committed to its continual enlargement, one is obligated to know one's members as far as possible. Several ministers may serve as colleagues on a church staff, thereby intensifying relationships with segments of the congregation. The multiple minister principle—a senior minister and associates—in large churches is preferable to the "closed corporation" idea of some who suggest limiting each church to a few hundred members. Some churches, because of their location or situation, will be small.

Beyond accountability for knowing persons in the faith community, what are the pastor's tasks in a church's systemic ministry? *The wise pastor sees shepherding possibilities, not only in personal counseling, but in preaching, worship experiences, calling, correspondence, and social encounters in the community.* The modern church overseer need not set up an unwieldy "ministering machine" and spend full time coordinating the coordinators of pastoral care. This would merely feed the subtle temptation to bolster "distance machinery" between oneself and the very persons one desires to serve under God.

A minister's responsibility should be defined in terms of the faith community's caring concerns, established in chapter 1, and in light of the following goals:

1. The pastor should *recognize the priority of personhood* in caring attitudes and actions. Just as we resent being manipulated and dictated to by others, the pastor realizes that people resist being treated as "things" and tire of being "used up" as expendable inventory in ecclesiastical production. Thus he or she will avoid duplicity, maintain openness, discipline emotions, and weigh words wisely in relationships. One will tend to leading, preaching, and teaching and seek to balance life through spiritual direction, Bible study, and prayer. Emphasis upon these main things in ministry is needed in our depersonalized culture. Wise ministers will avoid superficial opinions of persons and regard, with sensitivity, the difficult, often tragic situations of human existence.

2. The pastor should stimulate a *recovery of reverence* for God and for humanity through the celebration of worship, in one's own lifestyle, and in basic attitudes encouraged in others. Ours is not a religious world, but a brutal world of evil and brokenness. Persons suffer from a lost sense of

wonder in this technological age, when all miracles are being explained away, nature's secrets are exploited, and horizons are pushed beyond the stars. Worshipers have grown weary of preacher-centered churches, sustained by religious manipulation and pulpit huckstering. They have turned to modern mystery cults, like the New Age movement, the performing arts, sports, and nature worship, partly because some ministers have failed to put them in touch with the one true God.

3. The pastor serves as a spiritual catalyst in order to bring about the *realization of community* in church life. The contemporary churchgoer is suspicious of the pastor who constantly demands conforming cooperation and seeks to glue people together by involving everyone in everything all the time. A true faith community, which transcends the terrible loneliness of so many persons of all ages in our world, is a gift—the product of Christian life together. It is the kind of life that survives even Auschwitz-type persecution, as the journals of Dietrich Bonhoeffer and Ernest Gordon vividly attest.[21] No bonds of humankind on earth, beyond the ties of a healthy family, are so strong and sure and inspiring as those of the family of God. We, who have been "flung into existence" and tasted alienation's bitterness, need to belong to a vital fellowship of faith in order to transcend our fractured humanity.

4. The pastor should magnify the *relevance of faith in life* through preaching and personal communications with people. A Christian faith that is not workable in life is not a faith at all, but a cruel mockery. The Christian faith infuses human life with divine love, sustains one's vocational pilgrimage, supports life in trials and suffering, and sees one through the gates of splendor at death. People foundering in a wilderness of confusion need a relevant faith in God to grow on, to live by, and to hope with. The pastor who styles ministry through these objectives will present "the word of God in its fullness—the mystery . . . now disclosed to the saints . . . which is Christ in you, the hope of glory" (Col. 1:25–27). Such a community of faith may thus become a redemptive society in society.

3. The "Pastoral" Tasks of Responsible Laypersons

How, then, is the laity's role made specific? Pragmatic Westerners find it difficult to match a self-image of dynamic, hard-sell activism with tender, intimate tasks. Executives reason that Christ's spirit may work in religious matters but is ineffective in a tough-minded, competitive culture. Thus fast-trackers partition off "church affairs" from life's relationships. How different an attitude is conveyed by a West Side synagogue in New York City that combines spirituality and social action. The B'Nai Jeshurum congregation runs a soup kitchen and has forsworn large-scale renovations until a bigger homeless "suite" is completed. Former dean Ernest Gordon, of Princeton, recounted prisoner-of-war experiences in the "church without walls" near the River Kwai in Southeast Asia. There, men literally gave their lives for their friends. It was precisely the removal of "walls of partition" between persons, and between religionists and the world, that concerned Jesus Christ (Eph. 2:13–16). While the church's heart is inclined to God in worship, its eyes must see the suffering world approximately as it is, and its hands must unfold from prayer to service.

I believe that individuals can find dignity and meaning in concrete acts of love. So many people are engaged in a search for meaning in life. The paralyzing pessimism of existentialism, the loss of nerve and breakdown of the self in nihilism, and all types of escapism in world cultures indicate humanity's need for salvation and usefulness. A person's sense of meaning and worth may be found, as ethicist Helmut Thielicke has said, in "responsible action, in the *doing* of love, in the engagement. He who would know God and thus break through to the Absolute must first 'do the will of my Father in heaven.'"[22] Persons must believe that the Judeo-Christian message applies to every puzzling issue of life and find meaning in its service.

Laypersons can perform *pastoral* activities in the church. Ministry opportunities may be found in (1) guiding the members of a small Bible-study, self-improvement, or spirituality group; (2) greeting worshipers, receiving newcomers, and discipling believers in their adjustments to a new place; (3) calling in homes, social service centers, and hospitals; (4) praying for and staying in touch with absent members, such as military personnel, college students, nursing home residents, and individuals hospitalized for an extended period. The intercessory prayer ministry of parishioners for God's Kingdom, for each other, and for the world order reaps immeasurable harvests (John 14:14; Jas. 4:2–3, 5:16).

Some caregivers have placed themselves on call for the crises of life in their congregations. One urban church has a Good Samaritan Society composed of persons who are willing to risk ministry with overburdened persons by day or night. It is pledged to deal with the way things *are*. Its members take food into homes where persons are ill or jobless; furnish transportation for the physically challenged, preschool children, and aging persons; offer bilingual assistance as interpreters; work with juvenile court officers arranging foster homes for delinquents; visit prisoners; and seek to be serviceable in preventive ways through church agencies and community planning. Frequently, they offer what John Patton has called a "relationship beyond words" in doing concrete acts of ministry.

Retirement may open the door to pastoral activities for numerous men and women. A former civil servant of the government of India confessed: "I had a gentleman's agreement with Jesus Christ, when I met him twenty-eight years ago, that I would serve him in my daily work and give him all of my time upon retirement." Age influences participation in the church's caring concerns less than such factors as basic temperament, information about needs, health, time, sensitivity to one's neighbors, and willingness to do the truth.

The people of God can also perform pastoral activities in the world. Luther Youngdahl, a Christian statesman, once said: "Lay people in various segments of society are God's messengers for the releasing of grace and power for the healing of human life."[23] People who care—often "wounded healers" themselves—reach out to refugees from war-torn lands, international students and businesspersons, victims of sexual or physical abuse, AIDS sufferers, life's handicapped and mentally challenged citizens, unwed mothers, abusers of alcohol and drugs, and those growing old alone.

Sensitive Christians will detect the cries of those who are on the losing side in the struggle for existence. Those who become calloused to humanity's hurt are reminded that God hears humanity's crying. "He became their savior in all their distress. . . . In his love and in his pity he redeemed them . . . " (Isa. 63:8–9 NRSV). Some say that love is an "impossible possibility" in contemporary power-cultures and that justice is love's alternative in the social order. While society requires justice, love is still needed in human life. "We have never yet measured the *justice that is in love,* of which love is the only possible ground, the kind of love that undertakes to win back a lost creation in the only way there is to win it back, the pressure of its own hurt life leaning undefeated against the world."[24] Because God entered vicariously into humanity's hurt, his people are to share the earth's pain, while awaiting the day when there shall be "no more crying."

4. To Be Cared For

There is yet one other aspect of sharing pastoral caregiving—when we ourselves become the object of another's ministry. After all, do we need reminding that "pastors are people, too"?[25] What is it like when life's tide is running out, when things go out of control and caregivers stand in need of care themselves? After all, "patterns of participation" in pastoral care include those events when we personally need an understanding presence and to feel the blessing of a kinder world. Becoming the object of care — as a divorced person, a patient, a terminated pastor, a grieving spouse, yes, an alcoholic — is not easy, however. Ministers who have experienced spurious gifts of friendship, failed financial aid, betrayed intimacy, or outright rejection rightly suspect any proffered assistance. They distrust relationships that may hurt them again. Those who have once lived as a patron's pawn or who have suffered the misery of misunderstanding are reticent to trust a "helping hand." Indeed, "It is more blessed [to be able] to give than to [have to] receive," as Christ himself said (Acts 20:35).

One angry young pastor, who had been betrayed by a well-meaning confidant, grimaced with clenched fists: "I can't trust anyone any more!" Because some powerful helpers obligate the objects of their caring, persons may prefer to suffer alone rather than owe something to another.

When a person lives at the breaking point, it takes courage to open one's wounds and bleed in another's presence. To lay one's soul bare to a counselor, a physician, or a friend is not for the fainthearted. Discretion about disclosure is understandable. Persons who have fought old enemies on familiar battlegrounds may actually resent a peacemaker's presence. They are cautious about a new point of view or of becoming involved in deep relationships. Those who are feeling their way through a "minefield" may long for understanding and acceptance in religious vocation, yet prefer old conflicts to new commitments. Still, giving and receiving grace remains the heart of the Christian gospel. The Incarnation reminds us that acceptance of divine love releases a person from his or her lonely bondage. When one is "weak"— truly dependent upon care, human and divine — paradoxically, one becomes "stronger" (2 Cor. 12:10). One who accepts trustingly another's care bonds in a fellowship of the handicapped. To accept care from another is to be drawn into a community based not on proving oneself but on mutual trust and acceptance. Such gracious relationships are gifts which we are to trust and to receive.

Robert Frost captured the self-impoverishing style of life in "The Gift Outright." "The land was ours before we were the land's," he wrote of our American heritage. Yet many restrained themselves from receiving the gift.

> Something we were withholding made us weak
> Until we found out that it was ourselves
> We were withholding from our land of living
> And forthwith found salvation in surrender.[26]

Some mistaken believers hold that a *real* Christian, who trusts God, need never receive help from anybody. Yet God-experience does not enable an individual to declare independence from the human race. Often shame, or fear of exposure or reprisal or rejection, makes it difficult for an individual to disclose intimate needs to another person. But at least avenues of approach are possible. While every soul has its mystery, as Dostoyevski once wrote, men and women do desire strength for life's pilgrimage. So long as persons experience the "peril of hope," caregivers have a starting point, a place to begin.

A white-haired denominational executive, sitting in a handsome office, once related what it had been like for him to receive help from another. He had come home from World War I paralyzed, broken in body and spirit, to die. His Christian mother fed, bathed, and nursed him for many months. When he was stronger, he went to a government hospital. While there, several miles from the nearest city, a Christian layman who had also been in the war began visiting him. He told how the man and some young people from his church came every Sunday afternoon to see him. They brought him personal gifts and toilet articles. But more important—they gave him themselves! Through their refreshing moments of worship and confidential comradeship over the months, he learned to live again. Although his mother and the layman have both been dead many years, the Christian executive's life has been made rich with that fragrant memory. In such generous, unfussy ways, the church should cherish its ministers and offer Christ's healing to them.

III. The Courage to Care in Human Relationships

It's true! It takes courage to care, to risk effecting change in the life of a person, a family, or community of faith. Courage is that quality which keeps one going in the face of danger or discouragement. In pastoral care, courage implies being secure enough to risk oneself in a sticky situation or with a suffering person in a loving relationship. Those in what Paul Pruyser called "the transformational disciplines" or helping professions are "always faced with the 'messy' aspects of human life."[27] This is true in legal cases, in surgeries, in a church's financial affairs, in besieged lands in wartime, as well as common emergencies of life. Small wonder we shrink back when life is in flux, when things might "blow up" in our faces. Folks don't want to get involved.

A high-school student's response to a sermon she heard challenges such detachment. She confessed: "I have found many places in my own life where I keep a secret store of indifference as a sort of self-protection. . . . It takes courage to care. Caring is dangerous; it leaves you open to hurt and to looking a fool; and perhaps it is because they have been hurt so often that people are afraid to care."[28] Caring, which impels a person toward another human being in whom one *may* lose oneself, involves a risk. When one loves another person and invests in the relationship, that cherished person can injure a helper far more than someone whom he or she does not cherish. Those who are afraid to be hurt do not risk caring, for it is always costly business.

Caring is both *preventive* and *therapeutic*, if trouble comes. Love invests heavily in the welfare of family members, for example — bearing, believing, hoping, and enduring all things (1 Cor. 13:7). Many have been spared suffering by the preventive power of wise concern. On the other hand, real love listens attentively to the muffled signals beamed our way by people who want desperately to be heard and understood. What are those around us really trying to say with their words and ways? "If we maintain our distance, it will only be to perpetuate the shut-up-ness of our deeply troubled people until it must become the demonic spoken of by Kierkegaard and find itself expressed as 'shut-up-ness unfreely revealed.'"[29]

The family is potentially the primary caring community in any culture. Intrafamily relationships, from generation to generation, have the paradoxical power of preventing and producing tragic situations in life.[30] Parents who truly love their offspring will try to "train children in the right way" with the objective of self-discipline in view (Prov. 22:6 NRSV). Children learn what they are *to be* and *not to be* first from parent figures, then from their peers, their ministers and teachers, the laws of the community, and life in the "human jungle." The church, like the school, has a strategic opportunity to influence developing human lives "in light of who the [child] has been and with a vision of who the [child] can become."[31] Because parents are a child's first "priests," the home is central in personality development, in moral education, and in the socialization process.

It is now accepted generally that a child's earliest images and interpretations of God depend upon the symbolic resources of his parental relationships. Small children at home are still in "the dark" as far as the larger world is concerned. Their earliest ventures out of their cavelike environment, where the cave *is* the world, are with relatives, neighbors, or preschool workers. Following Robert Kegan's model of "the evolving self," Daniel Aleshire describes a two-year-old's emergence from his home environment.[32] At preschool, the child senses the world is larger than home. A little child is torn between wishing to be safe with family at home and wanting to discover the rest of the world. He or she may react with anxious symptoms, an occasional tantrum, even phobic behavior. Family time with children who spend each day in a childcare-type environment becomes crucially important.

With every child's need for love, security, consistency, and discipline in mind, let us look into the soul of Ned, a boy who at the age of ten was placed in a home for dependent children. The lad's mother had become separated from his alcoholic father when the boy was six years old. The woman was forced to institutionalize her son by court order, following repeated episodes of delinquency. On one occasion, he shared his frustrations and future plans with a Christian "parent substitute" whom we shall call Mr. P.

NED: I have heard several times that if you really want to go to college you can do it. It's a lot harder here because we don't have any encouragement from teachers, dorm parents, or leaders, or anything. Do you think I can go? I really want to go. [Silence.]

MR. P: Why do you think that it will be harder for you? [Pause.] Will college really be worth the effort?

NED: You see, it's this way. I want to go real bad. I've heard that it takes real good grades. You know that those stupid dorm parents make us get a least a C or they give us licks with that paddle! Some day I'm going to hit them back. I wish I could! . . . You know, I hate this place more than anything. Some of the boys run away from here, but I'm not, because you always get caught. Everyone in this school hates the place. We didn't want to be taken away from our parents; they made us come here. One day I'm going to get out of here and leave for good. I'll never come back. I guess that will be in a few years, because I only have two more years in high school. This is why I'm asking you about college. When you finish high school you have to go to work or go to college. I really want to go to college.

MR. P: Ned, you say that you want to go to college when you finish high school. . . .

NED: Yes, I want to get through with it as soon as possible. I want to make better grades, but I'm scared to. You see, when you make better grades or make too good grades, the other boys will hate you. The dorm parents let you have more privileges and the other boys begin to hate you. . . . I'm scared to make too good grades because they will fight with me. [He told of playing football and of the coach's suggestion of a possible scholarship.]

MR. P: Ned, you seem to have a real interest in college. This is good, but whether or not you go to college will in large measure be up to you.

NED: I feel that this is what I need, but it'll be real hard for me. I've heard several people who have come out here with their great beliefs and who want to help us poor things. They said that they would help me through college, but I hate them! I wish those old snobs would not even come out here! . . . Really, we don't want their pity. We know that we don't come from their old "good homes," but we're just as good as they are. . . .

Serious questions arise about Ned's future when we consider the emotional load he carries and his hostility toward life, himself, and all helping hands. A number of instructive things are revealed in this interview.

1. We have a glimpse of what parental failure can do. A youth who is alienated from parents finds it difficult to accept the offer of friendship from peers, authority figures, or those who clearly are interested in his or her welfare.
2. When love is lacking in a child's life he or she is insecure, fears rejection by everyone, and experiences low self-esteem. Even as we deplore Ned's plight we admire his pluck, his desire to amount to something in life.
3. Ned needed someone with whom he could share his inwardness and way of thinking about persons and problems, someone who would inspire his best. An older friend who dared to listen inspired Ned's courage to talk, to transcend his shut-up-ness. While young people need peer friendships and approval desperately, they also need adult friends. He shared his anxiety with a young adult who tried to understand his hostile feelings toward "old snobs." While he rejected patronage, Ned longed for an adult guarantor who had a solid and respected place in society. This clue guides the caregiver's concerns.
4. A love larger than all of life's hostility, fear, aggression, and suspicion is needed to accept this burdened youth and show him the Christian way of living. God's love, expressed through mature persons and through his Holy Spirit, can illuminate such a darkened life and inspire nobility in his soul.
5. While it takes courage for Christians to care in words, more persons are needed who will care wisely in their ways of living in the human community. This is something of what is meant by the startling New Testament statement: "Faith by itself, if it has no works, is dead" (Jas. 2:17).

Summary

We have explored the New Testament concept of the church as a redemptive society and the failure of many modern churches to achieve this caring ideal. The doctrine of the priesthood of believers was examined carefully and its implications for the pastoral roles of clergy and laypersons were noted. The performance and perversion of Christian concern were demonstrated clinically at the family level to insure that the principle of corporate ministry might find acceptance not merely in correct doctrine but in the doing of love. In the following chapter we shall consider the pastor's shaping influence upon the entire church's ministry through preaching and worship.

Notes

1. Carlyle Marney, *Structures of Prejudice* (Nashville: Abingdon Press, 1961), 200–15.
2. Pastor Alan Marr, for example, shares a team ministry at Westgate Community Church in Melbourne, Australia. In addition to traditional worship and education, the ministry sponsors a medical clinic for underprivileged ethnics; operates a job training center (including computer skills) for unemployed or underemployed persons; offers group support for adult children of alcoholics, divorced persons, single parents, and ex-mental patients; and sponsors summer camps for youth.
3. Charles V. Gerkin, *Prophetic Pastoral Practice: A Christian Vision of Life Together* (Nashville: Abingdon Press, 1991), 135–42. Also, see William M. Easum, *The Church Growth Handbook* (Nashville: Abingdon Press, 1990).
4. Robert McAfee Brown, *Making Peace in the Global Village* (Philadelphia: Westminster Press, 1981).
5. For contemporary challenges to *be* the church, see Paul A. Basden and David S. Dockery, eds., *The People of God: Essays on the Believers' Church* (Nashville: Broadman Press, 1991).
6. Kenneth L. Woodward, *et al.*, "A Time to Seek," *Newsweek* (December 17, 1990): 53.
7. Katarina Schuth, *Reason for the Hope* (Wilmington, DE: Michael Glazier, 1989), cited by Paul Wilkes, *The Atlantic* (December 1990): 62.
8. Martin Thornton, *Pastoral Theology: A Reorientation* (London; S.P.C.K., 1956), 69. See also chapters 1, 4, 5, and 21. This "reorientation" lacks the comprehensiveness of an earlier British study: Henry Balmforth, *et al.*, *An Introduction to Pastoral Theology* (London: Hodder and Stoughton, 1937). A more relevant discussion, in light of contemporary developments in Britain

and North America, was published by Alastair V. Campbell, *Rediscovering Pastoral Care* (Philadelphia: Westminster Press, 1981). Campbell now teaches Christian Ethics in New Zealand.

9. Wilhelm Pauck in H. Richard Niebuhr and Daniel Day Williams, eds., *The Ministry in Historical Perspectives* (New York: Harper & Row, 1956), 112.

10. Kenneth M. Carey, ed., *The Historic Episcopate*, 14, cited in T. F. Torrance, *Royal Priesthood* (Scottish Journal of Theology Occasional Paper No. 3, 1955), 35.

11. See H. J. Carpenter, "Minister, Ministry," in *A Theological Word Book of the Bible*, edited by Alan Richardson (New York: Macmillan, 1960), 146–51. Cf. Frank Stagg, *New Testament Theology* (Nashville: Broadman Press, 1962), 250–76.

12. Martin E. Marty, *The New Shape of American Religion* (New York: Harper & Row, 1958), 123.

13. See John H. Leith, *From Generation to Generation: The Renewal of the Church According to Its Own Theology and Practice* (Louisville: Westminster/John Knox Press, 1990).

14. Hendrik Kraemer, *A Theology of the Laity* (Philadelphia: Westminster Press, 1958), 143. Cf. Patton, *From Ministry to Theology*, 64–67.

15. Kenneth A. Briggs, "Baby Boomers: Boom or Bust for the Churches," *Progressions: A Lilly Endowment Occasional Report* (January 1990): 4–7; Cf. Wade Clark Roof and William McKinney, *American Mainline Religion: Its Changing Shape and Future* (New Brunswick, NJ: Rutgers University Press, 1987).

16. Woodward, *et al.*, "A Time to Seek," 50–56.

17. Edgar J. Elliston, ed., *Christian Relief and Development: Equipping Christian Workers for Effective Ministry* (Dallas: Word Books, 1989).

18. Quoted from Abbe Michonneau by Tom Allan, *The Face of My Parish* (New York: Harper & Row, n.d.), 67.

19. J. H. Fichter, *Social Relations in the Urban Parish* (Chicago: University of Chicago Press, 1954), 22, cited by Conor K. Ward, *Priest and People: A Study in the Sociology of Religion* (Liverpool, England: Liverpool University Press, 1961), 1–29 *et passim*.

20. Harriet G. Lerner, Ph.D., of the Menninger Clinics, *The Dance of Intimacy* (San Francisco: Harper & Row, 1989), 104.

21. Dietrich Bonhoeffer, *Life Together*, translated by John W. Doberstein (New York: Harper & Row, 1954); and Ernest Gordon, *Through the Valley of the Kwai* (New York: Harper & Row, 1962). Cf. Richard L. Rubenstein and John K. Roth, *Approaches to Auschwitz: The Holocaust and its Legacy* (Atlanta: John Knox Press, 1987).

22. Helmut Thielicke, *Nihilism: Its Origin and Nature—With a Christian Answer*, translated by John W. Doberstein (New York: Harper & Row, 1961), 162.

23. Luther W. Youngdahl, "The Layman's Responsibility in the Mission of the Church," *Religion in Life* 31 (Winter 1961–62): 90.
24. Paul Scherer, *For We Have This Treasure* (New York: Harper & Row, 1944), 80, emphasis supplied.
25. Gordon-Conwell Seminary graduates David B. Biebel and Howard W. Lawrence have edited *Pastors Are People Too* (Ventura, CA: Regal Books, 1986).
26. Robert Frost, *In the Clearing* (New York: Holt, Rinehart & Winston, 1962), 31. Used by permission.
27. Paul Pruyser, *Changing Views of the Human Condition* (Macon, GA: Mercer University Press, 1987), 7.
28. Quoted in Elton Trueblood, *The Yoke of Christ* (New York: Harper & Row, 1958), 73.
29. Ernest E. Bruder, "Having the Courage to Talk," *Pastoral Psychology* 13 (May 1962): 31.
30. See Edwin H. Friedman, *Generation to Generation: Family Process in Church and Synagogue* (New York: The Guilford Press, 1985).
31. Daniel O. Aleshire, *Faithcare: Ministering to All God's People through the Ages of Life* (Philadelphia: Westminster Press, 1988), 33.
32. Robert Kegan, *The Evolving Self: Problem and Process in Human Development* (Cambridge, MA: Harvard University Press, 1982). Aleshire, *Faithcare*, 77.

Suggested Reading

Brister, C. W. *Caring for the Caregivers: How to Help Ministers and Missionaries.* Nashville: Broadman Press, 1985. This book pulls back the curtain of privacy and permits laypersons to see the initiate struggles of vocational religious workers. It can enhance understanding and build bridges of co-ministry.
Corey, Marianne S. and Gerald Corey. *Becoming a Helper.* Pacific Grove, CA: Brooks/Cole, 1989. Examines careers in human services—motives, anxieties, stresses, and strategies for working with difficult persons.
Ellis, E. Earle. *Pauline Theology: Ministry and Society.* Grand Rapids: Wm. B. Eerdmans, 1989. A careful theological examination of spiritual gifts and their use in churches of all denominations.
Giles, Kevin. *Patterns of Ministry Among the First Christians.* San Francisco: HarperCollins, 1991. Shows how the earliest Christian churches were organized. Examines development of the roles of apostle, prophet, bishop, presbyter, and deacon.
Hobbs, Herschel H. *You Are Chosen: The Priesthood of All Believers.* San Francisco: Harper & Row, 1990. An examination of the Protestant concept of the corporate priesthood of believers by an elder statesman of the Free Church tradition.

Schaller, Lyle E. *The Pastor and the People,* rev. ed. Nashville: Abingdon Press, 1986. Schaller follows the career of imaginary minister Don Johnson at St. John's Church. Cf. *The Senior Minister.* Nashville: Abingdon Press, 1988; and related ministry studies.

Whitehead, James D. and Evelyn E. Whitehead. *The Promise of Partnership: Leadership and Ministry in an Adult Church.* San Francisco: HarperCollins, 1990. Analyzes the processes of partnership in Christian ministry—sharing power, managing conflict, and healing wounds of abused authority.

CHAPTER FIVE

PASTORAL ASPECTS OF PREACHING AND WORSHIP

In the Introduction, we met Libby Lyles, whose mother had suffered a massive stroke. Pastor Randy Stephens was forced to rethink the structure of his own faith even as he supported the Lyles family in its grief work. From the outset, the authentic Christian minister was called a *hope bearer*, one seeking to advance faith in a perplexed world. This brings to mind an occasion when Jesus Christ expressed a certain anxiety about his disciples' capacity for hope. "When the Son of Man comes, will he find faith on the earth?" (Luke 18:8). Would his servants have courage and steadfastness under all circumstances to hold to the promise of Christ's Coming?

The Master's concern reminds us that "the cure of souls is never merely a *method*, even a method derived from a doctrine, or a task for certain hours in the week, but . . . it involves *both* the faith we live by *and* all our daily activities and contacts."[1] Pastoral leaders are concerned with caregiving ministries by the entire community of faith in daily activities and contacts. Basic to such sharing is nurturance of "faith on the earth." In public worship, one touches the private dramas of peoples' lives — job loss, aging, family hurts, injustice, victimization by war, drug abuse — with the Gospel. One is compelled to address challenges to belief — faith and broken faith, trust and distrust, self and the larger community — and to aid the reconstruction of faith in peoples' lives.[2] Thus the prophetic and pastoral dimensions of ministry reinforce each other.

The purpose of this chapter is to (1) distinguish how life is undergirded and Christian service is informed through the pastor's public and private ministries; (2) characterize the pastoral preacher; and (3) focus the caring concerns of worship and preaching. The chronology of pastoral care flows from worship to calling, from preaching to counseling, from group work to witness and ministry. In turn, the private ministry informs and vitalizes preaching and worship. Frequently, a congregant departs from worship with a desire to talk with the preacher about some aspect of the sermon. Such a one may say, "You certainly spoke to me today, Pastor; I would like to talk with you about that subject sometime." A minister once preached on the theme of the daily providence of God. At the close of the service a woman who had been helped by the sermon said, "I certainly needed that message. Tomorrow we are moving to Colorado. This church and community have meant much to me and my family. We need to feel that we are moving within God's providence." Seldom does a pastor know or fully understand the private struggles, family dramas, relational issues, and vocational demands faced by all members of a faith community. Still, one's calling is to a holistic vision in public and private ministries.

I. The Public and Private Ministries

Christian history clarifies the dual dimensions of caregiving through (1) the enhancement of spiritual wellbeing (preventive or prophetic care); and (2) restoration of function when emergencies arise or dysfunction comes (therapeutic care). When ministers turn all their energies to one of these dimensions of pastoral work, they inevitably neglect the other. Both systemic and personal levels of concern are essential. Preventive care is linked primarily (though not exclusively) to the pastor's public ministry and to the people's responsibilities for extending the Christian faith into the structures of society.

The *preventive prophetic level* of concern is essential in order to avoid simplistic solutions to life's threats and crises, many of which are produced by grave social problems. Pastoral care of the individual person cannot be divorced from Christian strategy for family life and for a truly responsible society.[3] The pastor affirms community-minded foster care projects and members of the congregation who engage in the helping professions. The prophet-leader supports those who seek to alleviate social injustices and to prevent crime and inhumanity. In short, a pastor reinforces those who seek to live usefully in the world. One of the minister's greatest responsibilities is to assist publicly engaged members of the congregation to use their talents and strengths for the common good.

In an essay on leadership, educator John W. Gardner referred to "the discovery of talent in unexpected places," to releasing "the energies of every human being," and to "toning up the whole society" as individuals are encouraged to turn their talents toward constructive purposes.[4] Pastoral care participates in the drama of "hidden gifts discovered," and in the conservation of human talent for just causes in the earth. Encouraging persons who are potential centers of strength and witness requires as much pastoral imagination and skill as does ministering to persons in crises.

The *therapeutic* or *healing-supporting* level of pastoral care is primarily (though not exclusively) a private ministry with individuals, families, or small groups. Those who serve in Christ's stead extend the Christian *koinonia* to single persons and families who suffer life's tragic failures, traumas, and often unalterable situations. As a bridge between God and parishioners, the minister shares their private worlds of pain in intimate meetings and through intercessory prayer. Being "all things to all people" appears an impossible dream to the busy pastor. Getting ready for Sunday has more ego appeal than bearing dark burdens of hurt and loss and death. The bringer of eternal life to persons alienated from God cannot dismiss reconciling individuals in private "hells" of brokenness. For a pastor to rationalize that prophetic ministry is "best for me" and to specialize in proclamation does not exempt the congregation from the hard work of caregiving.

Admittedly, the pastoral tasks of preaching and worship are of a different order from intimate pastoral conversations. Yet both counseling and preaching are concerned with enhancing spiritual renewal and encouraging church growth. Some writers have sought to separate these functions by viewing the preacher as a prophet "on God's side" and the pastor as a priest "on humanity's side." Such a false dichotomy cannot be demonstrated from biblical theology. The New Testament bishop was both prophet and priest in the celebration of public worship and interpretation of personal commitments.[5] The testimony of the earliest Christian community in Jerusalem contained both prophetic utterance and "the apostles' teaching and fellowship ... breaking of bread and the prayers" (Acts 2:14-36, 41-42). The pastoral preacher thus renders a significant service by addressing the personal issues *(isness)* of people from within the categories *(oughtness)* of the Christian faith.

II. Bearers of Hope in a World of Peril

In the memorable phrasing of H. H. Farmer, the Christian pastor is a servant of the Word of God. As "bearer of the divine-human conversation," the minister leads the dialogue of worship and extends the relationships present in worship into "the sacrament of life."[6] The preacher addresses individuals *and* a congregation, each with separate interests and needs, yet with corporate concerns as the body of Christ. We may classify one sermon as "doctrinal," another "evangelistic," and a third "ethical"; yet we make pastoral suggestions in each sermon. The lectionary reading of the Scriptures is inclusive "in and out of season."

Theologian Elizabeth Achtemeier reminds us that authentic biblical preaching is essentially storytelling—a history of happenings through which God revealed himself to humankind. The content of preaching is not a collection of doctrines, ethical principles, pious precepts, or philosophical arguments. Rather, it is sacred history that gives us the essential shape of reality. God's story "shows us what is going on in the world, who the real power in our universe is, and what it is he is doing."[7] The divine Author helps us grasp the story's truth as real and to live obediently as citizens of God's new covenant Kingdom. Apart from biblical story there is no eternal life and no coming kingdom.

Harry Emerson Fosdick, a master of connecting biblical and human stories, once described preaching as counseling on a group scale. While preaching is much more than *that*, Fosdick was right when he determined that "every sermon should have for its main business the head-on constructive meeting of some problem which [is] puzzling minds, burdening consciences, [and] distracting lives." Furthermore, he realized that "no sermon which so met a real human difficulty, with light to throw on it and help to win a victory over it, could possibly be futile."[8] The popularity of self-help small groups (like Al-Anon) and self-help literature testifies to the remoteness and irrelevance to life-situations of much contemporary pulpit work. Some ministers have apparently lost the capacity to provide help for their members regarding the critical issues, dark shadows, even stark terrors, they often confront.

There has been some discussion among communicators about the "point of contact" in preaching—what in an individual is being addressed by the sermon. Relevance in preaching cannot be determined by human criteria alone. It is the Spirit of God, using the preacher's wisdom and the divine Word, that connects our preaching with life. The longer people listen and the closer they obey, the more they become like the One they worship.

Like the military chaplain speaking to sailors or soldiers on the eve of an engagement with the enemy, a preacher must be prepared to risk warfare on the morrow alongside the congregation. Leviathan, their formidable foe, awaits them in the turbulent seas and desert places of life (Isa. 27:1). Each warrior is ready; yet before the day's battle is done, those who remain will bear the burdens of the wounded and fallen. Some fighters become psychological victims in their exposure to the terrors of technological warfare. Others are overcome by battle fatigue. So it is in life. All worshipers do not face the same foes in the week ahead, but each member of the congregation needs assurance for the spiritual warfare ahead (Eph. 6:10–18).

Some preachers assume that if preaching is biblical it will be relevant; that if the Word of God is proclaimed it will find its mark in some needy heart. Such reasoning sounds feasible, but it may fail congregants in their search for a better way of life. Alan Richardson's *The Bible in the Age of Science* helps us to answer the twin issues of all relevant interpretation: "What *did* the Bible mean originally?" and "What *does* it mean today?"[9] Despite the preacher's concern, the person for whom a certain message is intended may miss the whole idea, or may be absent on the day of "her" or "his" sermon. In an account of a lawyer's suicide, the reporter said: "Mr. S. plunged to his death at 11 o'clock, Sunday morning—the exact time he had an appointment with his family to be in church." The sermon intended for that depressed man on that particular day was posthumous, not relevant, preaching. It came too late.

A preacher is addressing the congregation pastorally when keeping the burden of the Lord and problems of persons in tension in the dialogue of the sanctuary. One's objective is to shine a beam of healing light into the cancerous tissues of human existence. The wise pastor becomes a spiritual mentor precisely when dilemmas are faced, burdens are lifted, guilt is relieved, high purposes are forged, and hope is rekindled in the human heart. On a larger scale, one may turn the tide in an entire congregation that has lost its way—become listless, introverted or apathetic about life's great issues. For example, in an effort to inspire his faith community with fresh vision one minister offered a series of doctrinal sermons on the church—its origin, nature, true head, ministry, and mission. Under the general theme "The Fellowship of Confession," each sermon reflected profound prophetic importance.

What then is the content of pastoral preaching to be? Nothing less than the Word of God! It is precisely of thin, superficial sermons that people are weary. As they gather in worship to be reminded of that unseen world of the spirit, the faithful need to hear of "a God who does things for us, anticipates us, comes in quest of us, and carries us all the way."[10] Yet the interpreter of the Word has a great responsibility both to God and the people. A teacher sent from God must not misrepresent the divine-human situation through superficial utterances or misuse of sacred symbols. Preachers prostitute religion to unworthy purposes who offer God as an antidote to anxiety or as a sure path to health or personal success. Dysfunctional hope is dishonest "hope." God's Word comes as a gift, but also as a claim upon people's lives, requiring obedience.

The servant of the Word is to connect with the people, with the Scriptures, and with God. Without the Lord in one's life, the preacher has nothing of ultimate worth to offer hearers. Jesus reminded the disciples, "Apart from me you can do nothing" (John 15:5). A pastoral preacher who would lead others to sense the reality of God must be at home in the divine company. The burdened prophet prayed of his wife Agnes in Ibsen's tragedy *Brand:*

> Then return, with face aglow
> From His Presence, fair and free.
> Bear His glory down to me
> Worn with battle thrust and throe.[11]

When persons are struck dumb with grief, baffled by betrayal, crushed in their own clandestineness, stricken with illness, or enslaved by guilt, they need the assurance of a God who understands and cares for them.

Pastoral preaching is a powerful event in which one speaks for God in order to affect the life situation of other persons. The preacher takes into account worshipers' faith and broken faith, ambivalent feelings of anger and guilt, hope and anxious predicaments, then permits persons to connect imaginatively with God in the sermon. Speaking for the congregation enhances the possibility of making a difference in life situations with God's good news. The preacher includes peoples' needs, not alone in sermon delivery but in sermon preparation as well. Do they really understand the demanding processes of one's preaching craft, the quiet struggles of soul that go on in the minister's workshop? Dietrich Ritschl, a Barthian interpreter of preaching, has said the sermon is not the sole property of the preacher. It belongs to the congregation as well.[12] Imaginative ways of informing a congregation of one's sermon preparation process may be devised. The congregation can be trained to study biblical texts along with the pastor. Preachers, in turn, must listen to texts *on behalf of the people* by asking, "What is God's message for them in this passage on this particular occasion?" Ultimately, the preacher's goal is to be not cleverly contemporary but eternally relevant.

III. Pastoral Concerns in Worship

The service of worship is a sacramental event where God and worshipers meet. The church that ministers for the world's sake in mission, and for its own sake in nurture and caring, also ministers for God's sake in worship. A caring congregation, concerned for life's *ultimates* and its *immediacies,* must renew its vision and nurture its service in yieldedness to God. Because "life is difficult," as Scott Peck said, there is no substitute for a sense of the presence of God.[13] God alone provides the power to see life through. In Christian worship, the believer returns to the upstream region of life, participates in eternity, sounds the "Amen" of the church of the ages, faces the eschatological dimensions of existence, and consecrates life afresh in commitment.

The constellation of worship locates God at the center of all existence. The orbits of life move about him as planets orbit about the sun. Certain theologians have conceived God in a category "beyond personality," as being an ontological "ultimate reality" concealed in mystery as the "hidden God." Yet in Christian worship we remember that the God and Father of our Lord Jesus Christ has visited his people person-to-person with the gift of eternal life (John 1:1–18). Christ, while offering individual salvation, created a fellowship of new beings—the Church—a community of memory and of hope. The pastor and the people have this "treasure in jars of clay, to show that this all-surpassing power is from God and not from us." It is not to some mystical, ineffable light that worshipers respond, but to "the light of the knowledge of the glory of God in the face of Christ" (2 Cor. 4:6, 7). How, then, shall one proceed with the conduct of worship?

1. The Conduct of Worship

The role of the authorized, usually ordained, worship leader has varied in the branches of Christendom from age to age. In liturgical churches, the priest celebrates the service with a focus on symbols, spirituality, and Christian commitment.[14] While the biblical witness to worship is not liturgical, but rather direct, devotional, and disciplinary, the celebration of worship including the rites of Christian baptism and the Lord's Supper are taken for granted. In such informal communions as the Society of Friends, there is varied shape and action in relative formlessness. Each congregant is a minister and testifies as he or she is prompted by the Spirit in an otherwise unstructured service. And in free, nonliturgical churches, the preacher is central as God's representative. This priestly function occurs with weekly regularity as one mediates between the Almighty and people who desire to be more like God.

Liturgy and leadership of worship go together; thus the place to begin is to determine what is going on in the process. Religious devotees remember that their Creator comes first, is self-existing, all-powerful, holy, and redemptive; while they are of the contingent created order. In a theistic worldview, God reveals himself and requires humankind to respond in faithful obedience to him as the source of all being. The Greeks called humankind *anthropos*—"the upward-looking one." In response to the gods they envisioned, the Greeks offered *liturgy*, literally "the work of the people" in worship. The shape of their service included offerings, prayers, and meetings in sacred places.

Leaders of worship must ask themselves what motivates persons in their special work for God. The late Paul Pruyser, in A *Dynamic Psychology of Religion*, suggested four motivational reasons why people go to church.[15] One reason we worship is *imitation* of the Creator. People become like the gods (in this instance, God) they worship. The Passover meal in Hebrew history and modern Jewish worship identifies a special liberative act of God in freeing Israel from Egyptian bondage. And the Lord's supper connects Christian worshipers with Christ's atonement, even as baptism links them with his death, burial, and resurrection. Acts of worship are performed in remembrance and imitation of the Almighty, and easily slip into identification with the Creator.

Making things right between oneself and one's Maker involves *placation* or *restitution*, said Pruyser. One who has "missed the mark" by transgressing divine guidance seeks restoration of fellowship with the Maker. Ancient bloodletting of animals by a priest on peoples' behalf can be done symbolically through words of remembrance of Christ's atonement. Acts by which pastor and people may restore themselves include: prayers of confession, gifts for charity or missions, doing penance (the Catholic's way), by undertaking some task, or making restitution for some wrong.

Commemoration is a third important aspect of worship. In Judaism, there are events like the Passover, Feast of Lights, and Feast of Tabernacles to remember important elements of Jewish history. For Christians, the Lord's Supper reenacts Christ's death and for Protestants replaces the Roman Mass. Pastors who celebrate marriages and the ordinances, who officiate at funerals and memorial services, and who preside in gathered faith communities help people remember who they are, who God is, and who they should become.

The spontaneity, impulsivity, warmth, and fervor of worship denote giving God his due in *tribute*—joyous adoration of the Creator. OT worship was marked occasionally by singing, dancing, festooning a place of worship with flowers, as well as by solemn assemblies. NT worship began in *agape-feast* mealtime settings, but occasionally got out of hand with ecstatic speech and unregulated consumption of wine (see 1 Cor. 10–14 for problematic excesses in worship). A hymn writer described this self-forgetfulness in glad adoration as being "lost in wonder, love, and praise."

Worship, then, has room for many movements of the human spirit. While these observations do not exhaust our reasons for worship, they remind us of "the complexities of human need and motivation."[16]

Whatever the particular tradition, the weakness of much Protestant worship lies in its failure to be a truly corporate action, moving toward a single objective. Worship should be, in Dix's words, a "united and uniting action" toward God, a response to his judgment and grace and a stimulus to serviceable living in the world. The portrait of a congregation at worship— the chiming of the hour, hymns, prayers, offering, sermon, and parting blessing—is not a "still" but a motion picture. "Deep calls unto deep" in the call to worship, and each congregant is an active participant in the service of worship. A religious devotee shares the reading of Scripture, the pastoral prayer, the ministry of giving, and the message from God's Word. With the benediction ringing in one's heart, the worshiper departs blessed and determined to be a blessing. The worship leader's specific role will be determined by his or her particular community of faith, of order, of symbols, of language, of festivals, and of living. Yet each leader is to include all congregants in the service as far as possible.

Following are some suggestions that have general application regardless of the church's sociocultural situation, size, ethnic constituency, and particular communion:

1. The Christian pastor is to *teach the people concerning their joint roles in the celebration of worship.* One pastor periodically conducts in-the-pew training concerning the church ordinances. Then, during baptism or the Lord's Supper service, the people feel a personal sense of responsibility for connecting with God.[17] Informed congregants sense the rich heritage and symbolic significance of these cherished modes of remembrance and hope. Even as Christian persons experience God, not just "something," in such covenantal moments, they sense that God is experiencing them, too. Such expression becomes a token of one's gratitude, a mode of remembrance, an act of surrender, and a pledge of hope. It is a living covenant, ever new, between God and members of the community of faith.

Instruction regarding worship can also be carried on through family education and with children's groups at church. The attitude of reverence, for instance, is caught as well as taught and is demonstrated in the acts of life as well as in the house of God. Children learn to love God because he first loved them; thus they worship him in adoration and awe but not in guilt and fear.[18] Many ministers design a children's hymn, story, and prayer into the service to express an inclusive concern for everyone in worship.

To affirm with regularity the manifestation and mystery of God and the sacredness of life refreshes God's people "on their toilsome way." The ground of the sacred is involved with an order of things in which the worshiper experiences the reality of Someone known only in part yet trusted with complete devotion. Christian worship, theologically oriented and psychologically conditioned, calls for a verdict from each worshiper that will be carried into the daily round of life. Accordingly, the pastor will recognize the essential unity of all elements in the service and will prompt each congregant toward obedient action through participation.

2. This implies that the pastor will *recognize individual differences within the congregation and remember the participants' concerns in corporate worship.* Such knowledge requires imaginative identification, courage, and sensitivity. People come to worship from life with differences in age, gender, ethnicity, social roles, education, intellectual capacity, health, motivation, spiritual need, stress level, vocational situation, and interest. They return to "real life" situations following the worship service either burdened or blessed. Once, at the close of a service, a woman asked the opportunity to make a public statement. She shocked the minister by confessing that she had been most critical of him to numerous persons in the church. He had had no idea that the conclusion of the service would go that way, but was grateful for her moment of truth. Of course, each person present bears his or her own responsibility to worship the Father "in spirit and truth" (John 4:23).

3. The pastor acknowledges that *preaching occurs in a context of worship;* it is not an end in itself. One builds the hermeneutical bridge between life situations and biblical texts by asking specific questions. According to Elizabeth Achtemeier, these concerns may be grouped under four headings: (1) What would my people doubt to be true in this text? That is, what is hard for them to believe that becomes an obstacle to hearing? (2) What do my people need to know or be reminded of from this text? The sermon will answer their basic needs out of the Scriptures. (3) What inner longings, feelings, thoughts, or desires of my people connect with this text? The sermon will speak to these inner longings. And (4) if this text became true in my life, what would be the consequences?[19] The preacher imagines lots of possible sermonic approaches, then uses those most applicable to the congregation.

It helps us to recall that preaching in the biblical tradition was frequently a homily (*homilia*)—a discussion of or conversation upon a religious subject. It had the nature of discourse, often in narrative or story form, to help persons communicate with God. Harold Freeman, a teacher of preaching, says, "Too much contemporary expository preaching has failed to be creative, and too much contemporary preaching has failed to be biblical."[20] Among the varied forms of innovative preaching he advocates are: dramatic monologue, dialogue, narrative preaching, and drama and media helps. Despite attempts at creativeness, we acknowledge the final connection between God and people lies in mystery—in the purposes of his solemn will and the power of the Holy Spirit.

4. Pastor and people will attempt, constructively and imaginatively, *to relate their communion with God in worship to their conversations with persons in society.* In Book 12 of *The City of God,* Augustine wrote that "the two cities (the earthly and the heavenly, to wit) . . . are in the present world commingled, and as it were entangled together." The Christian is a citizen of two worlds, constantly threatened with the loss of the sacred, especially in this technological age. Gabriel Marcel, the philosopher, has said:

> In a world where technology is given absolute primacy, there inevitably develops a process of desacralization which attacks life and all its manifestations, . . . especially the family and everything connected with it.
>
> The only way one can hope to return toward the sacred is by turning away from the world, in order to find once again that simplicity . . . as well as the intimacy which is the privileged ground of the sacred.[21]

Marcel calls such turning from the world "conversion," not in the confessional sense, but in the value-judgment perspective of sensing once again what is vital in life. Indeed, worship points both to Christian conversion as decision and to the Christian life as the vocation of the people of God.

2. The Place of Worship

A second pastoral concern in worship is the *place* of religious practice, which is of a different order than the foregoing considerations. Christian ministers need to see clearly the function of architecture and symbolism in religious experience. Something of the spirit and soul of a congregation is revealed in the design of its worship center: its gatheredness, aspirations, hopes, reverence, symbolic life, and sense of mission. Steel, glass, tapestry, and stone, shaped into meaningful substance, have the capacity to hallow human aspirations and to reflect the glory of God. Architecture need not be ornate in order to communicate a church's character and theological identity or to facilitate the varied expressions of its life.

Max Weber has said that we live in a disenchanted world, in which matter is only matter and form is only form. Glass is glass, steel is steel, and stone is stone in our utilitarian culture. Modern church building designs seldom appear to point beyond themselves to God at the center of life. Church buildings are intended to be functional, even artistic, but there is a notable lack of unity in contemporary church architecture. Pastors and members of church building committees should remember that "in religious architecture, it is not stone and steel we are trying to reveal . . . but the transcendent, the invisible reality, even God."[22] A congregation's house of worship is a clue to its God-concept and a key to its own identity. It can reflect a fortress mentality, cradle community, or unleash the church for its mission on earth.

"How can the church-house help in ministry?" Consider this experience. A pastor once received a distraught young woman into his study who, a few minutes before, had contemplated leaping to her death from a bridge. "I looked from the swirling water below up to the steeple of your church," she confessed, "and I wondered what was beneath that cross." A church's architecture spoke to a potential suicide's despair and became an avenue of escape from death. The building is more than symbols, chapels, impersonal corridors, offices, and rooms. As a Christian training and worship center, the place of meeting mirrors human struggles and aspirations; it provides ministry resources; it offers salvation to the world; and it inspires excellence in mission.[23]

With this missional effect of worship in mind, some pastors are encouraging informal worship experiences entirely away from the church-base. One congregation in Florida, for example, has traditional Sunday morning worship with all conventional elements of liturgy in place. Two evenings each month, the congregation disperses into neighborhood homes for informal social-type gatherings. One evening a month, a congregational task force dresses casually and conducts informal worship in a regional shopping mall. Another evening, multicultural worship is encouraged as white ethnic Americans relate in music and devotions with African-Americans, Hispanics, and Asian-Americans. Basic worship concepts merge in synergetic, emergent approaches. *Place* mingles with *purpose* in an effort to touch lives for God in modern urban settings.

My own perspective is the Free Church tradition, in which the central focus of worship is the Word of God proclaimed and the Christian ordinances celebrated. I am sympathetic with Samuel Miller's claim that architecture dramatizes the dynamic interaction of God and persons and reflects the particular community's tradition. For example, I have been thrilled with the magnificent choirs, organ music, and preaching in cathedral-type urban worship centers. On the back side of nowhere in western Kenya, I have been inspired by worship in a stick hut among Masai believers. In Manhattan or San Francisco, skyscrapers, not crosses, dominate the skyline. Beyond the great Rift Valley, the mountains, not a tree-framed building, touch the horizon and remind worshipers of the Eternal.

From a pastoral perspective, the place of a church's meeting and the symbols of its sacred life should bring order to our chaotic existence. The elevated ceiling of its sanctuary should symbolize the majesty of God and the soul's highest aspirations of faith. The materials—glass, wood, tapestry, and stone—should convey the strength of God, reassure persons of his presence, and inspire each worshiper to reach beyond his or her own narrow limits. A church's doors should extend an abiding invitation to passersby to move from life's harried routine into a house of wondrous miracles. From its sturdy steps departing worshipers should go blessed into their homes and life's callings. If that ideal is realized, people need to hear the voice of God in preaching.

IV. A Pastoral Focus in Preaching

Christian preaching remains the most nearly normative activity of all Protestantism. Proclamation has a unique place in the world. While the "word of the cross" has always been "folly" to some, Christian ministers are under orders to herald the message of God in contemporary society (1 Cor. 1:18–21, 9:16; 2 Tim. 4:2). Many preachers, influenced by C. H. Dodd's *The Apostolic Preaching and Its Developments*, have concentrated upon *kerygma* (proclamation of the central gospel events) and *paraclesis* (exhortation) and have thereby neglected *homilia* (discussion of some theological subject) and *didache* (teaching). To the extent that this is true, Dodd has rendered us a disservice; for persons need all levels of Christian discourse. And proclamation has pastoral implications, for it focuses truth upon individuals.

Roy Pearson, a former president of Andover Newton Theological School, once proposed a fourfold agenda for preaching: "To celebrate the wonderful works of God; to contend for the faith delivered to the saints; to fill the hungry with good things; and to speak unto the children of Israel, that they go forward."[24] Pearson held that, ideally, every sermon ought to be a proclamation of the total gospel. Yet he confessed wisely that the gospel is too vast to be encompassed by a thousand sermons. Pastoral preaching, directed toward filling "the hungry with good things" and encouraging "the children of Israel," must be informed by "the wonderful works of God." Whatever the focus in a particular sermon might be, that "God was reconciling the world to himself in Christ" is determinative for all preaching for all time (2 Cor. 5:19).

The Christian preacher's goal is to challenge boldly all of human life with the truth of God's Word. God's story is placed alongside human stories so that existence is viewed in the context of salvation history. The preacher is concerned not merely to mirror the demonic depths of life destitute of hope, but to illuminate human darkness and despair with the light of life.

Christian preaching's concern holds the needs of persons in tension with those of the entire community of faith. George McCauley, S. J., has written of the community forming as well as community criticizing dimensions of the faith. It is not easy for one minister to represent Christ's community-wide vision, for we all have our blind spots. The pastor, noted Father McCauley, is

> charged with seeing . . . individual lives within the context of the whole; to bear the sometimes heavy burden of the community's tradition; to note the presence of inequality, division, and diversity; to create the conditions necessary for consensus; to foster a climate where reconciliation can occur; to judge the potentially demonic aspects of our "togetherness"; to ask whether the community we seek and attain is a specifically *Christian* community; to distinguish between his or her personal preferences and what community cohesion, maintenance, and critique require.[25]

One cannot possibly hope for approval from all of one's community all of the time in such an assignment. Thus charisma must give way to competence; charm must bow to character; good looks must search for wisdom; and skill must cry out for integrity. One's commitment to the divine calling of God is one's only certain anchor in the swirling, restless seas of Christian ministry.

How, then, shall one serve as prophet-priest in the pulpit? On one occasion, I was in the congregation of Riverside Church in New York City when the pastor, Robert J. McCracken, preached on "The Quest for Religious Certainty." The biblical text involved the experience of the woman of Sychar, who addressed her doubt to Jesus Christ at Jacob's well one noonday: "I know that Messiah (called Christ) is coming. When he comes, he will explain everything to us" (John 4:25). In the background was a recent air disaster, caused by a bomb explosion. A youth had sabotaged a U.S. plane on a domestic flight, killing all persons aboard, in order to murder his own mother and collect life insurance. Americans had been shocked by the affair. The members of that congregation needed certainty themselves! Pastor McCracken told of the necessity and universality of life's religious quest, its paradox in that Christ did not show us *all* things, and the certainty springing from a faith-love relationship with the living God. An expository sermon with pastoral intent countered mystery, tragedy, and sin and offered certitude in Christ.

Or consider the message "The Discipline of Disillusionment," preached by Wayne E. Oates to a national radio audience. He interpreted the "shaken world and unshaken kingdom" passage in Hebrews 12:26–29 as the need to have human illusions and doubts shaken to the foundations in order that "what cannot be shaken may remain." This was illustrated variously—illusions of marriage that must go before an "unshakeable covenant that rests in God" can be forged; disillusionments in the business world, in friendship, politics, and in love that must be disciplined. He concluded thus: "The unshakeableness of [God's] Kingdom is made more apparent than ever in the presence of the fragility of our own little schemes. The brightness of his hope is made more luminous in the darkness of our despair. The end result of our submission to the discipline of disillusionment is that we can give thanks for a Kingdom that cannot be shaken and offer to God acceptable worship with reverence and awe."[26] Such pastoral interpreters fill "the hungry with good things," so that they are nourished with the Word of God and the desire is stirred to live again.

Each Lord's Day the preacher addresses persons who are experiencing hazards and decisions, joys and sorrows, physical pain and mental anguish, conflicts of conscience and epochs of growth. In every congregation there are those who feel that their lives do not amount to much. Some have proof of their personal failure; others suspect that in quiet ways, life is slipping unchallenged through their fingers. Others feel trapped in a history they cannot change. The burdened are there hiding the secret sadness of sin and longing for escape from some blind alley. Some worshipers face uncertain futures. Most of them will go from church to bear great responsibilities in family, educational, vocational, and civic tasks. The sensitive minister will not be content to mumble inaudible prayers or chatter about mundane matters. Too much is at stake for casualness with the Holy! With its significance in mind, what factors characterize the pastoral/prophetic focus in preaching?

1. Christian preaching that is skillfully diagnostic and spiritually therapeutic reflects pastoral intent. Gaston Foote once interpreted the feeding of five thousand people, through Christ's miracle with a lad's loaves and fish

(John 6:9), in personal terms. Rather than discoursing upon miracles, he viewed our *little* and God's *much*. The problem addressed was the human tendency to live "on one's own," without reliance upon God. Said he: "This is more than a miracle. Jesus was doing something more than feeding five thousand people. He was explaining to his disciples and to us how we can take man's little and God's much, put them together and meet the problems of our day."[27] Such a sermon offers God's gracious Word afresh for healing and inspiration from within.

2. Pastoral preaching reveals God to persons, persons to themselves and prompts faith for the redemption and integration of personality. The preacher's own faith and love are herein revealed. Augustine once said: "What I live by, I impart." In this light, "It might be well at times to subject our preaching to . . . critical self-analysis to determine how much of it is a projection of [the preacher's] own inner needs."[28] The preacher occasionally projects personal anxieties and aggressions upon others, thereby engaging in diatribe rather than in authentic preaching. Words can wound, even as they have power to heal!

3. The pastoral interpreter illuminates human experience in each of the developmental epochs of life with Christian truth. Thus one shares the primary moments of life — birth, conversion, vocational choice, marriage, aging, death — and supports individuals when crises come.

4. Rather than moralizing upon particular subjects, the pastor's goal for hearers is the knowledge of Gospel truth, character strength, and personal responsibility. The objective is the *doing* of truth.

Years ago, I discovered the late Lewis J. Sherill's holistic wisdom in *The Struggle of the Soul*.[29] Reading that book as a pastor inspired me to address sermons to needs of life's seasons and to guide the "developmental tasks" that arise from infancy to death. One series of messages, carved from biblical texts, included these subjects and goals:

1. *Children of Desire* centered upon the central challenge of childhood — becoming an individual — and upon the family's readiness to receive a new infant and to participate in his or her personal growth.
2. *Striving for Maturity* focused the chief characteristics, claims upon, and choices of youth.
3. *Living Under Tension* addressed young adults' responsibilities, stress, and resources for growth.
4. A *Faith for Maturity* pointed those in the middle years toward a mature view of life, a Christian philosophy of history.

5. *Unto the Perfect Day* recognized the prospect of aging, changes including the need for simplification, and the church's role with its aging members.

6. *If I Should Die* pictured the biblical view of death and resurrection, permitting each listener to face the prospect of life's end on earth. Also, it viewed grief work in Christian perspective.

The response of a congregation to a pastor who takes seriously their relationships and responsibilities *here* and *now* is heartening. One sermon may not fit every need. Fortunately, the flock gathers with some degree of regularity week by week, and within an entire Christian year the preacher will have addressed the majority of members several times. One's multifaceted objective is to enhance the well-being of nuclear members, to call marginal members to commitment, to challenge false assumptions in the social order, and to empower each person for true Christian community (Mark 2:17; Rom. 12–14; 1 Cor. 12–14). The prophet-priest with such idealism will say some things that are neither popular nor easy for certain individuals to receive. A true pastor does not shrink from *confronting* the congregation with God's judgment-grace, even at the risk of being rebuffed in the process. One rejoices in *comforting* congregants with God's love and mercy when a gracious word is needed to get life going again. The worship leader's goal is useful living within the Kingdom of God.

Summary

The public and private ministries should be synthesized rather than separated in pastoral work. The prophet and the priest are not two different persons, for these tasks converge in the personality of the servant of the Word. The shape of a church's liturgy and the tasks of the worship leaders remain flexible, with the suggestion that they be appropriate to one's tradition, context, and cultural setting. Pastoral considerations in church architecture and worship leadership are general principles rather than categorical methods. A pastoral focus in preaching is viewed within a comprehensive context of four great concerns in Christian preaching. Each aspect or purpose is valid as the preacher addresses the faith community with the Word of God.

Finally, those who traditionally view going to church as the *end* of their Christian duty must rediscover the church's instrumental nature. Accordingly, worship is not the "end that crowns all" but the dynamic means to a larger purpose—life spent as a "living sacrifice" unto God. People are to go to church not to hear a grand finale at the week's close, but to sound anew the grand "Amen" of Christian faith upon the Lord's Day. Beginning life anew, they pledge to carry that faith into the rhythms of life during the week. Theirs is a fellowship of forgiveness and of hope for eternal life.

Notes

1. John T. McNeill, *A History of the Cure of Souls* (New York: Harper & Row, 1951), 87, emphasis supplied.
2. H. Richard Niebuhr, *Faith on Earth: An Inquiry into the Structure of Human Faith*, edited by Richard R. Niebuhr (New Haven: Yale University Press, 1989).
3. Harvey Seifert, "Prophetic/Pastoral Tension in Ministry," in Rodney J. Hunter, gen. ed., *Dictionary of Pastoral Care and Counseling* (Nashville: Abingdon Press, 1990), 963–66. For an integrated view of the family based on biblical truths and clinical insights, see Jack O. Balswick and Judith K. Balswick, *The Family: A Christian Perspective on the Contemporary Home* (Grand Rapids: Baker Book House, 1989); for a social science view, see Christopher Carlson, *Perspectives on the Family* (Belmont, CA: Wadsworth, 1990).
4. John W. Gardner, *Excellence* (New York: Harper & Row, 1961; Colophon paperback edition, 1962), 16–17, 33, 135–44. For examples of aid to marginalized persons, see Lisbeth B. Schorr, *Within Our Reach: Breaking the Cycle of Disadvantage* (New York: Doubleday Anchor Press, 1988).
5. Kevin Giles, *Patterns of Ministry Among the First Christians* (San Francisco: HarperCollins, 1991); Margaret A. Farley, *Personal Commitments: Beginning, Keeping, Changing* (San Francisco: Harper & Row, 1986); Lewis B. Smedes, *Caring and Commitment: Learning to Live the Love We Promise* (San Francisco: Harper & Row, 1988).
6. Douglas Horton, *The Meaning of Worship* (New York: Harper & Row, 1959), 72.
7. Elizabeth Achtemeier, *Preaching from the Old Testament* (Louisville: Westminster/John Knox Press, 1989), 13.
8. Harry E. Fosdick, *The Living of These Days* (New York: Harper & Row, 1956), 94. Cf. Edmund H. Linn, *Preaching as Counseling: The Unique Method of Harry Emerson Fosdick* (Valley Forge: Judson Press, 1966).
9. Alan Richardson, *The Bible in the Age of Science* (London: S.C.M. Press, 1961).
10. D. M. Baillie, *Out of Nazareth* (Edinburgh, Scotland: Saint Andrew Press, 1958), 15.
11. Quoted in Paul R. Clifford, *The Pastoral Calling* (London, England: Carey Kingsgate Press, 1959), 47.

12. Dietrich Ritschl, A *Theology of Proclamation* (Richmond, VA.: John Knox Press, 1960), 155. See Lutheran pastor F. Den Lueking's proposals in *Preaching: The Art of Connecting God and People* (Waco, TX: Word Books, 1985). Cf. Achtemeier's approach to sermon preparation in *Preaching from the Old Testament*, 39–60.

13. M. Scott Peck, *The Road Less Traveled* (New York: Simon and Schuster, 1978), 15.

14. See the significant study, Dom Gregory Dix, *The Shape of the Liturgy* (Naperville, IL: Alec R. Allenson, 1960). See John Tully Carmody and Denise L. Carmody, *Christian Uniqueness and Catholic Spirituality* (Mahwah, NJ: Paulist Press, 1990); also, Francis J. Moloney, *A Body Broken for a Broken People: Eucharist in the New Testament* (San Francisco: HarperCollins, 1991).

15. Paul Pruyser, *A Dynamic Psychology of Religion* (New York: Harper & Row, 1968), 176–78. Also see his "The Master Hand: Psychological Notes on Pastoral Blessing," in *The New Shape of Pastoral Theology*, edited by William B. Oglesby (Nashville: Abingdon Press, 1969), 352–66.

16. See William H. Willimon, *Worship as Pastoral Care* (Nashville: Abingdon Press, 1979), 62.

17. Martin Thielen tells how to teach a church to worship in *Getting Ready for Sunday: A Practical Guide for Worship Planning* (Nashville: Broadman Press, 1989), 231–32.

18. See Richard S. Hanson, *Worshipping with the Child* (Nashville: Abingdon Press, 1988); also, Charles E. Schaefer, *How to Talk to Children about Really Important Things* (San Francisco: Harper & Row, 1984).

19. Achtemeier, *Preaching from the Old Testament*, 54–55. Donald Macleod, *Word and Sacrament: A Preface to Preaching and Worship* (Englewood Cliffs, NJ: Prentice-Hall, 1960), discusses preaching within the context of worship, 93–118.

20. Harold Freeman, *Variety in Biblical Preaching* (Waco, TX: Word Books, 1987), 18.

21. Gabriel Marcel, "The Sacred in a Technological Age," *Theology Today* 19 (April 1962): 36–37.

22. Samuel H. Miller, "Sacred Space in a Secular Age," *Theology Today* 19 (July 1962): 216.

23. Jack Hayford, John Killinger, and Howard Stevenson in *Mastering Worship* (Portland, OR: Multnomah Press, 1990) show how ministers can help their people move from the divine circle of companionship to mission in the world.

24. Roy Pearson, *The Preacher: His Purpose and Practice* (Philadelphia: Westminster Press, 1963), of which one chapter appears as "The Purpose of Preaching," *Religion in Life* 32 (Spring 1963): cf. 278; see also 267–78.

25. George McCauley, S.J., *The God of the Group* (Niles, IL: Argus Communications, 1975), 87; cited in Willimon, *Worship as Pastoral Care*, 203–4.
26. Wayne E. Oates, "The Discipline of Disillusionment," *The Beam* (July 1963): 46.
27. Gaston Foote, "Man's Little and God's Much," sermon preached at First Methodist Church, Fort Worth, Texas, and printed for private circulation among members of that congregation.
28. Carl J. Schindler, *The Pastor as a Personal Counselor* (Philadelphia: Fortress Press, 1942), 136.
29. Lewis J. Sherill, *The Struggle of the Soul* (New York: Macmillan, 1952).

Suggested Reading

Achtemeier, Elizabeth. *Preaching from the Old Testament.* Louisville: Westminster/John Knox Press, 1989. In an approach to the Bible as the Community-creating Word, the author demonstrates use of the literature of the Old Testament for Christian preaching today.

Gerkin, Charles V. *Prophetic Pastoral Practice: A Christian Vision of Life Together.* Nashville: Abingdon Press, 1991. Proposes that pastors should embody and communicate the core values of Christianity, as these values are revealed in the Bible and in other primary texts of the Christian tradition.

Hanson, Richard S. *Worshiping with the Child.* Nashville: Abingdon Press, 1988. Helps adults understand the worshipful moments in a child's life and shows how to help children grow in their understanding and love of God.

Leisch, Barry. *People in the Presence of God: Models and Directions for Worship.* Grand Rapids: Zondervan Publishing House, 1988. Creative resources for persons interested in designing worship according to biblical models.

Segler, Franklin M. *Christian Worship: Its Theology and Practice.* Nashville: Broadman Press, 1967. A thorough presentation of the meaning of worship, including planning and conducting worship in Christian communities of faith.

Thielen, Martin. *Getting Ready for Sunday: A Practical Guide for Worship Planning.* Nashville: Broadman Press, 1989. Offers suggestions for shaping the worship service within the Free Church tradition. Clarifies the planning process.

Willimon, William H. *Worship as Pastoral Care.* Nashville: Abingdon Press, 1979. Emphasizes the worshiping community as the context for pastoral care. Relates Christian liturgy to life's common ventures and crises, as well as to celebrative events.

Wren, Brian. *What Language Shall I Borrow? God-Talk in Worship: A Male Response to Feminist Theology.* New York: Crossroad Books, 1989. A British hymn writer suggests creative worship ideas, deals with masculine vs. sexually inclusive language in worship, and seeks continuity with classic Christian faith. Challenges traditional orientations.

CHAPTER SIX

DIMENSIONS OF THE PASTOR'S CARING

I have said that a joint obligation rests upon the Christian pastor and the faith community of Jesus Christ to be a truly ministering church in the world. While a formal order of ministry is reflected in the New Testament, all Christians should participate in the worship, outreach, and pastoral dimensions of church life (2 Cor. 1). The effectiveness of a particular church's ministry will be determined largely by the encouragement and example of its official (ordained) leadership, as well as by the cooperative fellowship and support of its laity. Our question now becomes: What are some expressions of the ordained minister's work in the church that support the general ministry of the laity and reach out into the community?

Pioneer pastoral theologians like Anton Boisen, Seward Hiltner, Carroll Wise, Wayne Oates, and Paul Johnson interpreted the pastor's caring primarily, though not exclusively, in individualistic terms. Much of the focus was counseling anxious and distressed individuals. Freudian psychoanalytic theory was influential in an earlier era (although none of these thinkers was a pure Freudian), and Carl Rogers's client-centered therapy was much in vogue. The paradigm of pastoral care proposed here is a continuum in time, in context, and in depth. I begin with the faith community's humanity—the church has a human face—and its essential inward journey of worship as pastoral care. The transformation of worshipers in sacred space and time motivates them, ideally, to become pastoral workers in a pluralistic culture.

Leadership in the church's mission is shared, but the sharing is unequal. The pastor and ordained pastoral workers set the pace for ministries by all the nonordained (unofficial) caregivers in homes, schools, businesses, and workplaces in society. Rather than a medical model of sick parishioners coming to a religious health provider for counseling as *all* of pastoral care, I am proposing a holistic model for "one anothering" in a ministering church.

The inclusive process of pastoral care conceived here is a continuum in time and outreach. Through the week the minister encounters numerous persons in superficial contacts: in the church offices, before or following worship services, on city or village streets. A pastor crosses trails with some church members several times each week: in committee meetings, in hospital calling, or in private conversations. Public ministry with the *many* is extended in time and depth with the *few* in administration, teaching, visitation, correspondence, community contacts, and most intensely in personal counseling.

Here, we are considering the spectrum of pastoral relationships and resources that lies between contacts with the congregation in worship and conversations with an individual or family in counseling. This includes (1) administrative and group contacts; (2) calling and correspondence; (3) the pastoral uses of Christian literature; and (4) the pastor's prophetic influence within the larger community of concern. Principles of pastoral counseling and studies of caring events and relationships comprise the remaining chapters.

I. Leadership that Liberates Life

Whether a spiritual guide functions in a church setting, as a military or institutional chaplain, as a teacher, journalist, or church executive, his or her days are enmeshed in administrative processes. However idealized one's conception of the ministry was at the outset, a practitioner finds that to change settings or responsibilities will not cancel the obligations of administration. A teacher, for example, must continue to study, revise lectures, meet classes, confer with faculty committees, counsel with students, supervise their work, entertain visitors, conduct research, write for journals, correspond with others, lead off-campus conferences, maintain family time, and arrange times for meditation, recreation, and self-care—all within the week's work. For the minister, whatever one's particular context, some order must be brought out of the chaos of existence. Goals must be pursued and satisfactions built into life by spiritual pathfinders and their people.

To administer religious affairs is to make the services of oneself and one's people truly effective. The pastoral leader has been vested with the responsibility and authority to nurture and motivate the leadership potential within the congregation. Some groups, such as the Churches of Christ, view the minister as a stated preacher, minimize the pastor's "officialness," and charge a board of elders with church management. Those denominations with congregational polity have local church affairs strictly in the hands of the pastor, official committees, and the people. Presbyterial and episcopal forms of church government look to sessions, boards, assemblies, synods, and general conferences at a level beyond the local congregation for ultimate decisions and authority.

As a religious leader, whatever one's particular ecclesiastical identities and boundaries may be, one is tempted to set oneself at odds with the very people from whom one's authorization comes. An overbearing public image greatly influences one's pulpit work, priestly functions, and effectiveness among the people of God. In addition, one's use of power evokes community reactions, which influence a spouse's feelings and children's relationships. Perhaps the criticism most frequently leveled at some religious leaders today is that they tend toward authoritarianism.[1] Pinning the label is much easier than healing the malady, however. "He's a Mr. Greatheart in big things," observed someone about a religious leader, "but in administrative details he is a miserable failure." As ministers search their hearts in light of this perception, they should seek to democratize congregational decisions and be inclusive in church affairs. One may also influence laypersons to share decisions for the common good rather than dominate policies, and empower lay pastoral workers who are central to the church's mission.

Leadership that provides spiritual underpinning for the church's emerging ministries takes spiritual directorship seriously. One pastor affirmed his congregation thus: "It is a place where they let me lead." For some discouraged pastors, however, "doing battle" is the impression of each day's fatiguing hassles and demands. Success is measured in starting new ministries, body counts, overseeing decisions, financial power, and construction schedules. Rather than leading on a model of military combat, a people-centered spiritual director attends to what God is doing with individuals or in small-group events. A Maryland pastor observed, "Being a spiritual director doesn't mean . . . adding another item to our overextended job descriptions, but simply rearranging our perspective: seeing certain acts as eternal and not ephemeral, as essential and not accidental."[2] Life-on-the-run often bypasses peoples' deep insights and profound longings; there are so many other things clamoring for attention.

Effective pastoral administration attends to "quiet necessities" and liberates the talents and strength of laity through consultative direction, group decisions, and action. Becoming a leader in a Christian fellowship through whom the Holy Spirit can liberate each member to participate is a learning process. The minister and each member of the church staff need to have healthy interpersonal relations if they, in turn, expect church members to follow their leadership. Investing educational workers and committee members with responsibility and praising their well-done tasks is essential in this approach. Sharing the limelight of success and the pain of failure with the entire congregation is also necessary. An accountable, ordained leader takes neither full credit nor full blame for church affairs.[3] The minister's integrity and teachability serve as models for volunteer leaders. This ideal becomes specific as we consider the role of the church group leader.

II. The Work of the Small-Group Leader

One area of church life in which a Christian leader's controlling, conflict managing, and consensus-building powers appear frequently is small groups. A wise pastor should be familiar with the varieties of small groups in modern churches, educate capable volunteer leaders in group dynamic intricacies, and be available to share group life (Eph. 4:11-12). Here it is instructive to study the relation of Jesus and the Twelve in the Gospels. While the following guidelines for religious group process are addressed primarily to official leaders, they also apply to all persons who participate in church groups.

1. Small Groups in the Church

The church serves a useful purpose through the numerous relationships that its varied forms of group life make possible. Individuals function in key groups in the church much as they do in primary groups in society. The human sciences have demonstrated that a person's behavior and emotional needs are linked closely to family life and the primary groups of daily existence. One's identification with family members, close friends, and members of educational, religious, social, and vocational groups serves as a significant shaping influence upon personality. In many nations, tribal loyalties and language affect group behaviors, and in multicultural settings ethnic ties shape and color one's group identification.

One of the reasons why people attend a particular church is that they choose a faith community where they feel at home, in a group where they (1) experience acceptance and a sense of belonging; (2) get help through discipleship training; (3) develop their spiritual gifts; and (4) participate meaningfully in the church's life and work. *Belonging* is more essential than merely *attending,* both for the individual and for the common life of the entire church. In the light of its significance as a resource for religious development, as well as for Christian mission, creative group life should be appreciated and fostered as a means of pastoral care.

The term *group* designates any number of persons who are in dynamic relationship with one another, have some significant commonality, and assume some responsibility for one another. According to this definition, not every meeting of a few persons at church constitutes a true group. *Dynamic relationship* recognizes the flow of energy, feelings, and levels of communication occurring simultaneously between members in any effective group climate. The *common bond* may be task, gender, ethnicity, age, subject matter, goal, cause, belief, interest, and so on. The tie may be very strong for some, moderate or weak in others. *Assuming responsibility* for one's companions implies developing an altruistic "we-feeling" by group members. Such responsible participation is not the equivalent of warm-fuzzy "togetherness," which may be artificially arranged or imposed.

Kurt Lewin, a pioneer researcher in group dynamics, once said: "Relinquishing of a certain amount of freedom is a condition of membership in any group."[4] Life in church groups obligates participants to unity within diversity. To belong to a group implies that there will be a relative loss of freedom. One's individuality will be limited. The capacity to identify with and to share responsibility with others, however, contributes to the individual's own sense of esteem, spiritual growth, and inner freedom. A group member's self-discipline and sensitivity to others presupposes a sense of belonging to and commonality within the group. Priest-psychotherapist Wallace Clift describes the goal of spiritual group process as a journey into love, "in which we learn the truth about ourselves," grow in Godlikeness, and offer true acceptance to others.[5] Such searching of believers' hearts is not the end but a stage on the way to mission.

This leads us to ask, *"What kinds of small groups develop within the larger church structure?"* Mission-driven, rather than organization-driven churches create or recognize groups (1) for planning and consultation, with a task orientation; (2) for Christian education and guidance, with a teaching orientation; (3) for interpersonal discussion and problem-solving, with a therapeutic orientation; (4) for spiritual awakening and discipline, with a prayer and worship orientation; and (5) for fellowship and leisure time, with a play orientation. Specific groups may arise out of common concerns such as: women's rights; adult children of alcoholics; AIDS survivors; couples preparing for marriage; new church members; environmental ecology; persons surviving displacement, trauma, divorce, or death; persons in addictive or codependent relations; the elderly; and the like. Religious education groups have fostered faithcare and character growth throughout church history.

Some ministers have wondered about the practice of group counseling in a church setting. Perhaps they have read of this process in medical practice or know of some theory like Reality Therapy or Transactional Analysis.[6] Role playing, psychodrama, and Gestalt techniques are practiced widely in psychiatric and chemical dependency treatment centers today. It may be argued that "group therapy" is a medical term, implying professional treatment in a hospital setting. Spiritual leaders recognize, however, that "when the focus of attention is directed to what is happening to the members as a result of their participation in the life of a group . . . then 'therapy' is involved whether it is so designated or not."[7] Spiritual growth may occur in communities of faith that begin as Christian discipline, theological inquiry, common concerns, moral issues, problems of living, or administrative tasks, which develop therapeutic overtones during group processes.

This implies that church groups may be viewed from two perspectives: (1) the external or organizational view of the-church-as-groups; and (2) the internal or missional view of groups-as-the-church. Viewed externally, such fellowships may be designated as *primary* intimate groups of family members and close friends; or as *secondary* formal interest, age-graded, or task groups. Another way of viewing church groups externally is to see them as *informal* and *formal*. Persons are related informally in families, peer groups, talent, travel, or interest groupings, and the like. Whereas persons in designated church offices, such as the diaconate, or committees and organizations such as the Sunday school, are related in more formal fashion.

When the internal perspective is assumed, however, we turn from a substantial question about the group's nature or purpose to a dynamic process appraisal of essential group relationships. Here the question becomes not, "What kind of group is this?" but, "What is happening in this group? Will it have bearing in other relationships?" The leader's concern is with individual behavior—such as resistance, defensiveness, and projection—as well as with group morale, teamwork, and achievement. The simple question about the group's goals in light of the church's purpose is reconstructed into the not so simple question of what is happening to persons who participate in church groups. The leader's concern is that group members cannot be treated as *means* but must be seen as *ends* of infinite worth, who are potential instruments in God's hands. The group leader desires that individual members grow in the process *and* that the church's mission be faithfully pursued.

2. The Leader's Role in the Group Process

Some groups are the "givens" of religious fellowships, indigenous to church administration, religious education, family life, and Christian mission.

Other groups arise spontaneously out of internally felt needs. In any case, the pastoral worker or some leader will be recognized by each group, for *a group will be led by someone or ones!* Its leadership is a reflection upon the needs of its members at a given time and may change periodically. It can be hoped that the group will use its experiences to point beyond itself to spiritual growth of participants and to support the church's missional objectives. In this process the leader's role is vital.

While not a member of every group in the church's life, the pastor meets frequently with task units and small fellowships. As an official figure in any group, a minister's views may be sought with due respect, though he or she may not be an "expert" in the group's concerns. Still, pastoral care is as operative in group processes as it is in personal contacts and private counseling. In fact, one's counseling load is often linked to one's wisdom, sensitivity, and skill as a leader. *From a pastoral perspective, group behavior is purposeful:* (1) when a climate of trust and openness encourages personal initiative and participation; (2) when participants make a transition from individually held to group objectives; and (3) when the small unit faces its tasks in light of the entire church's mission and welfare.

Leading a small group in the church requires a measure of professional competence and skill.[8] The term *professional* is used here to indicate the leader's disciplined objectivity, which seeks the congregation's interests and goals above one's own needs and feelings. Frequently, a group feels the influence of a *natural* leader, a representative person whom the *formal* leader must deal with in guiding the group. The natural leader provides clues to the group's identity because he or she represents a history, or resources, or biases, or a position with which most members identify. The natural leader serves as a sounding board, as a group ego, and an indicator of the members' objectives, feelings, and differences. Group morale is linked to the formal leader's capacity for dealing with the natural leader, who may guide a group attack or try to "get" the leader. An official leader may ally with the natural power source, on the other hand, and as coleaders they may collaborate for the sake of group performance.

Some men and women have group leadership roles thrust upon them spontaneously; others are selected deliberately. In any case, leaders need to know how to plan and get started in the first sessions, how to clarify and summarize ideas, to set the tone, to handle diversity, to deal with problem situations, revise plans, and so on. The following principles are suggestive for leading a group in the church.

1. *The designated leader should understand the varied functions of group leadership.* While one may convene a group, it is not possible to control the

collective behavior, contributions, or performance of one's companions. The leader must learn to gauge the group's capacity for self-direction and the degree of leadership pressure needed at a given time. Some leaders function more as convenors and consultants, others as arbiters and facilitators. When resistance or conflict develop in group interaction, one must function as a mediator, interpreter, and peacemaker. At times, a leader plays "devil's advocate" in behalf of some disenfranchised or under-represented sector of the congregation.

The leader may be the group's friend or enemy, the object of their hero worship, or a scapegoat, receiving the blame for church problems. One may be temporarily disregarded in group discussion, or become the object of a direct attack. It is essential to maintain objectivity. So that the leader will not project his or her anxieties or hostilities, personal concerns may have to be bracketed, at least for the time being. Termination proceedings are the most severe form of group rejection of an employed leader.

2. *The leader should perceive clearly the purpose of the group.* In getting started, one helps the small unit formulate an idea of its identity, purpose, and goal. While such "housekeeping details" may appear mundane, establishing an agenda, defining realistic goals, setting limits, assessing resources, and structuring methods of action all assist group members to work together. Once their functional roles are clarified, the members' energies are released and directed toward the group's goal. As individuals accept the we-feeling of the group, they work more effectively to achieve their objective. Maturity comes with added responsibility.

3. *The leader should understand group dynamics and group process and assist each member to perceive the nature of group experience.* Each member retains personal autonomy; freedom to express ideas, beliefs, and expectations; and privacy—even as he or she "buys into" the group experience. The welfare of the group takes precedence over the welfare of the individual, so that each member experiences new relationships, social restraints, and disciplined ways of communicating in a group structure. Group development and socialization take time. Power and authority issues must be faced. Hopefully, groupthink will transcend polarization and leadership will be effective.[9] In this process, a Christian group has a clear advantage in that its communications do not depend upon raw competition or power but are grounded in love. The leader's chief concern is that productive ideas will be engendered and expressed, that self-interest will be transcended, and that Christian causes will advance through healthy group relationships.

4. *The official leader should know the group members and form an alliance with natural leaders when they emerge in a group.* The leader's strategy

is not to manipulate the group but to harness the creative forces in it, so that its true purpose can be achieved. This process is aided or impeded by its potentially natural flow of leadership. In the light of what has already been said about the significance of such persons, the convenor will rely upon members to build morale, relieve tension, and keep the group moving toward its goal. The official leader rejects group power networks at great risk. A crucial problem arises, however, when a natural leader brings out the destructiveness of a group. A subsequent case study will demonstrate how a pastor handled this problem in creative fashion. As the group forms and works together, a leader perceives that the members will not forego satisfactions unless they are replaced by other equally desirable satisfactions. Such knowledge is essential in group discipline.

5. *The pastoral leader should serve as a spiritual catalyst,* releasing the leadership qualities and talents of each group member. As the group develops cohesion and initiative, the leader's role changes from "guide" (expert, boss, authority) to "belonger" (member, participant, discussant). An effective leader depends upon the group for personal encouragement and development as a spiritual guide. The group's positive response strengthens one's capacity as a leader; or it may go the other way. The group may turn upon, abandon, or reject its leader. A group functions best when members of the small unit discipline their own ego needs and reach out to meet each other's needs. They are able to love each other and experience community because they have experienced God's love and forgiveness. Together, the Christian leader and group members function with mutual respect and restraint, provide security, and pursue their objectives in an atmosphere of Christian fidelity and mission. A minister leader thus grows along with the group in shared experience, spirituality, and "one anothering" skills.

3. The Shared Life of the Small Group

Christian life develops from infancy to maturity in shared group experiences in the church. Small, homogeneous groups are indispensable in Christian education. They make varied approaches to religious training and development possible. With adults, for example, Bible study may be approached through identification with religious stories and personalities. Innovative responses to a scriptural text may be preassigned to supplement the lecture method of instruction. And with children, role-playing of Bible characters, scenes, or incidents stimulates learning through improvisations, dialogue, actions, and participant understanding. Such group responsibility in teaching and learning aids members in carrying religious instruction from the church classroom into life's decisions and tasks. Passive, negative, or lonely members may be strengthened through participation with others. Those suffering the agony of divorce, addiction, homosexuality, psychiatric illness or depression, and physical or multiple handicaps may find support and friendship through sharing experiences with others in an environment of Christian concern.

What findings are available from actual church experience that can inform the pastor's participation in small groups? The following summary was prepared by a pastor who felt a particular concern for four teenage girls who were members of a church youth group. The pastor and young people were together during a vacation church school in which a thirty-minute discussion period followed the Bible lesson in each day's schedule. The pastoral leader introduced some pamphlets on controversial moral issues at the opening of school that catalyzed discussion, sharpened differences, and eventually led certain members to change.

Pastor Jimmy Ware described the four members for whom he was particularly concerned as follows:

> Ann is fourteen years of age, the older of two children. Her parents are inactive church members. She is obese and rather talkative. Ann is rebellious toward persons in authority and revealed much hostility toward her parents, especially her mother. She resented any kind of religious service. Ann is the leader of the group of girls.
>
> Beth is fourteen, the middle child of three. She appears to be about seventeen years of age. Beth is not as open with her hostility toward her parents as Ann, but she does resent the church.
>
> Kathy is fourteen and is the youngest of five children. Her father is an inactive Methodist and her mother is a leader in Plainview Church. She is openly hostile toward her mother and religion.
>
> Debbie is fourteen, the youngest child in her family. In the group, she is hostile but rather passive. Her father is not a professed Christian and her mother is a member of the Pilgrim church but attends the Methodist church.

Observe that Rev. Ware detected the natural leader of the group and knew details of family life, religious background, and some under the surface feelings in each of the girls.

The pastor taught the Bible lesson each day and functioned as designated leader of the "gripe (therapy) session" that followed. Here are some selections taken from his daily log of feelings and responses in the group.

First Day:

> [Jimmy Ware described the seating arrangement around a table.] The first day was spent with the group members testing me and trying to get me to

give them authoritative answers to their questions. Much hostility was expressed toward me in one form or another. [According to our definition, this preliminary meeting was not a "group" in the true sense.]

Second Day:

The seating arrangement changed [he described this]. Ann started the session with a bang, discussing subjects from parents to dancing. The discussion always found its way back to parents. About halfway through the session, Debbie, who had been quiet most of the time, agreed with the others that she could not talk with her mother any more. Tears came to her eyes; she coughed and bowed her head. While her head was down she wiped the tears from her eyes. [Ware dealt with Debbie's crying by not calling attention to it.] During the next three days, Beth and Kathy were not as verbal. Debbie was quiet and pleasant. In all the school activities, these three girls were more friendly and cheerful.

Fifth Day:

The seating arrangement changed today. [Ann moved closest to the pastor.] We had been discussing obscene literature the day before, and Ann had brought a pulp magazine to prove her point. The magazine was the object of discussion the first part of the session. She did not get the support she wanted from the group, so Ann dropped the subject. The rest of this session was spent in discussing the effects of pornographic literature upon one's sexual fantasies and social behavior.

The second week the seating stabilized; feelings were more positive. While Ann tried to dominate the group, the boys and girls did not let her. Leadership shifted more into the whole group's hands. During a spiritual commitment service at the close of school, Beth and Debbie made public professions of personal faith in Christ. In the final two sessions, the spirit of the group turned into rejoicing. Ann and Kathy became silent and thoughtful. Later Ann volunteered to serve as pianist for a Sunday school department on a regular basis. The pastor observed that her self-worth and personal grooming had improved following the vacation school. He followed up each of the other three girls with special needs, noting experiences at home, with their age group at church, and in community life. In sharing the life of a small youth group, Pastor Ware refused the role of an authoritarian personality in an effort to serve as a spiritual catalyst, eliciting the group's strength. This role was felt by the pastor to be facilitative but not passive. His introduction of literature in order to stimulate thought, discussion, and growth indicated that he rejected a laissez-faire style of avoiding all responsibility. When Rev. Ware was confronted the first day as an authority figure, he recognized this as a natural response of feelings carried over from certain family and social relations patterns. Rather than reacting judgmentally, he withstood their testing and handled their hostile feelings with Christian charity.

Jimmy Ware's concern for the group made him sensitive to expressions by each member, including the "problem" personalities. He recognized a significant turning point when the group moved from Ann's challenge of his leadership to a more democratic assumption of responsibility. Each member gained strength for living in this process, including two who professed their Christian faith publicly and four others who rededicated themselves to Christ during the commitment service. This pastor recognized the redemptive-therapeutic possibilities of shared life in small groups and grew from reflection upon these events. Such insight in leadership is instructive for all who lead small groups in the church.

III. Pastoral Calling and Communication

Changes in church leadership, like that illustrated with group process and practice, have also been reflected in pastoral calling. The charge is often heard in churches of different denominations that laity no longer see their ministers visiting private homes. Fast-lane lifestyles have changed us so much there seems little time for visitation like that enjoyed by our pastoral predecessors. Conditions shaping ministry are usually more complex than a pastor's personal preference, however.

Before fast-track lifestyles developed in metropolitan areas, getting around systematically to parishioners' homes seemed both feasible and essential. The minister in rural settings often traveled a circuit (as is still done in some mission fields), staying in the homes of hospitable hosts as one traveled. Calls were often spontaneous, social in nature, and unhurried. The agrarian economy geared its schedule to growing crops and livestock rather than to time clocks and commuter trains. Church programs were informal. Time was a universally available commodity.

1. Visitation Revisited: Going the Distance

In one generation, many ministers have moved with their people from a small town outlook to a globalized, economically interdependent world order. Church calendars are geared to round-the-clock industrial production schedules and to regional shopping centers where some businesses never close. Pastors have found themselves separated from their church members by demands of time, space, social roles, numberless interruptions, and countless concerns. Conceivably, a metropolitan pastor could have parishioners as patients in six or more widely separated hospitals simultaneously in a single city. Church programs have become more complex, requiring the pastor's presence in numerous evening meetings when one might otherwise be free for calling. Most of the nation's 75 million baby boomers are careerists, unavailable for daytime pastoral house calls. Visiting homes during the day may yield a few contacts with retirees, widows, or casually attired housewives who are unprepared (and often embarrassed) by an unannounced caller's visit. Many apartment buildings are "off limits" to solicitors, salespersons, and the like, including church emissaries. To see the family together demands that calling be done in the evenings when parents and children are at home. The tempo of school activities, sports contests, television programs, and civic affairs also militates against making time for calling.

Furthermore, some pastors, unwilling to undertake an apparently pedestrian task, rationalize that they have no time to waste in purposeless visitation. They find the plan of Richard Baxter, the seventeenth-century Puritan pastor, in Kidderminster, England, who practiced systematic oversight of the flock, inconceivable in the modern world. The prevailing attitude toward apartment and house-to-house calling is generally negative. Except for hospital calling, membership enlistment, and emergencies, most pastors prefer to be in the study, in a staff or committee meeting, counseling, attending a conference, or enjoying some relaxation. Married ministers try to spend some time with their own families, for they have covenants to keep in order to parent well, enjoy intimacy, and foster integrity in community life. Anxiety in navigating visitation, given church growth as a goal, leaves many ministers stressed-out in a chronic pursuit cycle.

A number of remedies have been prescribed for this apparent failure to live up to one's pastoral heritage of systematic, though often superficial, calling. One coping style is reactivity—getting swallowed up in busyness that blocks calm, intimate encounters with parishioners. Some ministers employ radio "spots" and television programs for communicating with members and attempting to reach outsiders. Others organize the laity for calling through programs like Evangelism Explosion; yet they themselves are available only in emergencies or difficult cases. Others set up a priority of calls—critical, essential, and so on—down to routine visits, which they tend to minimize. Of course, some still call upon their people with pastoral intent and with some degree of regularity. Others focus on in-house ministries *at church*: self-improvement groups, adult education, special lecture, and family-size athletic programs. Going the distance by making quality time for oversight of one's flock is not easy for modern shepherds.

Admittedly, contemporary ministers must conserve their time, talents, and energies for those things that are most needful. As "stewards of the mysteries of God," their time must be accounted for. Recognizing that the old ways don't work gives us an opportunity to examine excuses, like busy-ness and too few hours in the day, used to explain why ministers avoid call-ing today. Commitment to one's congregation means doing what it takes to keep in touch with one's flock. I feel, both from theological conviction and practical experience, that pastoral contacts with persons are essential to an effective Christian ministry. Simply ignoring this troublesome issue will not make it go away. We must go the distance.

2. Design for Pastoral Calling

The term *pastoral calling* has been employed to denote that vital aspect of ministry in which the religious leader's concern is communicated in a per-sonal way to one's people. Some writers have designated it as "precounsel-ing," others as "evangelism," with the result that many ministers dismiss the essential worth of visitation. It is quite possible that a calm visit will prompt deeper-level counseling relationships with some persons. However, not every pastoral call will be devoted to the discussion of emergencies or prob-lems. There is much to be said for a social visit by the pastoral family to new residents of a community, who have left cherished friends and familiar sur-roundings and may be overwhelmed with adjustments to the new environ-ment. Still, resistance to calling is real. To the extent one has not carved out a clear, healthy "I" in one's own family history, the more reluctance to being swallowed up by others in "togetherness visits" one feels.

The minister's loving interest in and concern for people form the basic motivation underlying private calling. There may or may not be some severe emergency or major crisis. However, one's ego must be intact enough to risk encounters with alien forces or deep needs. We should examine our motives in a particular relationship, which may lie more in the direction of reactivity, guilt, meeting someone's expectations, or our own needs for community approval rather than in real compassion.

All pastoral calling in a caring church need not be done by the senior minister. When a congregation's size and demands indicate a multiple staff ministry, colleagues should be sought who will share one's responsibilities. Staff members assigned one area of work—education, administration, or youth—may assume pastoral responsibilities for their volunteer workers, for example, as well as for some members. Large churches often designate some staff members as "church visitors"; or a retired minister responsible for visitation may be employed. A division of labor among staff members can be agreed upon at the time of employment and renegotiated along in staff meetings.[10] Members of the diaconate and church membership committee should be instructed in the conduct of pastoral, as well as other kinds of calls. They may accompany the minister or a staff member until they feel secure enough to establish depth relationships in visiting individually.

There are three major types of pastoral calls: (1) *routine* calls, in which the church's message and fellowship are carried faithfully to preselected persons and families; (2) *crucial* calling, in which Christian support is offered to those experiencing hospitalization, crisis, or emergency; and (3) *casual* contacts, in which the minister encounters persons in unstructured settings yet seeks to make such contacts vital. Pastoral calling may be accomplished by telephone, by visits in homes, hospitals, business houses, or wherever people are encountered in wayside contacts with pastoral intent. Home visits should be intentional, wisely scheduled (often by appointment), and faithfully conducted in order to give the pastor a feeling of direction and of achievement upon their completion.

Planning includes intelligent employment of the appointment system in urban churches, so that maximum use of time is made by both the minister and church members. The pastor's secretary or administrative assistant checks to clear a time when a family will be at home and available. Once the commitment is made to visit, the pastor should follow through or cancel the engagement. Rural area residents generally prefer the informality of spontaneous calls and would probably resent setting a specific time.

It would be erroneous to refer to *routine* visitation as "wasted time," for each call should perform some service. Calls in this category include: enlistment of newcomers, persons with special challenges or handicaps, senior adults, outpatients, and persons who have become isolated by choice or estranged in relationships.[11] The pastor also makes regular administrative, teaching, and occasional social calls, which affirm strong and faithful leaders as well as hurting and indifferent members. The skilled caller is trained to be used as people need to share significant concerns in their lives. Such a visit may provide an opportunity for a parishioner to talk with the preacher (for a change) and to share how he or she feels about some church matter. Even as one ministers to others, such visitation usually informs pastoral workers of needs and confirms them in Christian mission.

Think with me about some practical issues in calling. First, be intentional. There is little reason for compulsively visiting every home and apartment for visitation's sake. The pastor's concern is *depth* of relationship, not the multiplication of superficial contacts. One call may require fifteen minutes; another three-quarters of an hour. At home, a person generally risks being real, though some do keep up a facade. The pastor will attend to nonverbal clues, unintentional gestures, and remarks that reveal existing conditions in a home. While routine calling is not conducted for the purpose of increasing one's counseling load, some contacts will lead into private conferences or follow-up calls at another time. Much of what is said in the next chapter on the "dynamics of the pastoral conversation" should guide the pastor's face-to-face visits with people.

Then, be sociable. In some contexts it is customary to "take tea" or coffee, or to share a snack or full meal, a practice that is conducive to friendship and true intimacy between church families and the pastoral family. Christ is often represented in the Gospels as sharing a meal with old or new friends. Strong bonds of support may be formed among participants in such modern "love feasts"; they make no attempt to disguise their humanness from one another. Mealtime visits can focus friendships, overcome cultural barriers, transcend sticky cut-offs, and restore communication once it has been disrupted. Some routine visits fail because of the educational, spiritual, social, or emotional distance between pastoral workers and members of the church. Our goal is to make such routine contacts as productive as possible.

Then, be flexible. Calling in response to emergencies and crises cannot be scheduled in advance. Yet the pastor will be available to hurting people in times of sickness, prior to surgery, in family conflicts, at the birth of children, at moments of death, and in grief work.[12] Church members should be instructed to notify the church office of needs in situational crises. Ministers are as close to people as the telephone, though they will be encouraged to report needs at reasonable times, not when one is home at night. Grave emergencies may breach one's privacy. Such interruptions "go with the territory."

Many people who need spiritual direction in this anxious era deny that fact. They seldom come to a church building or counselor's office to discuss their problems. Congregations committed to people-centered outreach must discover ways to focus on target groups.[13] The Christian faith and fellowship must be taken to outsiders through ministries of compassion. Contemporary pastors should note that the brilliant preaching of persons like George A. Buttrick, Harry Emerson Fosdick, George W. Truett, and Henry Sloane Coffin of a generation past was linked vitally to pastoral wisdom and work. The careful preparation of sermons should be coupled with a wise pastoral understanding of one's congregation. Coffin, who as pastor of New York's Madison Avenue Presbyterian Church made approximately a hundred personal calls each month, once said: "As ministers of Christ we deem personal evangelism our primary duty. . . . In order to accomplish this we feel that we must be free to meet [persons] on their own ground, to understand their outlook upon life, to face with them their perplexities, to feel the force of their intellectual difficulties . . . that they may submit themselves unhampered to the easy yoke . . . of Jesus himself."[14]

While the Christian pastor's ministry grows more complex and demanding with the passing years, one's personal contacts should never become perfunctory. Above all, religious visitation should strengthen an individual's or a family's link with God.

3. Communicating Pastoral Concern

In chapter 4 we noted that Christian compassion penetrates human need at the level of daily life. The pastor's personal concern may be communicated through friendship with persons of all ages, public worship, preaching and prayers, one's spirit and availability to people; and by specific acts of ministry. Along with seeking social justice, which might prevent some crises from developing, a Christian minister has certain means for establishing contact with those who need the church's ministry. Using radio and television resources for worship or "spot" features may be negotiated on a fee basis with local media personnel. Specific religious programs are prepared by church groups for cable network presentation. Some ministers have contributed a newspaper feature column regularly to address issues people face week by week and to undergird life with Christian assurance. A number of other means—like correspondence and ministries of compassion by the congregation itself—communicate concern and do God's work here on earth.

1. *Pastoral correspondence* renders a specific ministry of friendship and encouragement and points beyond itself to conferences or counseling, if they become necessary. When moving to a new church assignment, for example, the minister can write a personal letter to each household in the congregation, voicing gratitude for the privilege of being their new minister and making himself or herself available in their common ventures and crises. We should write notes of appreciation to those who extend courtesies, hospitality, or give gifts to us or our family members. Occasions such as unique achievements, birthdays, anniversaries, commencements, or retirements offer opportunities to congratulate or salute one's people. Brief personal notes may be written by hand, correlated with a calendar through

the church office. More extensive messages may be typed or computer generated. Letters express the "power of the personal" in action. The birth of a child and crises such as illness, marriage failure, or death should be supported through correspondence as well as by visitation. All new members of the congregation should receive a pastoral letter personally extending the fellowship and ministry of the church to them.

I would caution the preoccupied pastor who may be tempted to care for such "burdensome details" with form cards or printed messages. Form religious notices, like "junk" mail, are received with little enthusiasm. They are considered promotional matter by recipients, rather than words of pastoral interest. New residents and seekers after mature faith tend to select the church that demonstrates concern for them and their children rather than as potential "grist for growth." The personal touch in incoming phone calls by a church receptionist and warm greetings to church visitors are both vital.

2. Pastoral care on a group scale may be accomplished by the *discriminating use of educational media materials* in the church. Issues like AIDS, moral decisions, vocational choice, spirituality, couple communication, sexuality, crime and violence, preparation for marriage, parenting, intergenerational family ties, estate planning, and grief work are subjects that may be faced creatively through selected media.[15] Educational media materials are ideal for religious development and training. Programs are easy to use by a group or single viewer in any setting. Video dramas, for example, can add variety to training sessions. Such learning tools enhance interest by showing examples that give meaning to abstract concepts. According to a U.S. Department of Health and Human Services publication on bereavement, an estimated 8 million Americans experience the death of an immediate family member each year. There are almost 800,000 new widows and widowers annually. Group use of media resources on grief and loss usually includes sharing time. Media presentations can probe quiet places of the spirit, like family conflict or death of a child, without personal confrontation. Dealing with such care issues in groups gives members a wider perspective and encourages support within the whole faith community.

3. Wise pastors learn to call on trusted parishioners who function as *communications centers and legitimizers* in the congregation. These are *natural* leaders, commonly held in high esteem by the faith community, but are not themselves official ministers in the church. In some instances, soon after the minister has moved to a new situation, certain manipulative members may create pressure on him or her to gain favor, shape decisions, or

control actions. Manipulators may be aging or wealthy or influential figures in the community power structure who seek to control the pastor through advice, threats, favors, or acts of "friendship." While we need not suspect the motives of powerful advisers, nor reject those with whom we disagree, we can read the emotional field and avoid intimate contacts with potentially destructive persons. Distancing is a common way to handle stress or anxiety without an emotional cutoff. Meantime, a supportive ally of the pastor may help all parties to work on relationship issues in a productive way.

The wise pastor learns to trust those reliable individuals who have demonstrated their worth as legitimate Christian leaders through the years. The lines of their existence will cross frequently in personal ties and professional relationships. Both as perceptive administrator and loving pastor, one will rely on these bonafide lay caregivers for prayer support, for reliable clues about people's needs and church conditions, for interpretation of one's own actions to others, and for comradeship in their joint Christian ministry.

IV. Strengthening Faith with Literature

It has been suggested that the church's ministry is to inform and strengthen the faith of Christians who face life's great responsibilities and decisions as well as its hazards and crises. Some parishioners, however, are beyond the pastor's immediate reach in preaching, calling, and small-group experiences. Some of the church's young people are away in college and university centers. Others are working in distant cities, training in technical schools, on assignment overseas, or away in military service. There is need for a Presence in such lives, a reminder not merely of home and friends but of life's great realities, of divine grace, and of resources for survival. The religious affections of such persons may be nurtured with carefully chosen literature.

It is not just that some members are half a world away and are beyond access. Others need to find their own stories disclosed in the Scriptures, biography, novels, and alternative renderings of their own experiences. The issues people face can cut them off from companionship: "a father who has lived too long, a child caught in drug dependence, a marriage somehow gone awry, a bounced check, a low examination grade, a failed committee, a lost faith, a fresh resolve, a gift inexplicable, a dazzling act of forgiveness, anger that energizes—or destroys—the stuff of life and faith and ministry."[16] One cut off in incredible loneliness said to me, "You have never had to live alone." As an elderly widow, she reads to stay in touch with a larger world. Identification with the strange convergencies of peoples' lives in history, the Scriptures, nonfiction, self-reports, and novels permits her to see her own life more clearly and put existence into kinder perspective.

The legacy of literature in our lives is beyond measure. Here, it is not my intent to propose specific titles of books as a diet of devotional, inspirational, caregiving, and therapeutic literature. That would be presumptuous, given the varieties of doctrinal convictions, educational levels, emotional health or disorders, pet issues, gender, race, age, culture, and professional concerns of a diverse audience. Two or three matters should be noted before I suggest criteria for a selection of religious loan-shelf books.

Many congregations have a book/media/resource exhibit in a well-lighted area of the parish hall or educational building. The booth may be set up with books and pamphlets for sale, staffed during appropriate days and hours, or as a "take one" free tract/literature center. Church libraries — with educational media, curriculum guides, books, and journals — make available the finest in current and classic religious resources. "Carenotes" may be stocked, with an attractive display stand, designed to "bring good news" to people who hurt.[17] These attractive small folders of six to eight pages in length have been prepared by specialists on almost fifty topics, like: "Finding Strength to Survive a Crisis or Tragedy," "Living Creatively With Chronic Illness," "Losing Someone Close," "Facing Cancer as a Family," "Doing Your Best as a Single Parent," and "Growing Old Without Fear."

Most churches in developed nations have excellent libraries that feature "books of the month," seasonal items, spirituality resources, the Christian year, childrens' literature, denominational curriculum pieces, standard Bible commentaries, different versions of the Scriptures, and classics of devotions and church history. Local writers and conference guests are featured in book displays. Autograph parties are often sponsored when a published conference speaker visits the church or community. Special discounted prices on books for church libraries or bulk orders may be arranged by one's denominational bookstore or publishing center.

Specific occasions may arise for giving books as presents, through prearranged church budget provisions. For example, gift books may be presented to couples whom the pastor is assisting in marriage preparation, to the grief-stricken, to the searching, and to the discouraged. Adoptive parents, divorced persons, AIDS victims, persons facing addictions or transitions, adult children of alcoholic parents, and survivors of sexual abuse need insights which transcend the past and lift vision to new heights. Robert Frost once spoke of an event that gave his life a *change of mood.*

Certain books have the capacity to help one bridge a cutoff relationship, to gain a new vantage point, to kindle compassion, or let the reader identify with another point of view. A writer can say it for us — putting feelings into black-and-white and ideas into words.

What criteria shall guide the minister's selection of loan and gift books? (1) We should recommend books with which we are well acquainted, sources that have spoken to our own concerns. We should not refer persons to reading sources indiscriminately. (2) The book should have a religious orientation or should assist the puzzled person to interpret his or her situation in the light of the Christian faith. (3) Problem-focused literature, such as psychiatric case studies, may injure a depressed, suicidal, or emotionally disturbed person. Particularly when a person is in therapy, a consultation with the therapist or physician should precede the recommendation of literature. (4) Laying the groundwork with a simple, basic discussion of hot issues should precede heavier, complex discussions of emotionally loaded matters. (5) The book should be gauged to the person's capacity, intellectual and spiritual, as well as to emotional needs. A book that is too technical or abstract may distort, not interpret, experience. (6) The book should have the capacity to stir the person's reflective ability. It should help the reader make sense out of life's tangled threads and point toward someone as a resource person with whom to share reactions. Such reading should show one the way to God.

Beyond the Bible itself, writings from the church fathers, such as Augustine's *Confessions,* devotional literature from the Middle Ages, Luther's letters, Shakespeare's dramas, Pascal's *Pensées,* Kierkegaard's *Either/Or,* Martin Buber's *I and Thou,* and classic works on spirituality — all aim to enrich daily living in the Kingdom of God.[18] Such literature may call a reader to praise or to prayer, to confession or renewal, to agony or to greater responsibility. When life is blinded by tears, when relationships are distanced, when guilt hangs about a person's neck like a stone, the wisdom of a writer may beam a shaft of light into one's awareness and stir life to productive relationships again.

V. The Larger Fellowship of Concern

Reading a book can clear up misunderstandings and supply missing pieces of information, but it is no substitute for face-to-face consultation with a competent caregiver. Persons bring all kinds of issues to ministers — spiritual, family, relational, legal, medical, vocational, you name it. Ethically oriented ministers prefer not to practice beyond the limits of their competence. Others simply prefer not to get entangled in therapeutic relationships with congregants. In considering this matter, each of us must decide the level of involvement with heavy emotional agendas with which we are comfortable. Avoiding malpractice or burnout ourselves is only one side of the equation. Our chief obligation is to have the finest professional help possible for people seeking help.

How can religious helpers provide quality services for culturally diverse populations? In earlier centuries, tribal priests and wise elders, both men and women, assumed responsibility for all medical, civic, relational, and religious matters. These healers were "all things to all persons," largely because there were few other sources of help available. Cultic wisdom, magic, and witchcraft persist in some underdeveloped cultures. Certain herbalists, shamans, and diviners still claim control of the unseen world with powers of life and death. Of course, professions have developed in most cultures and excellent educational and credentialing resources are prerequisite for physicians, educators, and psychotherapists, as well as for ministers.

Because of both the complexities of modern life and the "tunnel vision" of specialists, members of the helping professions now depend upon each other's expertise and aid. Specialization within the professions has created the necessity for consultation, referral, and group practice. Seminarians may be plagued with self-doubts and fear they will never be skilled enough to help deeply troubled people. Veteran clergy, on the other hand, may grow overly confident (even indifferent), thinking, "I can tackle anything." Experience under supervision teaches us to appraise our gifts and limits; then to work within a given range of persons seeking help.[19]

The twofold approach I suggest is: learn to work in a church/community system, and practice ethical procedures of consultation and referral.

1. Working within a System

One of the chief advantages of functioning within a church setting is the larger fellowship of concern in being priests to one another. Some skilled resource persons may be found in the local church membership. Paraprofessionals may be employed as staff members of neighboring churches and help when clear-cut answers are scarce in one's own faith community. A volunteer helper may have a greater redemptive influence upon a group than can the pastor—through identification of personal interest, availability, understanding, or similar gender, age, or cultural background. Like a vector in science, one personality exerts force of greater magnitude upon a certain church member than does another. When troubled, facing a decision, or in crisis, an individual turns for help to that wise person whom he or she trusts, who is available, who understands, listens, supports, and truly cares.

A division of labor has been necessitated not only among official church leaders and volunteers, but also between ministers and available persons in the helping professions. Interprofessional cooperation in helping persons cope with life's complexities must be made effective among practitioners at the community level. There have been misunderstandings and malpractices in the past. For example, ministers resent the tendency of some medical therapists to tamper with a person's beliefs or values, once a sufferer has been referred to them. Again, clergy and physicians frequently fail to communicate with each other even while ministering to and treating the same persons. Some psychiatrists, on the other hand, feel that religionists only palliate at best and may obstruct wellness by their pious stubbornness. This exclusiveness has usually been broken down when professional persons become acquainted, respect one another's credentials, and discuss their mutual concerns.

Things can go "sour" among practitioners of different faith groups within the same city. A Christian missionary, for example, was placed on a Muslim hit list because of his vigorous devotion to converting Third World nationals to faith in Christ. And bad blood can develop between representatives of different faith groups. "The Assemblies of God believers are good folks," said a denominational employee, affirming one faith group to a new acquaintance. His friend replied, "They're troublemakers here. We've had nothing but cut-throat competition since Rev. So-and-So set up headquarters here." Working within any context takes considerable wisdom, patience, and fortitude.

Certain principles guide a pastor's, priest's, or rabbi's relationships with community resource persons. First, interprofessional cooperation must be a two-way affair, founded upon shared ties of trust between practitioners. This implies that mental health workers, educators, physicians, and ministers are to determine how each group perceives its task and develop respect for what is distinctive in others. Getting to know the other person's perspective is disarming and usually leads to mutual confidence. Professionals, in turn, share mutual accountability for educating the community about their respective specialties and for modeling cooperation.

Second, community caregivers can admit their humanity and limits and call upon one another's resources when referral is indicated. Sometimes it is lack of education, experience, time, or empathy—as in AIDS cases, for example—that requires referral. Helpers can expend so much energy giving, supporting, cutting through red tape, and dealing with intractable situations that they get burned out. A hallmark of caring too much is a shift in the way we view the people we are called on to help.[20] Instead of feeling positive and concerned, one may feel unappreciated, used up, uncaring, or critical toward problem persons. Feeling *down* on oneself and one's parishioners—wanting distance from them or making derogatory remarks about them—is a clue to burnout. Referral to another helper need not be viewed as a pastoral failure. Rather, it is an opportunity to help persons focus their needs and obtain appropriate help. A team concept can also enable a battle weary pastor to leave the front lines for "R-and-R" before involving oneself with help-seekers again.

Third, some occasions call for particular resources or skills, and therefore for pastoral care by referral. This calls for community information as well as for the pastoral introductions to other persons or agencies. This leads to the pastor's question, "To whom shall we refer?" United Way Planning and Research Councils in the United States publish and update directories of community resources for most major metropolitan areas. A directory classifies by health category or specific need every conceivable civic, medical, governmental, educational, and social welfare service of the city or county. The index provides telephone numbers and contact persons in agencies from Alcoholics Anonymous, to child care and family services, Travelers' Aid Society, mental health resources, Red Cross, Salvation Army, substance abuse and crisis intervention centers, employment agencies, hospitals, to senior citizens, and Volunteers of America. The publications of local church councils and Community Councils provide essential sources of information for referral.

"Why should I refer my people away from God and the church, their best sources of spiritual help?" asks the minister. To which we reply: A pastor does not refer people *away from* God and the church. We simply put them in touch with the specialized help they need most. The pastor cannot expect a psychiatrist, for example, to be a lay evangelist, but we are free to ask directly about his or her values and attitude toward the religion of clients. It is just as erroneous for a psychiatrist to deny a patient a minister's counsel when help is indicated in some religious matter. The church majors in spiritual and moral matters. Thus referral is a mutual rather than a one-sided affair. The pastor helps as far as possible *and* depends upon the aid of others when it becomes necessary.

2. Referral Procedure

Suppose that a young woman who is an expectant mother out of wedlock turns to the church for guidance. She needs emotional support for her mixed feelings of regret, of being trapped, of hostility, and shame. She may feel that she does not want the child, that she has jeopardized her future and deeply injured her parents. She has questions about marriage, abortion, running away, staying at home, relinquishing for adoption, or entering a home for unwed mothers. Legal, medical, and financial considerations are involved, plus large blocs of time for her counsel and care. Shall the pastor arrange medical care and a private (possibly illegal) adoption for her unplanned baby? If a deformed child is born, who will provide for him or her, the young mother or the minister who assumed such great risks?

Several of these matters fall clearly into the specialized areas of other professional persons. More time, medical care, money, and legal aid will be required than the minister alone can supply. Clearly, one will not want to injure the young woman further. Neither will a minister do for a person what someone else in the community or adjacent city can do more effectively.[21] We can hear her confession, inspire her hope, stand with her and her stricken family, help them to clarify the future and call upon the resources that are most needful. Also, there is a ministry to the young man involved, and to his family.

The minister calls upon community resources, not in order to pass the buck, but because he or she wishes the best for all persons concerned. One may say to such a person: "Your situation calls for medical assistance, some legal work, and child care. Would you like for us to talk together with your family about getting this necessary assistance? You have come to me in confidence and I have no intention of betraying your trust. Yet matters will become more complex unless you decide soon upon a course of action." Once such a course of action is begun, the parties are free to move one step at a time. The parents are consulted. The pastor is free to contact professional persons, the young man's family, and to keep in touch with the girl and her family. In this way she will not feel that the minister has tried to "get rid" of her, or is too busy, judgmental, or embarrassed to see her.

A person who has been a resident in a home for unwed mothers, a patient in a psychiatric hospital, in prison, or has received therapy for substance abuse or addiction, does not need to be treated as a "case" upon returning home. An individual may be in consultative aftercare with a professional for months or even years. He or she may have great difficulty communicating with persons at home, in the church, and community. Yet the pastor should not reject such folk, distance relationships with them, or block them from church life. Hurt persons need the strengthening love and spiritual comradeship of Christian people, an opportunity to pick up life's pieces, relationships, and responsibilities again.

The minister's commitment to seek the finest help available for one's people and wise consultation for effective ministry prompt openness to a larger fellowship of concern. When going to a new community, we should meet persons in the helping professions, interpret our pastoral interests to them, and establish lines of communication and co-operation with them. We need to know where to go for help. In this way, we fulfill the law of Christ and extend the gospel into the world. With these resources in mind we turn to selected procedures and problems in pastoral care.

Summary

How shall we summarize all that has been said here? In chapter four, I mentioned Charles Gerkin's "centrifugal model" of caring tasks. The pastor works in the midst of a great variety of situations and contexts where issues are encountered, not in one office alone. Such movements beyond the inner circle of the church have been pictured in our consideration of administrative and group leadership processes, pastoral calling and correspondence, diagnostic and therapeutic uses of literature, and interprofessional cooperation. Such is the spectrum of caregiving between reaching the many in worship and sharing with one or a few persons in counseling. Our work in the next chapter will be to examine aspects of the pastoral counseling process.

Notes

1. Ronald M. Enroth, *Churches That Abuse: Help for Those Hurt by Legalism, Authoritarian Leadership, Manipulation, Excessive Discipline, Spititual Intimidation* (Grand Rapids: Zondervan Publishing House, 1992).
2. Eugene H. Peterson, *Working the Angles: The Shape of Pastoral Integrity* (Grand Rapids: Wm. B. Eerdmans, 1987), 106.
3. For a helpful discussion of ordination, see Thomas C. Oden, *Pastoral Theology: Essentials of Ministry* (San Francisco: Harper & Row, 1983), 26–34; also, see Wayne E. Oates, "The Marks of a Christian Leader," *Southwestern Journal of Theology* 29, no. 2 (Spring 1987): 19–22.
4. Kurt Lewin in G. W. Lewin, ed., *Resolving Social Conflicts* (New York: Harper & Row, 1948), 102.
5. Wallace Clift, *Journey into Love: Roadsigns Along the Way* (New York: Crossroad/Continuum, 1990).
6. Gerald Corey and others, *Group Techniques*, rev. ed. (Pacific Grove, CA: Brooks/Cole, 1988); also, see Jeremiah Donigian and Richard Malnati, *Critical Incidents in Group Therapy* (Pacific Grove, CA: Brooks/Cole, 1987).

7. Robert Leslie, "The Minister and Group Therapy," *Pastoral Psychology* 11 (November 1960): 51. Cf. also articles in *Pastoral Psychology* 6 (April 1955) devoted to the theme "Group Work in the Church."

8. See Marianne S. Corey and Gerald Corey, *Groups: Process and Practice,* 3d ed. (Pacific Grove, CA: Brooks/Cole, 1987), chapter 8, review of group process.

9. Donelson R. Forsyth, *Group Dynamics,* 2d ed. (Pacific Grove, CA: Brooks/Cole, 1990).

10. See Lyle E. Schaller, *The Multiple Staff and the Larger Church* (Nashville: Abingdon Press, 1980); also, Juanita Ivie and Donald W. Joiner, *Celebrate and Visit: An Every Member Visitation Program* (Nashville: Abingdon Press, 1991).

11. Herbert Anderson, *et al., Ministry to Outpatients: A New Challenge in Pastoral Care* (Philadelphia: Augsburg Fortress, 1990). Cf. C. Kirk Hadaway, *What Can We Do About Church Dropouts?* (Nashville: Abingdon Press, 1990).

12. David K. Switzer, *Pastoral Care Emergencies: Ministering to People in Crisis* (Mahwah, NJ: Paulist Press, 1989).

13. Pastors Calvin Ratz, Frank Tillapaugh, and Myron Augsburger share strategies in *Mastering Outreach and Evangelism* (Portland, OR: Multnomah Press, 1990).

14. Morgan P. Noyes, *et al., This Ministry: The Contribution of Henry Sloane Coffin* (New York: Charles Scribner's Sons, 1946), 11.

15. Catalogues of religious films and videos, with rental fees, are available through offices of major denominations; secular resources may be obtained from state and local mental health associations; departments of health; university film rental libraries; and commercial rental outlets.

16. Walter Brueggemann, *Power, Providence, and Personality: Biblical Insight into Life and Ministry* (Louisville: Westminster/John Knox Press, 1990), 22.

17. "Carenotes," One Caring Place, Abbey Press, St. Meinrad, IN 47577. Inquire about a sampler-pack of forty-eight titles before ordering in quantity.

18. See, for example, historian Glenn Hinson's introduction to the devotional classics, *Seekers After Mature Faith* (Waco, TX: Word Books, 1968).

19. See Gerald Corey, M. S. Corey, and Patrick Callanan, *Issues and Ethics in the Helping Professions,* 3d ed. (Pacific Grove, CA: Brooks/Cole, 1988), chapters 2, 9. Cf. H. Newton Malony, Thomas L. Needham, and Samuel Southard, *Clergy Malpractice* (Philadelphia: Westminster Press, 1986), 26–73.

20. H. J. Freudenberger and G. Richelson, *Burn-Out: How To Beat the High Cost of Success* (New York: Bantam Books, 1980), 154.

21. William B. Oglesby, Jr., "Referral," in Rodney J. Hunter, gen. ed., *Dictionary of Pastoral Care and Counseling* (Nashville: Abingdon Press, 1990), 1048–50.

See also, Howard Clinebell, *Basic Types of Pastoral Care and Counseling*, rev. ed. (Nashville: Abingdon Press, 1984), chapter 12 on "Referral Counseling."

Suggested Reading

Bennis, Warren. *On Becoming a Leader*. Reading, MA: Addison- Wesley, 1989. A distinguished professor of Business Administration at the University of Southern California relates stories of outstanding leaders and cites characteristics of effective leadership. A wise exposition.

Callahan, Kennon L. *Twelve Keys to an Effective Church*. San Francisco: Harper & Row, 1983; also, *The Leader's Guide*. Identifies twelve characteristics of growing churches and suggests ways congregations can increase ministry effectiveness. See also his *Effective Church Leadership: Building on the Twelve Keys*. San Francisco: Harper & Row, 1990, and the new, revised *Planning Workbook* for long-range church planning. San Francisco: Harper & Row, 1990.

Corey, Gerald, *et al. Group Techniques,* rev. ed. Pacific Grove, CA: Brooks/Cole, 1988. The authors advocate using techniques as means, not ends, in helping to generate therapeutic encounters between leaders and group members. See also, with Marianne S. Corey, *Groups: Process and Practice*, 3d ed. Pacific Grove, CA: Brooks/Cole, 1987. Covers all phases of group process, member functions, and leadership tasks.

Dale, Robert D. *Pastoral Leadership: A Handbook of Resources for Effective Congregational Leadership*. Nashville: Abingdon Press, 1986. The subtitle elucidates Dale's substance. This is his most important contribution to leadership in the church.

DePree, Max. *Leadership Is an Art*. New York: Dell Publishing Group, 1989. An industrialist shares stories and accrued wisdom from the marketplace with relevance for church leaders. Practical ground rules that work in the real world.

Forsyth, Donelson R. *Group Dynamics*, 2d ed. Pacific Grove, CA: Brooks/Cole, 1990. Offers case studies and examples of group dynamics in educational, industrial, judiciary, and interpersonal skill training settings. Focuses on leadership, power, conflict, and decision-making issues.

Schaller, Lyle E. *Create Your Own Future! Alternatives for the Long Range Planning Committee*. Nashville: Abingdon Press, 1991. Veteran church planner and consultant shows pastors how to plan effectively in a systemic context. Tells how to implement much-needed change.

Toffler, Alvin. *Powershift*. New York: Bantam Books, 1990. The author of *Future Shock* and *The Third Wave* completes his trilogy about dynamic cultural change with this global perspective on power as reflected in violence, money, and knowledge.

PART III

PROCEDURES AND PROBLEMS IN PASTORAL CARE

———

CHAPTER SEVEN

DYNAMICS OF THE CARING CONVERSATION

As *carriers* of religious faith into all the worlds of human living, Christian congregations witness to the possibility of personal and social transformation. Part of the pastor's congregational work of ministry is making Christian redemption credible in practical ways and helping the congregation to live in the light of the gospel. Christ's call to care and a congregation's promise to care join in a covenant of faithful obedience. The practical task becomes: How shall the pastor prepare a "witnessing colony of truth" as coworkers in support groups, hospital calling, intercessory prayer ministry, and outreach with the *left* hand, while at the same time preparing sermons, leading worship, counseling, conducting weddings and funerals, and growing a church with the *right* hand?

The ministry is all of one piece, like Christ's seamless garment, yet it seems a "gloriously impossible" calling. Here is where a perspectival view of ministry becomes not just handy but imperative. Whether pastors organize and teach, conduct worship and preach, or care and counsel—together pastor and congregation carry their faith into the world (Matt. 5:16). When we are persuaded of this theological purpose of ministry, we also become truer to the law of our own inner being. As indicated in pastor Bill Forrester's internalization of *calling* in chapter 3, we each need to be possessed by "a new purpose" for ministry—participating in the redemptive story of God.

With the community of faith's vocation in mind, we shall first clarify certain concepts and terms. Since informal calling in homes, hospitals, and so on, as well as more formal multiple-interview counseling sessions, partake of the nature of spiritual discourse, the designation *dynamics of the caring conversation* is being used in both an inclusive and an intensive sense. "Caring conversation" describes the contextual nature of the minister-person nexus, though the relationship may be that of pastor-parishioner, chaplain-patient, teacher-student, parent-child, or volunteer-neighbor. "Conversation" suggests the intensity of interpersonal dialogue, and includes such non-verbal factors as the manner of life of the conversationalists, levels of discourse, and their changing perceptions of each other. "Dynamics" suggests (1) the dimension of depth in human development; (2) the energetic forces at work when people talk together; (3) the presence of conflict and possibility of its resolution; as well as (4) the process of personal change that is possible through counseling. All caring interviews are not "counseling," in terms of time and intensity, but may partake of its nature in principle.

God's Word reminds us that his conversations with individuals are as old as the human story. As God's minister moves along the continuum of caring, from experiences with the *many* in worship to conversations with the *few* or *one* in counseling, we recognize that God himself continues his conversations with humankind. In the listening-responding dialogue of counseling, the caregiver functions as a facilitator of the divine-human conversation and as a catalyst, accelerating a counselee's spiritual change and growth. Both the public dialogue of the sanctuary and the private interview are essentially transactions with God. Critics who neglect or scorn counseling are profoundly mistaken about its nature, worth, and redemptive intent.

The particular character of caring conversations, as partaking of deep divine-human relationships, is illustrated in an Old Testament paradigm (Gen. 32:24–32). Jacob's wrestling with God's messenger at Jabbok typifies the process of spiritual growth through struggle and encounter. Jacob's history of deceit (he had outwitted Esau, Isaac, and Laban), strange dreams (such as the Bethel vision), and dread of meeting his brother are part of the background. When the news reached him that his alienated brother Esau was approaching, Jacob divided his flocks and family and sent them ahead. Like T. S. Eliot's "hollow man," Jacob remained alone at the camp, facing soul-size problems of old animosities and guilt feelings. At Bethel he had dreamed of God's nearness. Now, alone by the brook, he experienced the divine reality in an awful way. Before Jacob could face his brother, he had to give an account of himself to his Creator. An anonymous protagonist engaged Jacob in a mortal struggle that night. Rather than avoiding the encounter, Jacob grappled with God's messenger in the awful darkness and pled for a blessing. Not everything is told explicitly. Some things are hinted at or suggested. Jacob the deceiver's life was seen to be out of joint; yet he held onto the heavenly messenger until mercy was given. While this experience is set in antiquity, the pattern of the God-human encounter is clear and provides clues to the process of spiritual change through counseling today.

This brief but significant episode is an integral part of the spiritual biography of a person, plagued by his past, who worked through dark aspects of his life experience with pain and profit. Note the process: (1) A man with a shadowy record of failure in relationships faced a "D-Day" confrontation with his brother. (2) His wrestling with the dreadful mystery of existence was in reality a reckoning with God. In the process he discovered, not prowess or courage, but certain shameful truths about himself. (3) Jacob was highly motivated to unburden himself, to stay with God's messenger until he had assimilated his "shadow self" into conscious awareness. The blessing he pled for, which was granted, wrapped his spirit in a deep calm. At a theological level, that interaction was an experience of judgment and grace. (4) God's new covenant with Jacob supported his giving up secrets, coming out into the open, searching for integrity, and moving toward responsible behavior. (5) Jacob was equipped to live with a new sense of identity, a new name (Israel), fresh clarity of judgment, and hopefulness toward the future—all springing from his healthier relationship with God.

Aware of a new degree of emotional integration and empowerment, Jacob determined to make peace with his brother. Their reconciliation demonstrated new modes of relationship in the social order, which Jacob had learned through his encounter with God's messenger. As we consider the nature of contemporary pastoral counseling, it is possible to read too little or too much into this and other such conversations in the Bible. While the ancients held a more concrete view of personality than do present-day interpreters, their unburdening and assimilating past experiences, with support and equipping for life, parallels the counseling process today.

I. Types of Caring Conversations

The foregoing paradigm pictures the religious counselor's frame of reference and chief concerns: a burdened person (or family unit) seeking relief; a trained, socially sanctioned caregiver; and their spiritual discourse before God. With limited resources of time and information, a minister cannot know all about those who come for help. Much like military commanders in the heat of battle, modern pastors must possess situational awareness in order to foster relevant Christian ministry. Developing time-limited counseling skills requires considerable wisdom—gaining insight into oneself, learning from experience, using community networks, as well as tracking issues in the divine-human conversation.[1] The biblical paradigm provides a model for modern spiritual guides: (1) helping persons unburden loads,

(2) supporting them in the process, and (3) equipping them for relation-ships and tasks now and in the future.

From the outset it has been acknowledged that the minister and congregation have both prophetic and pastoral functions to perform in the world. While winning persons to salvation in Christ is crucial, strengthening them for Christian living and enabling them to serve God effectively in the social order is just as crucial. Because ministers are both heralds and guides of God's good news, we are to grow churches *and* persons.[2] Pastoral counseling moves salvation from otherworldly preoccupations of what we are saved *to* "out there someday," to what Christ saves us *from* now: meaninglessness, addictions, family abuse, anxiety, depression, erotic and hostile impulses, self-defeating behaviors. For too long, noted African-American pastor Vaughn Walker, "the evangelistic call has emphasized saving souls without an equal regard for saving people."[3] Pastoral vision sees beyond a kingdom on a corner, inside brick and mortar, to deep needs—broken marriages, substance abuse, underemployment, classism, sexism, homelessness, poor health services, limited educational opportunities, and people needing empowerment in their search for a significant life.

Strugglers turn to Christian guides for help mid the pressures of life, even as they turn initially from life in sin to Jesus Christ for salvation. Conversations of a pastoral nature and intent are thus crucial for relating the implications of the gospel to life. Yet all caring conversations are not identical.

In order to be discriminating, I am suggesting a threefold typology to distinguish levels of caring conversations in congregational life: (1) precounseling interviews, (2) peer counseling dialogues, and (3) more formal pastoral counseling. At mid-century, the late Seward Hiltner distinguished *counseling* interviews from other pastoral contacts that are *precounseling* in nature.[4] This distinction involves the discussants who share in therapeutic conversation, limited time frame or brief duration of encounters, the degree of intensity of relationship, as well as the intent of individuals engaged in spiritual discourse. Given the faith community's sense of ultimacy, even incidental encounters are potentially significant.

Precounseling interviews converge at key points of commonality. They partake of the nature of private discourse, but are usually semiprivate chats, conferences, consultations, or telephone visits between concerned parties. Precounseling conversations may be distinguished by (1) their relatively brief duration; (2) the initiative and availability which the helper often takes in such interviews; (3) the varied settings in which they occur; and (4) the fact that such visits consist chiefly of acute or current concerns.

Here is a grandmother requesting prayer by the pastor or church representative for a grandson overseas in military service. A mother weeps quietly during an after-worship report to her minister that her teenager has been hospitalized temporarily for abusing drugs. A single young executive invites her Sunday school teacher to a salad lunch with the explanation: "I need to talk with someone about something that's come up at work." Hiltner saw such sharing as *that,* which goes before counseling, in a penultimate sense.

Peer counseling designates the work of trained laypersons who walk alongside of people and provide friendship, support, or guidance when needed. Eldercare centers are relying on trained senior citizens, for example, to listen to residents for needs that are harder to get hold of than physical needs — like depression, grief, or hopelessness.[5] A Mennonite congregation in Bristol, Indiana, was stunned by a series of divorces among its members. An elder, Elizabeth Stauffer, noted: "In the past, divorce was regarded as very much an unforgivable sin. We've not really learned to live with it redemptively. I think [we're] learning, but twenty years ago we wouldn't have known how. The divorcing persons would have left the church."[6]

In an effort to meet the need, the congregation followed the Stephen Ministries program, an interfaith plan in which twenty members received fifty hours of training so they might provide a form of low-key, individual counseling. To date, more than twenty people in the congregation have received long-term supportive care from Stephen ministers. Mennonites in the past were good at helping one another in physical ways. Now they are learning to give care in other ways.

The "power of two" puts a face and supportive listeners with folks in all walks of life. Lay Christians are coming to recognize that all encounters where the human condition is laid bare and truth is shared are potentially eventful.

This keystone of *significance* in the human religious search is reflected in a first-time meeting between Marcy, a twenty-two-year-old, single-again city dweller, and Jeff, a visitor enjoying a swimming pool party at an apartment complex. Marcy had a beer in her hand as she picked up conversation with Jeff. They exchanged introductions at poolside, surrounded by folks on floats, swimmers, and loungers. She observed that Jeff's party-goers were "not running around yelling and drinking," and asked if they were a church group. That led into a brief religious history of why Marcy did not go to church.

MARCY: I've always been different than most religious people, I guess. I need to ask a lot of questions, and most people in churches don't like for you to do that. They think you're a heretic or something.

JEFF: That's too bad. It shouldn't be like that. Churches aren't supposed to be that way.

MARCY: Yeah. I've always done a lot of thinking about God and life. I've also read of lot of philosophy, too. That's helped me some. A lot of people don't like agnostic philosophers. Some of them may not believe like a Christian does, but that doesn't mean they don't have anything good to say.... Guys like Sartre ... are not against Christians. They just view life from a different point of view, and a lot of things they say are very helpful. [Marcy elaborated how certain wise persons had helped her answer some serious questions.] My life has been a real nightmare, and that forces you to stop and look at things.

JEFF: When you say it's been a "nightmare," can you tell me more of what you mean? [Marcy shared about her "very religious" upbringing, broken relationships with men, violation of her value system with "drinking and partying," grave doubts, along with her profound spiritual hunger.]

MARCY: Even when my boyfriend and I were going to church, I felt like there was always something else besides what we believed that I needed to know. I couldn't ever tell what it was, but it bothered me that it always seemed "out there." And I never knew if I could even find a way to discover what was "out there." This feeling has always perplexed me. [Their conversation ranged from her report that a neighbor had called her a blasphemer for raising so many questions, to talk of her ex-husband who was too pious, to what might be a good church for her to attend, "in case I ever do go to a church."]

Marcy's pain at a party oozed out with a caring stranger—someone who listened to her feelings of shame, failure, and loss of a Dream; who noted her longing to feel valued as a person, even with questions and doubts; and who spotted her loneliness and need for companionship, including a faith community that really cared. Marcy longed for acceptance and a way through to God, "out there," so that he could help her with self-doubts, guilt, anger, and grief, and nurture hope back into her spirit. This visit in a casual setting was not counseling in a formal sense; yet it was significant. It points up the store we must set in peer counseling and the value of proper training for it.[7]

So that the pastor's "left hand may know what the right hand is doing," we should distinguish precounseling visits, emergency calls, and short-term caring conversations from formal, multiple-interview counseling. Calls to the church office in one day may vary from an elderly woman whose husband has fallen and broken his hip, to a report of an automobile accident in which a popular church youth has been killed. Such burdens come wrapped in time-limited costumes rather than in long-term intrapsychic conflicts. An individual's need for handling some emergency, for spiritual strength, and for clarification of direction may be as urgent in a single-interview contact as in multiple-interview counseling. Speaking the truth in such moments is God's way of guiding us.

Pastoral theologian Brian Childs tells how pastors and peer counselors may assess the possible outcomes of brief interviews:

1. Is there a clear presenting (focal relational) problem?
2. Has the person experienced healthy relationships in the past?
3. Can the counselee relate flexibly with the helper?
4. Is the individual bright and psychologically minded?
5. Is there motivation for change, not just symptom relief?[8]

Based on the experience of Peter Sifneos and others, Childs says a counselor should have positive responses to each of these criteria in order for brief counseling to be effective.

Coupling such diagnostic variables with theological wisdom can help persons dealing with basic *being* (ontological) issues in counseling.

1. Does the counselee link his or her experience with God as "a severe mercy"?[9] As you listen, explore: "Is my counselee open to the hand of God (Providence) in this event?"
2. Is there a powerful religious stimulus present to help set the person's house in order, to forgive, to form a new covenant with someone, to go on with the project of living?
3. Will the counselee bond with a support group that will reinforce positive, adaptive behavior? Without hopeful theological grounding, brief counseling may be in vain.

Conversations with persons that precede formal pastoral counseling in time and depth include: (1) social contacts in the marketplace, fitness center, hospital, and elsewhere; (2) supportive calls, often accompanied by prayer, in the hospital or home; (3) teaching interviews, frequently initiated by the pastor in order to prepare persons for church membership or for marriage, to interpret some ecclesiastical or doctrinal matter, or conversations that are disciplinary in intent; (4) confessional disclosures in which a person reveals feelings of guilt, powerlessness, anger, anxiety, or need for faith in a single conversation; and (5) consultative talks with staff members, fellow ministers, or other professionals in behalf of some person or family.

A more formal counseling relationship is recognized when the pastor and an individual who has come for help appraise their past conversations and agree to establish a structured, longer-term counseling situation. This covenantal shift in relationship should be clarified by both participants in the sharing process. Following an exploratory discussion of what seems important, lasting no more than one hour, a more extended, multiple-interview relationship may be agreed upon. The connection is structured so that the counselee has major responsibility for continuing the interviews, for terminating them, or reopening them at any time. While ideas for structuring formal interviews came initially from psychotherapists, defining the counseling relationship and time frame is a requisite for Christian helpers as well.[10] Structuring the counseling situation involves scheduling time periods to work through the counselee's concerns (though the number of sessions may remain open-ended); agreeing upon a place of discreet privacy for the meetings, such as the minister's church office; and clarifying the counselee's expectations, initiative, and responsibility as well as the minister's function as counselor. Both of them invest heavily in the interactive (contracting) process, though ultimate responsibility for change rests with the counselee.

Frequently, a systemic process is involved. Even as they collaborate in an effort to help the counselee, the person's family may turn to the pastor for help. Psychological testing or a medical examination may be indicated. An unemployed or terminated individual may require a career assessment or skilled on-the-job training. Networking, with the possibility of professional collaboration and referral, should be held open, if such specialized resources are needed. With this typology in mind, we now consider pastoral counseling's distinctiveness.

II. The Nature of Pastoral Counseling

We come now to address three practical questions. First, given all the schools of psychotherapy and counseling that have emerged in this century, what is distinctive about *pastoral* counseling?[11] Second, is Christian counseling by the clergy actually "pastoral psychotherapy," as some have said? Third, can it be demonstrated from records of caring events that spiritual direction actually points persons to God? Following an examination of these issues, we shall trace identifiable phases of the pastoral counseling process.

1. Distinctive Elements of Pastoral Counseling

What distinguishes pastoral counseling from other kinds of counseling today? *First,* pastoral conversations presuppose the God-human dialogue of existence, though theological issues per se may not be raised by the counselee. Any human concern is an accepted issue for pastoral counseling. When life's ultimacies are laid bare before a representative of the Christian faith, the conversationalists find themselves in the presence of God (Matt. 18:20). It is unnecessary for them to *do* or to *say* something "religious," for the entire relationship partakes inherently of religious experience. Such counseling is a means of implementing the expectancy inherent in the Christian life. To a degree, pastoral counseling may be viewed as a form of prayer—a conversation with God in the presence of another.

Second, pastoral counseling may be distinguished from other kinds of counseling (educational, psychological, medical, and so forth) on the contextual grounds of a religious orientation and set of assumptions.[12] While employing principles common to other professional counselors, ministers generally stand on biblical-theological ground and bring a profound sense of Christian hope to care-seekers. Whether one intends it or not, some persons endow the religious healer with special authority—even magical expectations—which may tempt one to charlatanism. Intense relationships with authority figures stir feelings from childhood. Without intending to, we may become the object of one person's sexual fantasies, another's hostility, another's shame, and another's dependency. Early on, the pastor may have to assist the person in clarifying his or her specific expectations and employment of the counseling process.

For example, a man who had been operating a small contracting business declared bankruptcy. Because his family had been accustomed to a substantial income, they continued personal expenditures as usual. When ready cash and credit sources had been exhausted, the family lost everything. Eventually, the man turned to his pastor in a period of depression, feeling not only financial failure but a sense of hopelessness. After two or three brief conversations, it became clear that the man was trying to use the minister as a financial guarantor to gain refinancing for another business venture. Progress was made in their relationship with the passing of time between interviews, telling the investor the truth, and with clarification of the pastor's function as a spiritual guide. The man was directed to a certified financial planner in the community who could help him regain his financial bearings. Meanwhile, the pastor supported the man's search for self-worth and responsibility before God. In this instance, the pastor declined to cosign a large collateral loan at a local bank.

Third, pastoral counseling may be distinguished by the kind of ministry it attempts to perform in relation to what is distinctive among other professional counselors. Fundamentally, *pastoral counseling may be viewed as the process of conversations between a responsible minister and a concerned individual or intimate group, with the intent of enabling such persons to work through their concerns to a constructive course of action.* Such a process view of pastoral counseling magnifies the relationship itself rather than a technique per se. Pastoral counselors are eclectic in that they find clues in varied approaches to personality theory and to therapeutic methods. Their single-minded task is to provide both healing intervention and spiritual direction, pointing Christians to effective discipleship in the social order. Salvation and health or *wholeness* are the pastoral counselor's specialties. "The word is not of primary importance," noted theologian John B. Cobb, Jr. "What is of primary importance is that pastoral counselors are clear as to what constitutes *genuine* health or wholeness or salvation and that . . . they relate their vision to the cumulative wisdom of the biblical and Christian traditions."[13] Rather than using some borrowed "technique" or false hope *on* counselees, honest pastoral counselors prefer to share an empathic relationship and to speak the truth hopefully *with* them.

While listening acceptingly to the counselee's feelings, the pastor's mediatorial function is to reflect the mind of Christ as well as the person's own feelings back to her or him in the interviews. Our goal is that the one seeking help come to grips with the past, if *that* is in question; develop insight into current feelings and experiences; and discover the power of the future for purposive, hopeful living. In this respect, pastoral counseling must move beyond a purely nondirective posture, with confidence in its unique goals and tasks.

In order to understand how to get started in the hard work of counseling, let us contrast brief excerpts from two interviews. The first pastor attempts to control the conversation and to manipulate the counselee, whereas the second is more accepting and responsive to the person's feelings. Though these illustrations overstate the case, the point should be clear.

1. A *directive-manipulative approach*

(The minister's office was the setting for this conversation.):

MRS. P.: For sometime now things haven't been going very well at home [Mrs. P. begins to weep softly].

PASTOR: Come now, Mrs. P., I am sure that things aren't as bad as they seem, and I feel sure we can find help in God's Word.

MRS. P.: Pastor, you just don't know how bad it is.

PASTOR: I certainly think you have done the right thing, coming to your pastor, I mean. Let's talk about it honestly and openly. Why don't you just start at the beginning and tell me everything.

MRS. P.: I just had to talk to someone . . .

Here, the counselor's insensitivity, shamanistic sense of power, and need to control the interview are obvious. He unconsciously belittles Mrs. P.'s feelings, reassures her prematurely, and suggests that she tell "everything" in one interview. Rather than joining Mrs. P. on her spiritual journey, he stiff-arms her with "things aren't so bad." To his credit, he is willing to listen to her story, though on a fact-gathering basis. A manipulative counselor may help, but may also damage counselees with such repressive tactics and superficial relationships.

2. An accepting-responsive approach

(The following excerpts of conversation transpired in a general hospital setting.):

BRUCE: It's like this truck hitting me. Man, it knocked all the evil inside me out of me and I feel clean inside. When we suffer the evil goes out of us. [Bruce described how badly his leg was injured in a truck accident.] When they asked me if my leg was broken, I said, "Broke, broke, broke," and it was. I told 'em to turn it back up toward heaven.

MINISTER: You feel that your suffering is for a purpose then?

BRUCE: . . . I really have caught a hard time in life. I don't know why my wife would leave me like this, just when I need her so much . . . alone . . . with nobody to care. She don't love me; she just loves herself. She thinks I'm nuts.

MINISTER: What would cause her to think *that* and leave?

BRUCE: Because I was in a mental hospital . . . that's before we got married. [He continued his explanation at some length.]

In this pastoral intervention, there is a clear effort to "get with" and stay with the patient's feelings. The man expresses several things, but depression and dependency are paramount. Until Bruce builds trust in persons—human and divine—his conversations will provide primarily release of strong emotions rather than clear perception of reality. He may draw human support rather than developing faith in the providence of God. Fortunately, the minister encouraged Bruce to use their times together for spiritual growth and visited him on twelve occasions during his process of recovering from the accident.

As far as time, the person's condition, and circumstances permit, the pastoral counselor will listen patiently, respond reflectively, and comment carefully, all so that the counselee may clarify his or her feelings, develop realistic hopes, and assume responsibility for life's decisions and tasks. Pastoral counseling is prudently permissive and persuasive, accepting and confronting, humble and teachable, yet truly wise in the ways of grace. It is urgent, involved, and tiring work. The uniqueness of Christian counseling lies in the use which the participants make of the self-confrontation occurring at any moment in the relationship, and of the illumination—human and divine—given in their face-to-face meetings.

2. Pastoral Counseling and Psychotherapy

In his comparative study of psychotherapies a generation ago, psychiatrist Jerome Frank noted three features essential to such endeavors: (1) a trained, socially sanctioned healer, whose healing powers are accepted by the sufferer and by society; (2) a sufferer who seeks relief at the hands of a healer; and (3) a structured series of contacts between the healer and sufferer, through which the healer tries to produce changes in the sufferer's emotional state, attitudes, and behavior.[14] Psychiatrists are medical therapists and use physical and chemical adjuncts, like hospitalization and prescribed medication, along with individual and group therapy. Their practice is built on a medical education and presupposes a physician-patient relationship, secular setting, and fee basis of treatment. Psychotherapists are guided by ethical standards of practice, both in their guilds and under law, and are subject to suit for malpractice.

The healing influences in all forms of psychotherapy rely on relationships of trust, words, acts, and rituals in which healers and sufferers, including groups, participate. All modern psychotherapies, noted Frank, originated in two historical traditions of healing—one religious, the other naturalistic or scientific. This is not the occasion to debate the issue of whether or not religious conversions and conversations are, in fact, psychotherapy (that is, healing of the self). Relationships among the disciplines of psychology, psychiatry, pastoral counseling, social work, and their sub-branches remain in flux and are governed by their respective credentialing bodies, as well by the practitioners themselves.

I have long maintained that the work pastoral counselors do should be *therapeutic* (in the sense of healing or of spiritual wellness), but should not be called *therapy* in a secular sense. It has become quite commonplace for ordained ministers to offer counseling and therapeutic services in centers separate from Christian contexts and traditions. They are obligated in such instances to be duly credentialed, often licensed by the state, paid by third-party insurance fees, and to function ethically as psychotherapists. Full-time pastoral care and counseling specialists may serve on a church staff. They must decide who they are and the tradition or theoretical basis of their practice.

Theologian John B. Cobb has sage wisdom for all who function in these fields. He both cautions and guides religious counselors:

> For pastoral counseling to carry forward genuinely the ancient tradition of the care of souls, it must separate itself further from secular therapy. Therapy can too easily be based on a model of restoring people to the capacity to function satisfactorily in society as it now exists. That can be a proper moment in pastoral counseling, certainly, but it cannot provide the basic model. The goal of pastoral counseling needs to be something like growth in grace, the strengthening of Christian existence, enabling Christians to be more effective disciples, or salvation. Such a goal will enable pastoral counseling to be spiritual direction as much as it is therapy.[15]

While secular therapists look primarily to the "healing forces of life" within their patients for recovery, pastoral counselors rely upon the character and power of God to effect constructive changes in counselees. All healing forces are God-given initially. In Luke 17:21, Jesus implies that sensitivity to the presence of God *within you* is the clue to his coming for anyone. Healers and seekers alike must *see* the reality of God saving people in their very midst.

The primary goals of pastoral counseling are (1) to share the faith journey as persons unburden their feelings and come to grips with reality; (2) to support persons who seek spiritual resources during some crisis, decision, or growth phase of life; and (3) to equip counselees to face reality, make constructive character change, become more decisive, or grow in intimacy —human and divine. Unburdening one's soul in the classic sense of soul care precedes making headway on the journey of faith. While all religious counseling may not follow this paradigm in three-step fashion, counselors in reflecting on their work sense that uncovering the self (discovering the past) precedes healthy venturing again.

These goals for pastoral counseling are predicated upon a relatively enduring relationship of trust between the minister and the people. Diagnostic evaluation of the counselee's situation, spiritual resources, regressions, plateaus, and growth is influenced by their prior acquaintance and durable relationship. Because ministers face many time demands, they will limit counseling with one person or family unit to four to six sessions on a specific issue. This number is arbitrary but realistic, given the limited training of nonspecialist pastors.[16] Many helping events are confined to one or two interviews. After an evaluation hour, the minister decides whether to covenant (contract) for a specific number of sessions or to refer the help-seeker(s) to someone else for care. Once the number of sessions has been agreed upon by both parties, stick to the bargain. Time management is a key component of the therapeutic relationship.

With such criteria in mind, it is clear that some troubled persons are inaccessible to pastoral counseling. Rather than facing their problems, they "act out" conflicts through addictive, abusive, neurotic, even religiously masked behavior. While they do not need *labels*, persons whose destructive or compulsive behavior invites social disapproval or rejection actually need help. If an individual's behavior is appraised by family, work associates, friends, or minister as being grossly inappropriate or bizarre, a medical consultation is in order. The man who hates the world, the woman who is eccentrically detached from life, or the recently converted young person with too many scruples may be hiding personality disorders behind masks.[17] The degree of social or emotional disorder is the clue to urgency in seeking medical advice. A person in a prolonged period of depression, the delusional individual who feels constantly mistreated or persecuted, the person who avoids all social contact and sits staring at the walls of one room, or the person who becomes religiously "out of character" through obsessive Bible reading, compulsive praying, crying, and so on—each may require time and skill beyond the limits of pastoral practice. Referral for medical or other consultation, in cooperation with the person's family, is appropriate in such instances.[18]

How then does counseling by responsible ministers differ from the psychotherapeutic interventions of physicians trained as psychiatrists? *First,* as noted earlier, while pastoral conversations should be therapeutic (healing) in the redemptive sense, a minister's work is not "treatment of patients" in a medical sense. *Second,* while aware of unconscious drives in counselees, the parish pastor or priest relates to persons primarily at conscious levels of experience and conflict; a psychiatrist, on the other hand, is prepared to cope with unconscious dimensions of experience. This medical professional is trained to diagnose aberrations of attitude and conduct, to explore deep levels of intrapsychic conflict, to work in a hospital environment, and to "tease out" mechanisms of defense like identification, projection, transference, and countertransference with patients. Hypnosis, drugs, and various forms of shock and group therapy are standard treatment modalities in medical settings. Meanwhile, research remains to be made into religious assumptions about divine Providence and prayer, the effect of faith on "dated emotions," the influence of forgiveness upon unconsciously motivated regressive behavior, the dynamics of compassion and self-hate, and the power of Christian hope over despair.

Third, while Christian counseling and psychotherapy are both social, collaborative, and growth-oriented, the former is directed to persons who are relatively free to carry out their constructive strivings; the psychiatrist is trained to treat those whose defenses are so shattered that they are temporarily immobilized by illness. *Fourth,* while home, work, and church settings are unrestricted by pastoral counselors, an institutional setting provides controls and limits for the person who may be dangerous either to himself or to others.[19] *Fifth,* as a physician, the psychiatrist has several years of clinical preparation for the task, plus the resources of medical diagnosis, team treatment, and varied forms of therapy at hand.

While aware of a patient's religious ideation and possible aberrations, the medical therapist's goal is to help patients gain insight into the nature of their bondage and to acquire ego controls over unconscious impulses. The physician labors in order that the patient's illness may become a gateway to health. The pastoral counselor, on the other hand, attends to counselees' God-images and sense of how God works in the world and helps them to do life. The focus is on meaningful connections with other persons and the significance of the Christian faith as the integrating center of life. Both the clergy and Christian psychiatrists are concerned with strengthening families, improving spiritual-mental health in society, and lowering the prevalence of abusive behaviors, along with controlling crime and violence. They are interested in the recovery of health, but are also concerned with preventing problems in family living and providing social programs to enrich our lives. Many such programs, with appropriate networking in the public and private sector, are already "within our reach."[20]

3. *The Power of Pastoral Counseling*

We noted in chapter 3 that the church is always in the process of being born and reborn within the arena formed by purposeful communication among Christians. Counseling, wherein heart-to-heart talk is shared in an environment of respect and trust, has become a vital concern of all who live at the center of religious communications. Yet talking is as old as the human race. God created humankind in his own image for companionship, for communion; thus to converse is to be both human and Godlike. The words of persons struggling for the moment of healing have long been disclosed in the prayers, soliloquies, and dialogues of the Bible and great literature. Psalm 42 discloses the conversation between the stronger and weaker selves within one psalmist: "Why are you downcast, O my soul? Why so disturbed within me?" (42:5). The stronger self responds: "Put your hope in God; for I will yet praise him, my Savior and my God." The act of talking to oneself is a solitary experience, reserved in our thinking for the lonely person, the self-defeated, the innocent child, and the troubled citizen of earth.

Talking with a trusted caring person breaks the lonely monologue of existence. Counseling becomes "the axe for the frozen sea inside us," to quote Franz Kafka. Monologue breaks into dialogue with someone who desires to understand. The depths of the overburdened one meet the depths of a helpful guide who listens with perceptive, liberating love. As in prayer, so in counseling God grants the sufferer his steadfast love, provides a way to face one's own finitude, and encourages commitment to the future. Spiritual self-discovery and affirmation come not in "mere talk" alone but in meeting God in another's presence. In this respect, ministers dare not take their conversations with others lightly. It is precisely in the pastoral conversation that pastoral care focuses divine truth upon specific human needs.

Talking to oneself can do little more than confirm one's need for community and to be heard. Sharing with a responsible listener opens a self-talk person to the possibility of community, reality, and the truth. Language is a vital part of being human and of experiencing others as persons. For some, small talk is enough. Language is a convenient facade for holding other people at bay. The superficially humorous person, the shy or withdrawn person, the orally aggressive talker, and the flighty conversationalist are each basically insecure individuals. Thus they dare not exchange the coin of conversation in depth for fear of losing control or of being discovered in their weakness. Others, with tremendous burdens of shame, temptation, or hostility, fear that the truth will come out if they share with another. Of course, many persons long to share their stories with someone who knows the God story, who will help them unburden their souls, and face the future with hope.

Trained pastoral counselors know that merely getting people to talk is not sufficient. In fact, prolonged talking may be dangerous if the person is deeply depressed. He or she might self-talk into suicide! Again, we know the "presenting" problem—the thing or things that the counselee speaks about in the beginning—may be only the preface to much deeper concerns. People tend to send up "trial balloons" initially to test the minister's acceptance and good faith. The pastoral conversationalists will recognize that a moment of truth has come when the counselee's self-revelation is made explicit. Until that time, the person may use the relationship to gain sympathy in a situation, to "dump" feelings, to be seductive, or to manipulate the minister in ways other than as a counselor. Purposefulness in growth counseling and support in crisis counseling begin when self-discovery *in truth* begins. Ideally, self-disclosure moves toward self-awareness, self-acceptance, divine empowerment, and responsible behavior within the community.

The power of pastoral counseling must be measured in its capacity for helping people find *ultimate* meaning amid *temporal* existence. Two research reports help us view temporality through theological eyes. Charles E. Brown investigated notions of time among disturbed psychiatric patients and their pastoral counselors. He observed that interventions that helped persons face not simply the past but their own future "end time" proved most helpful. "*Authentic existence,* he wrote, "*is clearly eschatological existence,* i.e., existence characterized by *acceptance of the past, openness in the present, and commitment to the future.*"[21] It is the power of the future in human existence that impressed Brown and his colleagues in their search for wellness.

A generation earlier, Wayne E. Oates, who spent so much of his career ministering with deeply troubled people, expressed similar assumptions about the cruciality of time in giving care. He wrote: "Pastoral counseling . . . takes place either implicitly or explicitly within the commonwealth of eternal life as we know it in Jesus Christ. The way of life we have known in times past, the decisive turnings in our way of life called for in the living present, and the consideration of the end of our existence, our destiny—all these come to focus in the spiritual conversation known as pastoral counseling."[22] Time-limited counseling, like a camera's telephoto lens, draws what lies out in the distance into clearer focus. What is *now* is not everything. As the apostle Paul expressed it, "Our present sufferings are not worth comparing with the glory that will be revealed in us" (Rom. 8:18–27). God—not our present constraints, crises, or conflicts—is guiding history to its climax. That is reason for hope!

We readily acknowledge that talking things over with a minister may not help. Memories of failures haunt some would-be helpers—the counselee who went from a pastoral interview into a psychotic episode, or to prison for some act, or deeper into an addiction, who finalized divorce, or took a life—the counselee's own or that of another. Few failures of pastoral counseling have ever been published, partly because ministers are reticent about revealing their mistakes. Some common hazards and examples of clinical issues appear in the *Clinical Handbook of Pastoral Counseling.* The editors present effective caring events with commentary, issues of assessment in varied situations, and approaches to facilitating psychospiritual healing and growth.[23] While humbling, a minister's failures may teach her or him more than constant success.

Thus far, several principles have been implied that should guide the minister's conversations with others. Believing in the integrity of counseling, we are to (1) approach this aspect of pastoral care, not with a hit-or-miss attitude, but with clinical skill and redemptive intent; (2) cherish persons created in God's image for whom Christ died; (3) structure the counseling relationship with the individual or family unit so that our times, meeting places, and mutual tasks during the conversations will be clear; (4) rely upon the counselee's capacity for decision-making and responsible action as far as the situation permits; and (5) commit time with counselees with the due regard for the best interests of all the congregation. Rather than moving beyond our depth or time constraints, risking damage to a sufferer or ourselves, we may refer certain counselees to trusted professional colleagues. The cardinal principle that all pastoral conversations partake of religious experience both heightens and intensifies the counseling relationship.

With the power of pastoral counseling in mind, we now examine certain phases of the counseling process.

III. Counseling as Relationship and Process

We sense the near madness of codependency in dysfunctional families in events reported by a pastor named Steve. Ronn and Vicki, a young unmarried couple living together in his parents' home, had been involved in an intergenerational quarrel and requested an appointment. Steve knew their backgrounds from previous associations at church. They had been engaged for about three months. Ronn, eighteen, dropped out of high school and was not employed. Vicki, also unemployed, had moved in with Ronn and his family several months before; now Ronn's parents had asked her to move out. They faced consequences of a forced *change.* Before their engagement, Ronn had been heavily involved in the abuse of drugs and alcohol. They asked to meet Steve at his office that evening and arrived on time.

The emotionally loaded situation that brought about their conversation began when Ronn and Vicki questioned Ronn's parents about problems of other family members. Ronn's brother was involved in buying and selling illegal drugs. His sister, recently separated from her husband, had invited her boyfriend to move with her back into the family's home. It was a "boomeranger" situation, as adult kids returned temporarily to the family nest—an explosion waiting to happen. Ronn's parents verbally attacked his brother, Jack, and sister, Janice. In outraged, displaced anger, Jack got angry at Ronn and physically assaulted him. It was from the fray of battle in a very dysfunctional family system that Ronn and Vicki sought help. They were hurt, angry, and confused.

After hearing the above events summarized, the pastor spoke of the future.

STEVE: What do you two plan to do in the near future concerning marriage, jobs, and so forth?

RONN: Well, we plan on getting married as soon as we can afford it.

VICKI: We just don't know when we will be able.

STEVE: Have you been looking for jobs?

VICKI: Sort of. We have had a lot of other stuff we have needed to do lately. The offers that I have had have not been what I've wanted. [They spoke of the two of them getting involved with other young people at church, and how great it had been finding acceptance in the community of faith. Ronn attributed his deliverance from substance abuse—"all that junk"—to Vicki's rescuing efforts.]

VICKI: You would not believe how bad it was. That is why I'm afraid to leave him alone now. I'm afraid he'll drink or something and get started again.

STEVE: So you try to be with him all the time.

VICKI: Yes. [Begins to cry.] I don't want to lose him. [They explained that she has agreed to move back with her parents following the blowup at Ronn's house. She feels forced out and anxious in her codependency with Ronn.]

STEVE: To be honest, living in the same house with your parents is just asking for trouble. Lots of "fires" can break out. [At this point, both Vicki and Ronn confessed to sexual secrets. They lived "as if" they were married. Both of them felt "real guilty about it, knew it was wrong," and seemed relieved it wasn't a secret anymore.]

RONN: I feel like God is still mad at us.

VICKI: We have asked forgiveness, but still. . . .

STEVE: The Bible tells us that if we confess our sin to God he is faithful and just to forgive us. He doesn't hold sin over our head. You can be assured that God has forgiven you. Put that behind you and go on. . . .

These excerpts from Steve's early pastoral practice document phases of the counseling process. We may observe, parenthetically, that Steve failed to note how women may be trapped by male violence. The crisis in Ronn's family involved codependency, violent behavior, substance abuse, as well as cohabitation. Steve had much to learn about the nature of family violence and its impact on people's lives.[24]

The phases of the pastoral counseling process move forward, through ups and downs, somewhat in linear fashion: (1) experiences of pastoral caring prior to counseling; (2) entering the counselee's private world through trusting, intentional self-disclosure; (3) appraisal of the person's (or family unit's) situation; (4) sharing their plight in Christian perspective; and (5) termination of counseling and resumption of less formal associations again. Since we have previously explored varied dimensions of the pastor's caring, including appraisal and referral, we shall focus on the counseling process proper.

1. Pastoral Caring Prior to Counseling

Keep in mind that pastor-parishioner relations often involve emotionally loaded issues that come in every shape and form. For example, at two o'clock one morning a minister received a telephone message from the sister of Beth James, a member of his congregation. Calling from a midtown hospital, the sister reported that Beth had just come from the delivery room and had been told that her baby was dead at birth. "Would it help if I came on to the hospital immediately?" the minister inquired. She said that it would, so he made a brief hospital call in order to assure the young couple of God's reality and presence in their loss and sorrow. The pastor anchored his care in the truth: "He who did not spare his own Son, but gave him up for us all—how will he not also, along with him, graciously give us all things?" (Rom. 8:32).

From that experience a counseling relationship was born between the young couple and their minister. Following the child's burial and the mother's return home from the hospital, the pastor had several counseling conversations with Joe and Beth James. They told of their childhood religious backgrounds, of their indifference to God as young adults, and of their interpretation of the child's death as a religious experience. In time, the participants in these interviews grew closer to God and to each other as they sought to interpret both the child's death and their own Christian responsibility in life. Also, the young husband and wife were drawn into the church's fellowship and ministry. Rather than rejecting God, through the counseling periods they affirmed his presence in their lives and their desire to serve him more adequately through the church.

An individual's reaching out to the minister may come quietly as someone says after a worship service, or in a casual moment: "I've been wanting to discuss a matter with you for some while now." If it is not convenient to share at that time, the minister may suggest a time and place for their meeting. The help-seeker will be free to disclose matters without fear of exposure or of imposing on the minister's time. Upon other occasions, the cry for help may come like a 911 call, suddenly, almost violently. The minister may learn that a person is threatening suicide or that an abused wife is leaving her alcoholic husband. A young person in the church may have been apprehended in a crime, with family dreams for their child shattered by one delinquent episode. Such forces push people to their minister for help.

2. Entering the Counselee's Private World

Formal counseling usually begins with an exploratory interview initiated by the person or couple seeking help. In Ronn's and Vicki's case, above, the pastor *joined* them as a young adult himself in their conflicted hopefulness for a good outcome to bad circumstances. Family therapists indicate the value of "joining" a family or single person by sharing points of commonality with them. *Joining* implies both attending to and attempting to understand the other person(s), while seeing the shape of our own bondage and fragile hopes in the lives before us. It gives outsiders a feeling of moving inside with the caregiver.

People facing hot issues, who want out of emergencies, may try to put a "sophisticated spin" on their self-presentations in the initial interview. Such hidden agendas require skillful management throughout the relationship. Through joining, the pastor assures the care-seeker of his or her value, though, as with Ronn and Vicki, some may feel "like God is still mad at us." The *unspoken influence*, initially, is valuing those who need to conceal as well as to reveal how bad it really is. Thus the pastor's diagnostic antennae are working through observation of physical features, like posture and eye contact; voice tone (for symptoms of depression, anger, or violence); as well as directed listening with open-ended probes for clarification.

Along with the need to "look good" in a minister's presence is the fear of talking too much, of becoming too well known by another. A person may say, for example, "Some people talk too much, like I've been doing here. I'm sorry for bursting out like that. I hope you'll forgive me." Fear of rejection, reprisal, or exposure may persist deep within. A person may live a lie through the pretense of sharing. When a counselee feels that he or she has divulged too much, the pastor should reassure the person of their confidential relationship. As a point of professional ethics, the minister will be certain not to divulge such privileged communication nor use personal information in a deliberately hurtful manner.

Another unspoken influence on the process is the counselee's reticence to reveal secrets to another person. "It is not easy to bleed in another person's presence," a lawyer who was my counselee said to me. Self-disclosure is painful for some people. Highly defended or protective individuals may have been betrayed previously by other persons (including other ministers), so check out their previous "helpers." Ronn and Vicki lived together "in sin" in their own view; yet they could not verbalize easily their mixed feelings about financial dependence on their parents, fear of violence, family rejection, vocational impotence, and guilt toward God. In contrast, other persons may demonstrate a parading posture, masking reality with a dramatic need to impress the minister with their unique situation or peculiar history.

I have said that beneath-the-surface forces such as needing to be nice, fear of self-disclosure, and one's tempo of relatedness operate as hidden agendas in counseling relationships. Another key diagnostic factor is the private meanings individuals assign to religious symbols, God-images (usually carried from childhood), and theological concepts. Closely related are ethnic and cultural taboos, superstitions, powerful prejudices, and resistance to growth or change. What meaning, for example, does the counselee assign to such remarks as, "I feel that my daughter has become my *cross* because of the way I treated her years ago," or "I can't *trust* anyone any more," or "My *prayers* don't seem to get out of this room?" "I think that I have committed the *unpardonable sin*." "I don't have anything left to *live* for since daddy *died*." "The *devil* has really gotten into me lately." "Why does God *punish* us like this?" or "My *faith* is all I've got"?

Ronn responded to the pastor's word about divine forgiveness thus: "I thought God stayed mad at you when you sinned. What you said really helps." Both Ronn and Vicki felt powerless; still, they sought a way through to God. Depth communication is unclear until religious language is assigned meaning by the participants in the interviews. Semantic problems are more complex for ministers who serve in other lands or with other ethnic groups, and for chaplains who work with mentally deficient or deeply troubled patients, in eldercare, in prisons, and in specialized settings like AIDS centers. Acquaintance with the counselee's cultural subgroup, religious tradition, intelligence level, and unique nomenclature or manner of expression will help the minister to perceive a person's private world with greater clarity.

Another nonverbal force at work in pastoral counseling is the kind of *hopes* or *expectations* the burdened person holds in relation to the minister. The church pictures divine Providence to attendees; yet Providence does not guarantee protection from evil and suffering. Some seekers expect the minister to "patch up" everything from academic failure and premarital pregnancy to general nervousness and amnesia. Yet we are not miracle-workers. Ronn and Vicki hoped pastor Steve might become a family peace-maker or, if that failed, then God's "doc" to cure their sick families. The pastor's ministry of family reconciliation is valuable. Perhaps it is most worthwhile in those faith communities where counselees can experience acceptance and feel they belong to an extended spiritual family. Helping a person to clarify realistically what he or she hopes for and in whom they are placing their hope is a valuable part of the counseling process.

In history taking the counselor learns important information from a person's past. The genogram aids this process in family therapy.[25] It reveals intergenerational information over at least three to four generations: lands of origin of one's ancestors; intermarriage across national or ethnic bound-aries; embarrassing or shame-full relatives; as well as one's religious, voca-tional, and medical background. While the diagnostic process is still in its early stages, if the person's condition, upon appraisal, merits specialized medical or other attention, the wise pastor will guide him or her to the best possible sources of help. On the other hand, as the counselor truly joins the help-seeker and enters his or her world, the healing process has already begun. Their shared conversations and the healing presence of God in the intervals between their interviews form significant links in the process of restoration and coping with life.

3. Sharing the Person's Plight and Pilgrimage

Pastoral counseling is essentially a time-limited process in which a Chris-tian minister shares an individual's plight (focal problem) intensively and temporarily until the person works through essential issues and resumes life's full responsibilities again. Their sessions together will involve slow, difficult, yet most significant work. Feedback from the therapist to the counselee is encouraged as part of each session.

While the relationship itself is crucial for the counselee's support or growth, what specific resources are open to participants in counseling con-versations? Pastoral intervention consists chiefly of listening and respond-ing to human stories, of sharing pain, of fathoming hidden depths (with appropriate questions) for clarification, of defining reality in a humane way, and of providing trustworthy spiritual direction. Nonthreatening questions may be asked in order (1) to clarify information; (2) to enable the inquirer to express his or her thoughts or feelings; (3) to facilitate transitions; and (4) to lift up reality so that the counselee may foresee possible consequences of personal behaviors or planned courses of action.

In order to assess another's life-situation or, as in pastor Steve's visit with Ronn and Vicki, a couple's plight, it is helpful to ask oneself key questions and review them in retrospect. They will function as diagnostic guideposts as the conversations move along.

First, what is this person or family unit seeking? The pastor summarized his findings related to what Ronn and Vicki expected thus: They needed someone to listen to them. They were hurting and needed to release those feelings. Second, they wanted advice as to how to handle a sticky situation. Ronn was angry at his parents for ignoring the problems of his brother and sister. He was upset at his own over-reaction to his mother's demand that Vicki move back with her parents. Both Ronn and Vicki needed help to face their relational emergency. Third, they expected feedback, including suggestions from Steve about what to do. They also wanted his support in a time of shame and confusion, and guidance about a future course of behavior.

Second, what functions am I as a Christian minister performing in this counseling process? Steve sensed his functions shifting several times during the conversation. As pastor, he felt his primary responsibility was to communicate both his own concern and the care of God for the couple in a dysfunctional family experience. As priest, he heard their confessions and offered words of forgiveness in God's name. This was done in the power of the Spirit, taking sin seriously, not as "cheap grace." As an adviser, Steve felt inadequate because of the complexity of their dysfunctional family systems and the fact that all of the other persons (variable components of the systemic process) were outside his grasp.

"I feel my overall effectiveness could have been greater had I been more experienced," he observed. Yet Steve sensed he had provided spiritual direction for the young couple and that their presence in the church fellowship would strengthen their resolves.

Third, what theological issues are obvious in this conversation? The pastor determined that several theological issues arose during his visit with Ronn and Vicki: the purpose of God for human existence; the providence of God for his creation; the nature of sin and divine forgiveness; the need for spiritual growth; and possibilities in the future for them and their families.

Though he failed to communicate it, Steve might have assured the pair that, while their lives had spun out of control, God was in control of the situation. Romans 8:28 still stands. God would work through the situation to bring about good things. Both Ronn and Vicki held God-images of an "I gotcha," punitive judge who was "still mad" at them. They had each confessed their shame to a vengeful God, yet continued to experience poor self-worth. Steve stressed the seriousness of sin to them and the power of a grace-full God to forgive completely.

How they would function in the future was up for grabs. Both Ronn and Vicki expressed a desire to grow in the church's nurturing fellowship. The pastor affirmed their start on the path of spiritual growth. At least they left his presence more hopeful by far than when the session began.

Fourth, what dysfunctions are obvious that merit address? Here, the pastor was less clear because of absentee family members, presence of substance abuse and law violations in drug trafficking, extent of damage to their hope in God, and the full shape of their God-images. Fortunately, they remained in the church and were strengthened to face their vocational, ethical, and emotional struggles.

Beyond listening, the minister's resources include (1) one's identity as God's person and theological education for ministry; (2) the fact that one represents a community of Christian faith, love, and hope; (3) one's authentic, unsentimental interest in the care-seeking person or family unit; (4) therapeutic employment of prayer and the Word of God in relation to the person's concerns; (5) a theodicy of evil and suffering for pastoral practice; and (6) devotion to the eternal kingdom of God beyond the tragic struggles of humankind. A pastor's entire ministry is oriented toward illuminating those values and relationships which shall endure for eternity (Heb. 11:27, 12:1–2, 13:14). Beyond the counseling sessions proper, the minister continues to support the person through prayer, personal interest, and the church's empowering fellowship.

4. Termination of the Counseling Relationship

Leave-taking is quite significant in pastoral counseling, for the minister and the individual continue their associations in a larger framework of church and community life. Pastors and priests are less free than secular psychotherapists to terminate counseling relationships. Neither do they have a fee-taking basis for assisting the person to value their times together and to assume responsibility in life.[26] Some interviews are discontinued when a person fails to appear for an appointment and does not mention counseling again. The pastor may elect to close out the relationship at this point, or to contact the counselee with a supportive note or phone call. Ideally, the participants terminate their relationship in good faith when their agreed-upon goals have been accomplished. As the person gains wisdom and strength for living, he or she "drops" the pastor *as counselor*. Their relationship shifts once again to pastor-parishioner contacts in the church and community setting.

While I have briefly mentioned the matter of *special feelings* (dependency, transference, and so on) that may arise in pastoral counseling, and which are treated in full-length works on this subject, attention should be paid to one matter. When a person's life has been laid bare before a minister, he or she may feel either quite close to or quite distanced from the pastor. Some defensive counselees even leave the church. A grateful counselee may invite the pastor into his or her home, give personal gifts, or find other appropriate ways for expressing gratitude. The minister can aid the person's adjustment back into church life (1) by receiving a gift, if offered, with appreciation; (2) by directing the individual's transferred feelings of affection or hostility Godward; and (3) by providing specific ways and means for the growing person to serve God in life. While *sharing* the pain of estrangements, brokenness, addictions, angers, and disappointments with help-seekers, true counselors do not *bear* the world's pain. God alone is the ultimate burden bearer.

IV. Ultimate Concerns

In conclusion, I would like to mention two aspects of pastoral conversations that are of paramount significance to ministers. One has to do with *acceptance* in counseling. The other deals with the *unique contribution of counseling* in modern church life. *Acceptance* in pastoral conversations in no way cancels our ethical idealism. *Oughtness* is bracketed temporarily in order to absorb the impact of life's *isness*. True believers are expected and empowered to live with spiritual excellence in the world (John 1:12–13). Christians are provided a new vantage point and rich resources for life's pilgrimage. Yet their relationships in our flawed world are not free from conflicts, missteps, and inner agonies (Rom. 7:4–8:38). While Jesus Christ intercedes "in the presence of God on our behalf," those who minister in his stead seek to undergird and guide God's people in the transactions of life (Heb. 9:24).

There is a bipolar tension in the minister's life between (1) the need to be an authority figure, a convincer, persuading persons toward ethical ideals; and (2) the necessity to function flexibly as a coworker with God and persons, permitting individuals freedom to grow (or to fail) and to affirm faith for themselves under God. In pastoral work, God's *claim* (judgment) and *gift* (grace) go together. His wrath is the other side of his love; one is not experienced without at least sensing the other. A pastor's acceptance implies, neither ethical naiveté nor sentimentality, but discriminating awareness of human sin, divine Providence, and humankind's need for the mercy and grace of God.

Ministers communicate acceptance or rejection both verbally and non-verbally in their attitudes and encounters. The feeling-tone of an interview will be influenced by the graciousness of the pastor's greeting, by one's attentiveness, spirit of kindness or sternness, mood of sincerity or superficiality, and willingness to understand the person's plight *from within* his own perspective. A counselee who feels the minister's rancor or rejection will have great difficulty expressing himself or herself in a way that will prove redemptive. Life is already *under judgment;* one turns to God's representative in order to go forward under the divine mercy.

In addressing the question of ultimate concerns, *what is achieved in counseling that cannot be achieved elsewhere in church life?* Is it not enough for a person to share in the worship and witness of a fellowship of truth without expecting to confer with some minister? Stanley Hauerwas and William Willimon debunk sentimental pastoral counseling in favor of rejuvenating believers as "resident aliens" in an unchristian world.[27] People become well, they hold, by participating in the story of God. Of course, we all favor wellness in members who will build up the church by whatever means it takes. Their critique is justified if it challenges the American pastoral counseling *system* that has become bogged down in financial and legal exigencies, but must not exempt pastors from caring conversations in the *parish domain.*

Building up the church, when viewed from an *administrative* perspective, includes enlarging the budget, improving the physical plant, and increasing the membership. Church growth is essential for authentic congregations, but it is a beginning not an end in itself. In viewing the building up of the church from a *pastoral* perspective, ministers are obligated to cherish the faithful adherents *and* the tortured people who comprise the congregation. Carroll Wise once noted, "When the pastor helps one person he is helping many others. . . . Indeed, one of the functions of pastoral counseling is helping to remove barriers to fellowship, and thus in a real way creating a sense of Christian community."[28] As barriers to belief, to hope, and to the future are removed through caring conversations, persons are freed to *do the truth* and to serve God more effectively in the world.

The core of effectiveness of pastoral counseling lies, in large measure, in the church's ability to nurture hope in God, whatever life's circumstances.[29] Because grace and hope function on both personal and systemic planes, pastor's concerns for their peoples' lives in *base* communities of home/school/work must parallel their passion to build up the *faith* community. After all, getting a person or family into the church fellowship and worship is the *front*, not final, end of ministry. The church's rituals, beliefs, and organizational framework help care-seekers gain control of chaotic, mysterious, sometimes unmanageable events and emotions; offer them comradeship on the journey of faith; and help them grasp a sense of direction and mastery in life.

When we recall the personal interviews of Jesus, the time the Lord took for one man or one woman in trouble, crisis, or decision, we will cherish personal conversations afresh in our own ministries. In counseling, as in all other aspects of our high calling, the Christian pastor labors and lives anticipating the life everlasting. Our lively hope is well-expressed by Mr. Stand-fast in Bunyan's *Pilgrim's Progress:* "I have formerly lived by hear-say and faith, but now I go where I shall live by sight, and shall be with Him in whose company I delight myself."[30] This hope is the Christian pastor's confidence.

Notes

1. While reading counseling interviews with comments in books (for example, Brian H. Childs, *Short-Term Pastoral Counseling: A Guide* [Nashville: Abingdon Press, 1990]; and David Switzer's *Pastoral Care Emergencies: Ministering to People in Crisis* [Mahwah, NJ: Paulist Press, 1989]) offers valuable, essential guidance, there is no substitute for supervised clinical experience in learning to practice counseling skills.

2. See William M. Easum, *The Church Growth Handbook* (Nashville: Abingdon Press, 1990); Kirk Hadaway, *Church Growth Principles: Separating Fact from Fiction* (Nashville: Broadman Press, 1991); Roy C. Nichols, *Doing the Gospel: Local Congregations in Ministry* (Nashville: Abingdon Press, 1990); Tex Sample, *U.S. Lifestyles and Mainline Churches* (Louisville: Westminster/John Knox Press, 1990).

3. T. Vaughn Walker, "Relevant Christian Ministry for the 21st Century," *Black Church Development* (November/December 1990).

4. See Seward Hiltner, *Pastoral Counseling* (Nashville: Abingdon Press, 1949), 125–48. The trend for pastoral counseling to determine its own fundamental theory and distinctive practice, with appreciation for advances in other disciplines, is demonstrated by comparing the above with works such as C. W. Brister, *The Promise of Counseling* (San Francisco: Harper & Row, 1978); Gary R. Collins, *Innovative Approaches to Counseling* (Waco, TX:

Word Books, 1986); Richard Dayringer, *The Heart of Pastoral Counseling* (Grand Rapids: Zondervan Publishing House, 1989); and Howard W. Stone and William M. Clements, eds., *Handbook for Basic Types of Pastoral Care and Counseling* (Nashville: Abingdon Press, 1991).

5. Hugh Downs, "The Power of Two," "20/20," ABC-TV News (February 8, 1991), report on a California peer counseling project.

6. *Progressions* report on "New Ministries: The Transformation of Caring," A Lilly Endowment Report (January 1991): 9.

7. See, for example, C. W. Brister, *Take Care* (Nashville: Broadman Press, 1978); Howard Clinebell, *Well Being: A Personal Plan for Exploring and Enriching the Seven Dimensions of Life* (HarperCollins, 1992); Marcus D. Bryant, *The Art of Christian Caring* (St. Louis: Bethany Press, 1979); Milton Mayeroff, *On Caring* (New York: Harper & Row, 1972); Stanley J. Menking, *Helping Laity Help Others* (Philadelphia: Westminster Press, 1984); Howard Stone, *The Caring Church: A Guide for Lay Pastoral Care* (San Francisco: Harper & Row, 1983); and William J. Rademacher, *Lay Ministry* (New York: Crossroad/Continuum, 1991).

8. Peter E. Sifneos, *Short-Term Dynamic Psychotherapy*, 2d ed. (New York: Plenum Medical Book Co., 1987), 27; cited in Childs, *Short-Term Pastoral Counseling*, 44, 137.

9. Sheldon Vanauken, *A Severe Mercy* (San Francisco: Harper & Row, 1977). Cf. William B. Oglesby, *Biblical Themes for Pastoral Care* (Nashville: Abingdon Press, 1980), 13–44.

10. Gregory P. Bauer and Joseph C. Kobos, for example, propose seven principles for defining time-limited counseling tasks in *Brief Therapy: Short-Term Psychodynamic Intervention* (Northvale, NJ: Jason Aronson, 1987), 6–9. A Focal Relational Problem (FRP) is first established; then all of the helper's and counselee's energies are kept in focus to address that issue.

11. For examples of diversity, cf. Jay E. Adams, *Lectures on Counseling* (Grand Rapids: Baker Book House, 1978) with Carroll A. Wise, *Pastoral Psychotherapy: Theory and Practice* (New York: Jason Aronson, 1980).

12. An empirical study of the significance of context in counseling was reported by Seward Hiltner and Lowell G. Colston in *The Context of Pastoral Counseling* (Nashville: Abingdon Press, 1961). Colston, working in a church setting, found that the faith community accelerated the salvific or healing process.

13. John B. Cobb, Jr., "Pastoral Counseling and Theology," in *Handbook for Basic Types of Pastoral Care and Counseling*, edited by Howard W. Stone and William M. Clements (Nashville: Abingdon Press, 1991), 39.

14. Jerome D. Frank, M.D., *Persuasion and Healing: A Comparative Study of Psychotherapy* (Baltimore: The Johns Hopkins Press, 1961), 2–3.

15. Cobb, in Stone and Clements, *Handbook for Basic Types of Pastoral Care*, 39.

16. Charles W. Taylor, *The Skilled Pastor: Counseling as the Practice of Theology* (Minneapolis: Fortress Press, 1991), pp. 137–41.

17. Wayne E. Oates, *Behind the Masks: Personality Disorders in Religious Behavior* (Philadelphia: Westminster Press, 1987).

18. Ron DelBene, *From the Heart: Stories of a Pastor's Walk with His People* (Nashville: Upper Room Books, 1991), lists help-giving organizations, 93–109.

19. Bill Blackburn, *What You Should Know About Suicide* (Waco, TX: Word Books, 1982).

20. See Lisbeth B. Schorr with Daniel Schorr, *Within Our Reach: Breaking the Cycle of Disadvantage* (New York: Doubleday/Anchor Press, 1988).

21. Charles E. Brown, *Time as a Determinant in Pastoral Processes: An Examination of the Conception of Time in the Works of Sigmund Freud and John Macquarrie and in Selected Cases of Pastoral Care with Implications for Pastoral Theology and Pastoral Counseling,* unpublished Ph.D. dissertation (Princeton, NJ: Princeton Theological Seminary, 1982), 446-47; cited in Childs, *Short-Term Pastoral Counseling,* 33. (Italics are Brown's.)

22. Wayne E. Oates, *Protestant Pastoral Counseling* (Philadelphia: Westminster Press, 1962), 164–65, 183–88.

23. Robert J. Wicks, Richard D. Parsons, and Donald E. Capps, eds., *Clinical Handbook of Pastoral Counseling* (Mahwah, NJ: Paulist Press, 1985), *et passim.*

24. See Marie M. Fortune and Judith Hertze, "A Commentary on Religious Issues in Family Violence," in *Sexual Assault and Abuse: A Handbook for Clergy and Religious Professionals,* edited by Mary D. Pellauer, *et al.* (San Francisco: HarperCollins, 1991 ed.), 67–83. Also, see Fortune's *Sexual Violence: The Unmentionable Sin* (New York: Pilgrim Press, 1983).

25. See Monica McGoldrick and Randy Gerson, *Genograms in Family Assessment* (New York: W. W. Norton, 1985).

26. An exception is the freestanding pastoral counseling center, unaffiliated with a particular congregation or denominational group, dependent on fees for professional services.

27. Stanley Hauerwas and William H. Willimon, *Resident Aliens: A Provocative Christian Assessment of Culture and Ministry for People Who Know That Something Is Wrong* (Nashville: Abingdon Press, 1989), 142.

28. Carroll A. Wise, *Psychiatry and the Bible* (New York: Harper & Row, 1956), 131-32.

29. Pastoral theologian Andrew Lester is in the process of publishing findings on hopefulness and hopelessness in his counseling practice.

30. John Bunyan, *Pilgrim's Progress,* edited by J. B. Wharey (Oxford: Clarendon Press, 1929), 326.

Suggested Reading

Brister, C. W. *The Promise of Counseling*. San Francisco: Harper & Row, 1978. Examines counseling from the viewpoint of biblical faith, Protestant theology, and contemporary behavioral science. Offers practical approaches for helping troubled people in particular circumstances.

Childs, Brian H. *Short-Term Pastoral Counseling: A Guide*. Nashville: Abingdon Press, 1990. Shows how the pastor and a counselee agree to work on one specific problem during no more than ten sessions. Integrates the practice of short-term psychotherapy with pastoral work in the church.

Glaz, Maxine and Jeanne S. Moessner, eds. *Women in Travail and Transition: A New Pastoral Care*. Minneapolis: Augsburg/Fortress Publishers, 1991. Nine women collaborate to explore how women's life experience both requires and models a new systematic pastoral care.

Oates, Wayne E. *The Presence of God in Pastoral Counseling*. Waco, TX: Word Books, 1986. Also, *Pastoral Counseling*. Philadelphia: Westminister Press, 1974. Shows how to recognize God's presence as the central dynamic in pastoral counseling. Reflects deep roots in both theology and psychology.

Stone, Howard W. and William M. Clements, eds. *Handbook for Basic Types of Pastoral Care and Counseling*. Nashville: Abingdon Press, 1991. Essays honoring Howard Clinebell on the theory and practice of pastoral care and counseling. A basic resource book.

Taylor, Charles W. *The Skilled Pastor: Counseling as the Practice of Theology*. Minneapolis: Fortress Press, 1991. Proposes a "Metanoia Model" of specific skills and theological assessment for behavioral change through pastoral counseling.

Wimberly, Edward P. *African American Pastoral Care*. Nashville: Abingdon Press, 1991. Places caregiving in context with the narrative aspects of preaching and worship in the life of a congregation. Proposes unfolding, linking, thickening, and twisting as narrative counseling techniques.

CHAPTER EIGHT

SHARING THE PRIMARY MOMENTS OF LIFE

Christian ministers share personal and collective experiences with their people on multiple levels, all simultaneously, within a complex maze of relationships. These levels of relationship include: (1) the career of the human self as it develops over time; (2) the person and his or her family unit in a base community matrix; and (3) the cosmic context of our existence as sojourners on planet Earth. It is within social systems—marked by particular features of geography, ethnicity, economics, and political stability or turmoil—that communities of faith grow or fail to thrive. Part of our challenge in leading and caring for folks entwined in complex social systems is that life moves and changes, so people don't stay "put" or "fixed." Bridget McKeever said it well: "Even when we seem to effect some healing and to engender new life, the fragile plant transplanted back into the stony ground of the old system soon withers."[1] Our assignment is larger than we initially imagined. The church must care for *both* a person throughout his or her life span *and* the ecology in which he or she is embedded. How does this assignment take shape in local communities of faith? I call such congregational ministry: sharing the primary moments of life.

We share "life on the road" from its inception in infancy to discovering the reality of death. A Christian couple, for example, looks to the church for support during those years when children are being added to the family circle. The birth of a child, so intrinsic to family experience, remains one of life's primary moments in which persons are open to the rituals of pastoral care. In like fashion, the minister shares life's spiritual renewal, transitions within vocation, the commitments of adulthood, and the process of aging with people. Through a faith community of imagination and hope, the minister serves as a spiritual guide with whom persons may identify and participate meaningfully in the Christian pilgrimage (Ps. 40:2; 1 Tim. 4:12).

We who share pastoral ministry often possess only a peephole view of our congregant's lives. Pastors see parishioners one or two hours a week in formal worship settings, where faces look much alike. Yet these persons come to church from a social matrix of relationships representing varied values, with educational and class differences, each bearing a sense of personal frustration, failure, faith, or fulfillment in life. Furthermore, ordinary people must be viewed in a "cosmic context" if their problems and possibilities are to be perceived correctly. People come to church looking for a God they can trust and a minister who is authentic and believable.

Once we become alert to life's systemic webs and to what Kierkegaard called the stages along life's way, we will address pastoral care to human complexities in the real world. Some phases of human development — preadolescence, the middle years, and old age, for example — are not discussed here. For reasons of space, I have selected for discussion five primary moments of life. The pastoral conversations appearing in chapters 8 and 9 do not in every case convey an ideal approach, but they do illustrate Christian concern in selected events.

Life's primary moments in congregational ministry do not always appear in a neat cycle. Life refuses to meet the tidy expectations of those who accept responsibility for others. For example, a minister in a rural setting may find that the congregation is composed primarily of senior adults; major pastoral assignments may come at the "reality of death" end of the lifespan. A baby-boom generation church with multiple options in programs and ministries may attract children and their parents in large numbers but fail to attract senior adults. Although a minister is available to everyone in the church and community, some who are suffering "shipwreck" may avoid the prophetic orator or weak shepherd and share their concerns with a friend or a stranger. One church family may resent a minister's presence in a set of circumstances in which another household is greatly dependent on pastoral care. Again, what one individual experiences reverently in spiritual terms another may look upon lightly with irreligious eyes. Such factors influence the effectiveness of the congregational ministry.

The Christian pastor and congregation are enmeshed in life's relationships, decisions, risks, and pressures day by day. Young and old church members alike feel that their minister either accepts and prizes them in their daily struggles or rejects them and remains aloof from life's tough realities. At best, they will experience the religious leader as one possessing a discriminating understanding of the human lifespan, who applies Bible principles to real life situations, and who charts clear pathways between God and ordinary people.[2] In each key moment of life, the pastor and the people share a common conviction that they may "receive mercy and find grace to help us in our time of need" (Heb. 4:15–16). With this faith, the caring pastor participates meaningfully in the moving dramas of life.

I. The Beginning of Life

It has been observed that, "It is as the new parent first holds the infant that the parental soul most yearns for the 'ideal' and seeks a worthy 'dream.'"[3] The process of becoming parents is freighted with questions and complexities. Parenthood drives many young adults to seek God as they face complicated times. Thus childbirth is akin to religious experience, whether or not the parents assign religious significance to the event. A Protestant chaplain's survey of maternity patients in a metropolitan hospital revealed that about one-half of the interviewees interpreted their childbirth experiences spiritually. In biblical thought, the birth of a child was viewed as a divine blessing and as an occasion for a festival of joy and dedication. Naming the child and inaugurating certain "rites of passage" in the family have had religious significance from ancient times (cf. Gen. 33:5; Ps. 127:3; Luke 2:21–52). God's representative, usually a priest, presided at the dedicatory rituals and strengthened the parents for their new child-rearing responsibilities. The event of parenthood is thus a prime occasion for pastoral attention.

Pastoral care of children and young people properly begins with the minister's concern for their parents even before the children are born. Because children reflect the kind of social-spiritual context in which they grow up, the home and church share a joint responsibility in preparing persons for parenthood. Parents and others who work with children in the church must be genuine persons "in a genuine milieu" themselves in order to develop a child with a healthy personality.[4] Spiritually immature or emotionally deprived adults frequently fail to nourish their offspring with loving discipline, whereas homes in which durable relationships of love and trust abound provide a creative atmosphere for proper personality development. Delinquent or irresponsible children develop most often in homes or institutions that are dysfunctional or negligent in some way. For example, when lightning strikes in husband-wife conflicts, it often strikes *through* the children in that home. Thus churches should enlist potential parents prior to the birth of children and seek to prepare them for their new family tasks.

A young married couple's preparation for parenthood should be under-taken with the same honesty and seriousness as was their original prepara-tion for marriage. Parenting is hard work. A pastoral group for new parents in the church, perhaps meeting once a month, could provide an atmo-sphere for discussing topics such as (1) the changing family in our culture; (2) biblical guidelines on such core issues as sexual development, honesty, and discipline; (3) how children learn about God; (4) the child with physical challenges or exceptional abilities; and (5) the shared ministry of church and parents to children. Videotaped equipping modules, small-group expe-riences, visits at the birth of a child, sermons on key family issues, pastoral letters, the ritual of parent-child dedication services, and provision of cur-rent resources in the church media center—all reflect congregational con-cern for families.

Parents-to-be need to prepare realistically for a baby's coming so that there may be *psychic space* in the family's life for the new arrival. If there are other children, they may help to arrange the nursery at home and should be instructed about the baby's place in the rhythm of family life.[5] While the family does not construct all its hopes, relationships, and loyalties entirely around an infant, family members will pace their lifestyles to the interior timing of the young child. In a poignant moment in an Old Testa-ment family's journey, a wise father responded to those who wanted him to travel faster: "I [will] move along slowly at the pace ... of the children" (Gen. 33:14). Pacing home activities and relations is a necessary aspect of the family's preparation for and acceptance of God's gift of new life.

Life's beginning provides specific occasions for an interprofessional family ministry by members of the community's health team. Needs may arise at a child's birth that prompt the joint efforts of ministers, physicians, lawyers, and social workers. This is often the case with infants born into a marginal-ized socioeconomic system who need medical care and decent food, shel-ter, and safety. A team ministry is also necessitated among professionals when childbirth involves a tragedy. Such was the case in the experience that follows.

Mr. and Mrs. Nelson Latham were members of a large church in which she had served for a time as a member of the staff. When it became evident that their first child was to be born, she resigned the position and prepared for the child's coming. They had married late in life. Mrs. Latham was almost forty at the time of the child's birth. There had been no medical evi-dence of trouble during the woman's prenatal care, thus her physician was surprised when a hydrocephaloid son was born. He knew how difficult it would be when the couple learned that their child was deformed and would probably not survive. Thus he enlisted a seminarian involved in clinical pastoral education in the hospital to break the sad news to the couple along with him. In this instance, an occasion of potential jubilation became a time of mourning when the malformed infant died.

The minister-in-training shared the couple's spontaneous sorrow, arranged for the child's burial at their request, and stood with them during that tragic period in their lives. He also notified the Lathams' pastor, so that they might have his spiritual ministry in the days ahead, and supported certain hospital staff members who had become involved emotionally with the couple during their loss and grief. Through appropriate pastoral care, the Lathams were able to share some disturbing questions about their religious experience with the minister, to express their grief, and to face the future with new faith and devotion. In addition, the young minister learned that a physician was also a member of the human race and that their shared ministry had made the Lathams' tragic experience more tolerable for the doctor. Small wonder that people observe young adults returning to religious communities when they have children.

The beginning of life involves varied kinds of experiences in pastoral work. Normally, a child's birth is an occasion for communal rejoicing and for a public ritual of family consecration to God. My own Free Church tradition encourages the dedication of the parents and infant upon the occasion of a child's birth, but rejects infant baptism because of the cardinal Baptist principle of the integrity of the individual in matters of religion. Clergy of sacramental traditions administer baptism to infants as a "rite of identification" with the family's faith, name, and spiritual sponsorship.[6]

Whatever the minister's particular faith, a chief obligation at life's beginning is to undergird parents for their new risks and responsibilities.

A church representative usually visits a new mother after the safe arrival of her child in the hospital. Physicians remind us that nature permits her to "let down" a bit after an infant's delivery. Faced with new tasks, a mother may appear exhausted or depressed rather than exuberant during a postdelivery pastoral visit. Such is the case when multiple births—like twins or triplets—pose an economic crisis or major burden to the new parents. In calling, the pastor will be alert to a new mother's mood as well as to her expressed concerns. Through appropriate Scripture selections and prayer, the caller will seek to inspire hope in God for life's new tasks and relationships. (See, for example, Gen. 16:11, 21:1–7; 1 Kings 13:2; Isa. 9:6; Ps. 27:10; Prov. 8:32; Matt. 1:21, 18:1–6, 19:13–15, 21:16; Mark 10:13–16; Luke 18:15–17.)

Successful attending depends not only upon the pastor's intention but upon the new parents' receptivity or sense of need, and upon the gracious action of the Holy Spirit. The following conversation indicated that the shutter of each soul was open wide to God's help because of the existential situation. After learning that the Colvins' son was born with a slight ortho-pedic defect, pastor Bill Bateson called upon the couple in the maternity ward of a small-town clinic. The nurse assured him that things were clear for his call and noted that Mr. Colvin was with his wife at the time. They greeted each other as follows.

PASTOR: Well, good afternoon, folks [shaking father's hand]! How's the new mother today?

MRS. C.: Hi, Brother Bateson. Oh, I'm just fine [her voice was weak]. We have that big boy we've been waiting for [smiling].

PASTOR: Wonderful! What is his name?

MRS. C.: We named him Mark, pastor. I've liked "Mark" for years, and it's a Bible name, too.

JOHN C: With a short name like Mark, maybe he won't ever get a nickname like some of the kids in our family. We hope that everyone will just call him "Mark" [pause].

PASTOR: It's a big accomplishment to have a fine son here and to give him a good name. How is the young man doing since his arrival?

MRS. C: Okay, I guess. When they first brought him in here, having Mark beside me seemed almost too good to be true. We had waited for him so long. He hasn't cried a bit when he's been in here. The nurses say he's a good baby. [Her remarks revealed some strain and reserve.]

JOHN C: [hesitantly]: Did anyone tell you about Mark's feet, Brother Bateson?

PASTOR: About his feet?

JOHN C: Yeah, the doctor explained to us that his feet were turned around somehow from the way they should have been when Mark was born.

MRS. C: We noticed it the first time the nurse brought him in. Dr. Wills had already told us that his feet were turned wrong inside me.

PASTOR: Oh?

JOHN C: It's not bad, but they are turned around like this [demonstrated with his hands]. Dr. Wills says that in a few months we will have to take him to St. Louis for orthopedic surgery. [Pause.] I don't know just how they do it, but he says they can be turned around straight in a couple of years. It's going to take several operations, though.

MRS. C: He said that Mark will have to wear special shoes for a few years in order to support his ankles but that he ought to get along fine and will be able to run and play like other children.

The pastor felt their ambivalence—gladness in their first son's birth, yet sadness because of the bone defect. They did not reflect guilt or hostility toward God, merely concern about the child's welfare. Pastor Bateson sensed some undisclosed negative feelings and gave the Colvins an opportunity to express them. He knew that they were concerned and desired to lift up their concerns to God in prayer.

PASTOR: Well, you folks have experienced both a great blessing and a new concern in Mark's coming. We are fortunate to live in a day when surgery is available for the correction of such problems. This still doesn't eliminate your concern, however, does it?

MRS. C: We just hate to think that the little fellow will have to be in a cast most of the time for the next two years.

JOHN C: He'll probably be late in learning to walk. But we think he'll be all right [pause].

PASTOR: Jerri [takes mother's hand] and John, may we pray together and ask God's guidance and strength for you. [He thanked God for Mark's safe arrival and for the doctor's wisdom in suggesting that the defect be corrected early, and asks for spiritual strength for the Colvins. His prayer caught the flavor of their mixed feelings, pointing them to God.]

Had the pastor been uninformed or called routinely with some quip about the Colvins' "bouncing baby boy," he might have missed their true feelings and failed to support them in their need. Again, he could have made too much of the matter, intensifying the couple's anxiety about what people might think or stirring hostility toward God. Instead, his acceptance, warm interest, and genuine sharing of their pride and their plight helped the couple to think realistically and rely upon God's strength for the events ahead.

Once children are born, churches will strengthen Christian homes in appropriate nurture and discipline of their offspring. As young parents try to rear children in responsible and wise ways, based upon good information rather than tradition, they are exposed to many conflicts and insecurities. Perceptions of one's child-rearing responsibilities come from memories of childhood, from the models provided by relatives and friends, from reading, discussion, personal mistakes, and the advice of professionals and other parents.[7] Young adults are often tempted to reject their own backgrounds and to distance themselves from their elders in the differentiation-of-self process. As novice parents reflect upon their elders' foibles, they may secretly fear failure themselves and desire guidance from the church. Mistaken ideas change slowly through experience and new vision of truth.

Once a pastor called upon a family of newcomers in the community. As he approached the house, he heard a child's cries. When he rang the doorbell, a young mother with a baby perched on one hip and a sobbing son at her knees came to the door. Obviously bothered, she explained the tearful situation and added: "Daddy always said, 'Spare the rod and spoil the child.' But I always feel guilty when I whip Jimmy. He's not really a bad child, just meddlesome." The minister listened, then replied that he, too, was a parent and understood that there were no magic answers to disciplining children. He asked the mother if she had read anything on the subject of parenting. When she responded negatively, he suggested titles of church library books that might help.[8] The pastor expressed a desire to follow up with this family, to assess problem behaviors, and to provide more resources on parenting. While young parents are not to be left to the mercy of every "wind of doctrine," merely telling them what to do is not a cure-all either. Those who minister to young parents and through them to their children cannot expect perfection from the guardians of life's beginnings. Pastors can, however, assist parents to avoid some obvious dangers, can stand with them even in colossal failures, and can help them to achieve family strengths based upon a mature Christian faith.

II. The Renewal of Life

Ministers who share life's beginnings and growth may help to clarify the meaning of faith in childhood for parents and youth workers in the church. What, for example, can Christianity mean to the infant or young child who responds primarily to the touch of gentle hands and the tone of one's voice rather than to ideas? Daniel O. Aleshire's *Faithcare: Ministering to All God's People through the Ages of Life* tells how parents may guide a child's religious development at home.[9] Grownups mirror the meaning of God to youngsters first through relationships, then through example, and later through instruction. Children learn love through adults' timed responses to their frequent needs; later, through recognizing God's love for them.

Qualities of soul that parents incarnate, like faith, love, and hope, as well as the spirit of the home, are caught by children and reflected in their maturing relationships. The studies of Erik Erikson and others indicate that a person's capacity for *basic trust* or mistrust originates in early child-hood. Trust of oneself and others, beginning with an infant's dependence upon powerful providers, is essential to both health and salvation in the future. Erikson's developmental perspective on human life provides refer-ence points for measuring growth and ritual functions in religion. He warned parents and caregivers, however, not to abuse phasic expectations or ritual structures and, thereby "take the game out of growing up."[10] What is true of trust is also true in moral growth and conscience development. A child's conscience develops as he or she internalizes the moral voice of par-ents, teachers, peers, culture, and God.[11] Also, one comes to think of one-self as "good" or "bad" and to respect or disrespect oneself according to the esteem in which she or he is held by parents and significant others. Home and church thus collaborate in pointing youth to a personal faith in the liv-ing God.

Pastors, parents, and church workers have the common aim of leading young people to make a meaningful Christian commitment and to identify formally with the church at the appropriate time in life. Such Christian iden-tification is linked to God's gracious action and the individual's response. Conversion—the renewal of life—is to be viewed dynamically in terms of the individual's mental ability, spiritual sensitivity, emotional maturity, and sense of personal accountability to God in Christ. The chronological *age* of Christian decision is not uniform.[12] The general *stage* of development for Christian commitment is timed to the individual's recognition of God as our Source—he is behind it all—spiritual awareness, notion of sin, and per-sonal identification with Jesus Christ in a faith community.

Protestants generally view the renewal of life as the gracious gift of God rather than as the achievement of an individual. Both divine and human determinants are involved in religious experience, whether the pattern is conversion in free churches or confirmation in those practicing infant bap-tism. The Christian faith must be at work in a person's home and commu-nity experiences before it becomes valid in life. Psychiatrist Earl Loomis was correct about adult influence: "The member of a religious community must find his *faith and practice* a part of his total life if it is to 'take' with his children."[13] Salvation, while involving Christian education, is a transaction with God and can never be treated as a matter of nurture alone. However, people do not jump out of the skin of their developmental history by means of a vast forgetfulness when they become Christians. They still have a past, a present, and a future, but Christ enables them to face their history and destiny with courage.

The family's indelible influence upon a person's religious experience is mirrored in the following conversation. A minister once called upon a young man who had presented himself for church membership but attended church only spasmodically thereafter. At first, the youth resisted the pastor's offer of interest and help.

PRESTON: There are some things that I have to get straightened out between me and my dad and my brother before I can give my heart wholly to God.

PASTOR: I don't know what you have reference to, but it may help to share this with someone.

PRESTON: I figure there are some things that a man has to do by himself.

PASTOR: Most things are better solved when you allow someone else to share them with you. [Pause.]

PRESTON: Well . . . it's my dad. Every time I need him, he just isn't there. It seems that things are just never right between us. Just about the time I think things are going all right, my brother comes back and things are right back where they were before.

PASTOR: Is it that you want things to be right between your dad and yourself?

PRESTON: Yes, but he never takes my side. You know, I'm under a two-year suspended sentence for some trouble that I got into because of my brother.

PASTOR: Someone told me that you were trying to protect your brother. [The youth told how he had stood trial for his brother, who had stolen a car and then fled to the West Coast.]

PRESTON: My lawyer advised me under the circumstances to plead guilty and throw myself on the mercy of the court. My dad didn't say a word for me. He just sat there. My aunt did say something for me, so did my mother. But nobody else believed me or stood up for me.

PASTOR: I know that it is hard for you to talk about things that mean so much and yet hurt so deeply.

PRESTON: I can try and try and do everything I can, but I just can't seem to make things right between us. [He started crying at this point.]

PASTOR: Is this what you think has to be straightened out before you really give your heart to God?

PRESTON: Yes. I don't believe that I can live for God and feel this way toward my dad and my brother.

PASTOR: Preston, if you will let God help you, he will.

The minister longed to see Preston and his young wife serving God in the church and enjoying life together as a family. The young adult felt that his dad had failed him, and that he could not have God's acceptance as long as he resented his father so deeply. Preston's God-relationship had been influenced indelibly by his shame response over an invalid mother and public humiliation by his father. Intensive pastoral work is required to lead such a shame-based person to Christian commitment and to active church membership.

Given the biblical fact that salvation is both a point of decision and a process of development, many observers feel that a weakness of evangelism of the past was that it stopped too soon (Rom. 13:11; Phil. 2:12). Religious instruction was neglected once a Christian commitment had been made. *The church's appropriate pastoral concern in life's renewal is that the individual be disciplined into a community of love and hope as well as into the content of the church's faith.* Pastoral work with those who have committed themselves to Christ includes: (1) Christian baptism; (2) a meaningful ritual of reception into the church membership; (3) discipleship instruction; (4) a memorable first communion service; (5) strengthening their ties of faith and friendship; and (6) providing opportunities for serviceable living through the church's ministry in the world. Caring for "life on the threshold" is thus a crucial aspect of evangelism.

Discipleship or catechetical classes, meeting in four- or six-week series through the year, provide a strategic opportunity for the minister and new members to become acquainted personally. Literature has been designed for use in such groups by most denominations.[14] By its very nature, a discipleship class anticipates discussion of the church's history, beliefs, and organization, and of the new believer's questions, anxieties, feelings of incorporation into the faith community, and age-specific opportunities for service. Some churches expect all those coming into their fellowship to attend such sessions. Others provide separate groups for children and adults when suitable teachers are available.

Answering questions of a doctrinal or personal nature is a vital aspect of pastoral care of the new member. Informed congregants act from inner strength and wisdom rather than from group conformity and shallow judgments alone. This is illustrated in the case of a woman who had presented herself for membership in a Baptist church. Following a worship service, she asked the minister: "Am I going to have to get into *that* thing [pointing to the baptistry] and get myself all wet? Why do you folks dunk everybody under the water?"

The pastor explained that immersion is a symbolic and dramatic ritual picturing one's Christian experience. "A person who links life by faith to Christ is buried symbolically with him 'by baptism into death.' The baptized believer thus identifies with Christ's death and resurrection and pledges that in the future he or she shall 'walk in newness of life.'" Rather than censure the woman, the minister pictured immersion as her obedient identification with Christ and the church, and as a dramatic witness to her experience of eternal life (cf. Rom. 6:4–11; Gal. 3:27).

While new members are pleased to receive a confirming letter of welcome from the pastor, they need the social warmth of meaningful friendships and groups in the church. Children need to meet those who will teach their age groups in Sunday school and young people need the comradeship of their peers. Some new believers' faith may falter; doubts may arise. It is important for them to understand that, "We move between doubt and trust, but both ends of that spectrum are included in faith."[15] Our struggles can lead us to greater commitment. In reality, the entire congregation is responsible for receiving new members into its fellowship. The minister helps by making such receptions personal, warm, and tangible.

III. The Callings of Life

Like religious commitments, decisions concerning one's daily work are interrelated with the developing sense of identity in human personality. Some interpreters distinguish "calling" as God's gracious election through the gospel to the Christian life, and "vocation" within his providence as both daily work and the "'whole' of [human] existence presupposed by God's 'calling.' "[16] I am aware of these distinctions but use the terms *calling* and *vocation* interchangably in this discussion. The community of faith can help give form to one's sense of vocation, which is subject to changes along the way. People who feel powerless to affect the world around them often turn to religion as part of their larger search for meaning.

Vocation is our sense that life needs us even as we depend on "more than ourselves" to sort things out and contribute meaningfully to life. Frederick Buechner has provided a useful explanation of *vocation* that reflects this duality of direction.

It comes from the Latin *vocare*, to call, and means the work one is called to by God.

There are all different kinds of voices calling you to all different kinds of work, and the problem is to find out which is the voice of God rather than of Society, say, or the Superego, or Self-Interest.

By and large a good rule for finding out is this. The kind of work God usually calls you to is the kind of work (a) that you need most to do and (b) that the world most needs to have done. If you really get a kick out of your work, you've presumably met requirement (a), but if your work is writing TV deodorant commercials, the chances are you've missed requirement (b). On the other hand, if your work is being a doctor in a leper colony, you have probably met requirement (b), but if most of the time you're bored and depressed by it, the chances are you have not only bypassed (a) but probably aren't helping your patients much either.

Neither the hair shirt nor the soft berth will do. The place God calls you to is the place where your deep gladness and the world's deep hunger meet.[17]

In commenting on this deeply satisfying need to feel needed, Sharon Parks notes the young adult's hunger to hear, above other voices, the voice of God. Through the discovery process, one's faith community can rejoice that the individual has found his or her niche—what God wishes for *them* and for the *world*. The service of religion as mentor for those listening for God's voice is to point life to the open road of ambiguity, risk, and passionate search. Men and women who had "this job thing fixed" often find themselves "on the road again." Mentoring communities of faith can provide befrienders and hopers for persons trapped in the "wash" of job dismissals, company buyouts, corporate relocations, and executive displacements. Hearing God's voice for vocation requires a vision not merely of job retraining but of advancing the Kingdom of God. Job seekers need more than the next paycheck. They need to understand "the commonwealth to which we belong is in heaven" (Phil. 3:20–21, Goodspeed).

A *concrete place for ministers to begin in vocational guidance is with the youth of the church.* Adolescents, who are experiencing so many changes— physical, emotional, and social—are generally receptive to rap sessions and guidance in the area of life's work. Young adults face issues of sexual identity and interpersonal intimacy along with satisfactory career selection. Their parents' judgments usually influence their job interests, though not in the sense of identical family apprenticeships and work functions. A boy whose father has been successful in agriculture, for example, may not wish to remain on the farm. A banker's daughter may reject her father's vocation for herself in favor of law, education, business, or medicine. Erik Erikson has theorized that the special growth problem of late adolescence is the establishment of one's identity, and that youth's special danger is "self-confusion" or role confusion. Biff, in Arthur Miller's *Death of a Salesman*, reflected such decisional paralysis and vocational perplexity: "I just can't take hold, Mom; I can't take hold of some kind of life." With boyhood past and the central core of personality confused, the growth crisis involved may require more than vocational guidance. Such instability may require professional psychotherapy.

Given culture's recognition of "womanspirit rising," young women are deeply involved in a search for identity, meaning, and vocation in life. They are torn frequently between conflicting desires to marry and establish a home, yet find a suitable occupation and pursue additional education to that end. Education is viewed as the "ticket" to creative selfhood; nonetheless, countless women in marginalized situations face uncertain futures.

A young adult once revealed her struggle with self-definition and life's direction to her minister.

PASTOR: This is your last year in high school, isn't it? Where have you thought about going to college?

ALICE: Well, I really haven't done too much thinking about it. In fact, I don't imagine I'll be going to college at all. [Pause.] Mother and Daddy don't seem to be interested in my going to college.

PASTOR: You mean they don't care whether you go or not?

ALICE: I guess they care all right. [Pause.] I know they can afford it, but they won't say they want me to go. They just want me to make up my own mind about the future.

PASTOR: You think that they don't care whether you go to college or not.

ALICE: Well, I just don't know. [Long pause.] I don't guess it's *them* all together. I'm really not sure I want to go to college. In fact, I don't want to get out of high school now.

PASTOR: You don't want to graduate?

ALICE: Oh yes, I want to graduate, but I don't want to leave high school. I know it sounds funny. I know you think I'm silly.

PASTOR: You don't want to leave because of your friends there? [This was only an educated guess.]

ALICE: That's it partly. Another thing is that I'll have to make a decision about what I'm going to do.

PASTOR: You mean about whether or not to go to college?

ALICE: Yes, in a way. You know, I've been going steady with Tim for about a year and a half now. [She looked at the floor.] Well, he wants to marry me when he gets through college.

PASTOR: Oh?

ALICE: He plans to finish in three more years. I know that will be a long time and that I could go on to college during this time. But I'm afraid I won't get to live.

PASTOR: Get to live?

ALICE: Well, you know—have a family and a life, and all that. I've been going to school all my life and I don't want to waste three more years by just going to school. Anything could happen, and I'd never get to do anything but go to school. Do you see what I mean?

PASTOR: Yes, I'm trying to understand. Still, I challenge you to become all that you can be. Don't slam the door on your future just because of family or community pressure.

Alice was described by her minister as a beautiful high school senior who had been elected to numerous honors by her fellow students. The school counselor told her pastor that, while Alice had great intellectual potential, her grades had been affected adversely by numerous extracurricular activities. Her ambivalence about finishing school and the future involved ambiguous feelings about women's true vocational options, her role as a homemaker and mother, insecurity in having to form new friendships and make a new start at college, and anxiety over possible loss of intimacy with her boyfriend. Alice was searching almost desperately for meaning in her feminine experience.

Such conversations reveal that a young person's career concerns are many-faceted, frequently compounded by questions of basic identity and objectives in life. They lack accrued wisdom and guidance in decision-making. Achieving differentiation of the self and moving from dependence upon parents and others to more secure self-reliance is a major aspect of vocational reflection. Young people need to trust their own giftedness and convictions about a career, while respecting the opinions of parents and judgments of others. Skilled information may be provided through tests in cooperation with public school guidance personnel and through literature supplying occupational information. Ultimately, a Christian's vocation is one aspect of total stewardship of life unto God (1 Cor. 10:31). When one seeks divine direction in life's calling, one may also be assured of God's providential care in efforts to get a job and make a good vocational adjustment. In getting started, one may do a little of this and a little of that just to earn money. Along with experience, the job seeker learns to "rejoice in hope" because of God's personal touch and the reality of his eternal kingdom.

The Christian pastor is uniquely suited to counsel with those who are interested in religious vocations. Today, many mid-careerists feel compelled to "the work that God calls us to do"; yet they are unclear about church-related careers. A minister can answer questions about educational requirements, job opportunities, cross-cultural issues, the joys and frustrations of religious occupations, and about the determinative quality of God's will in such vocational decisions. Some counselees will question their spiritual gifts, wondering if they truly prize people and are properly motivated for the Christian ministry.[18] Others feel ashamed because of a questionable past, deprived because of family abuse or brokenness, or anxious because of a previous job failure in another field. In the contemporary Church, there is much ambiguity about gender issues and the place of women in the creative and redemptive activity of God. Obedience that leads one to Christian service must cross many barriers.

A minister once talked with a young couple who were considering a church-related calling. The wife, Karen, was concerned about her husband's past.

KAREN: What about David's past?

PASTOR: What do you mean, Karen?

KAREN: Well, do you think his past will hurt if he is ever pastor of a church? What if somebody should find out about it?

PASTOR: I have heard that David has a "past," but I have never inquired about it. Nor do I feel that I need to know it, for to me it is just that—a *past*.

DAVID: I appreciate your attitude in this matter, but what about others? I'm always afraid it might hurt my work in a church. [The pastor suggested three ways a person might regard the past: parade it, hide it, or face it realistically as one forgiven by God and the community.]

PASTOR: Perhaps the healthiest approach would be to regard this part of your life as past and over with, no longer to be recalled nor feared. It need not be paraded; nor should you be afraid of being found out.

DAVID: What would I say if somebody in a church asked me about it?

PASTOR: You might say, "Yes, that is the way I was before Christ came into my life. But now that I am forgiven I have a new life in Christ." If your people sense that you are not afraid of your past, then I doubt that they will be too concerned with it either.

Unresolved guilt can become an intolerable burden in a person's life. As a model, the approach suggested to this young couple was helpful. However, such a confessional conversation may be the time for reconstruction of meaning, in light of past experiences, rather than for premature reassurance. The young man had sought divine pardon for his past but was uncertain about human forgiveness.[19] While David was covert about his guilt, his wife had the courage to open the subject for discussion and a possible solution. Or anxiety may have prompted her question. The pastor knew that healthy-mindedness moves beyond "what lies behind" and faces "what lies ahead" in life's journey (Phil. 3:13). Karen and David needed to experience this truth for themselves.

James Archer has written a guide for counselors attending persons who face vocational decisions and career choices.[20] Persons with disabilities caused by disease, accident, or war, mental retardation, retired citizens, widows and divorcees, the under-employed, ex-convicts, addicts, and former psychiatric patients may seek pastoral intervention in the search for meaningful existence. While the church may not be called on frequently, vocational decisions and needs are usually complex when they do appear. How may the minister assist such individuals when they turn to the church for help? Specialists suggest that one (1) obtain full information about the applicant; (2) cooperate with community agencies that exist for such purposes and with employers who help persons with special challenges; (3) act with honesty in each case; and (4) be a true pastor—a spiritual guide—to the person and his or her family.

IV. The Commitments of Life

Thus far, the pastor's care and ritual functions have been examined in three significant areas: birth and childhood, religious experience, and vocational selection. The choice of a marriage companion is another reference point of life in which church members look to their ministers for spiritual guidance and officiating at weddings. The term "commitments of life" refers in this context to entering and sustaining the covenant of marriage. The commitment concept could be applied broadly to numerous covenants from forming personal friendships, to sharing a community of persons, or indeed, fidelity to God. It is directed here to the Christian minister's functions in the experience of marriage—its origin, stresses, failures, community frameworks, and future.

Lovers change, and love changes. Commitments help hold life together when romantic love no longer prevails. Yet two commitments often collide, and people do break their promises.[21] Sharing love and commitment in faith communities is risky, sometimes painful, business.

Our consideration might proceed on the premise that every adult will be married some day, or at least hopes to marry. With the givens of world population distribution in mind, however, marriage is not an option for many people. Numerous adults, by choice or circumstance, are destined for singleness. Accordingly, churches acknowledge their responsibility to single adults such as professional students, careerists, and widows and divorced persons who are "single again." Life is not easy for the older unmarried person. Occasionally, the community fails to understand why a certain man or woman remains single. Because of his or her status and solitary situation, the single adult may feel left out of church "family programs," and thus deserves special pastoral interest. Also, the widowed, unwed parents, and divorced adults in the second half of life require skillful shepherding. Given the complexity of today's family systems, the church's youth merit spiritual direction and careful preparation in mate selection and marriage.

Preparation for marriage is a lifetime concern. People are prepared for marriage not only through casual and entertaining sex education, childhood family intimacy, social discourse, observation, reading, and formal instruction, but through all of life's experiences. The capacity to love develops from infancy and has many facets: emotional, social, spiritual, biological and volitional. Marriage preparation is thus an area for lively cooperation between homes, schools, social agencies, and churches; between parents, teachers, community workers, and ministers. Children and adolescents gain strength to love and inner serenity for the risks and responsibilities of marriage through all of life's relationships. Most of them hope to establish what Harry Stack Sullivan called a fully "human repertory of interpersonal relations," including marriage, in adulthood. It is commonplace to speak of the need to "work at" marriage. The assumption is, notes Margaret Farley, "that we *do* have some power to make choices that will sustain our committed loves."[22]

Divorce statistics indicate that many who intend to fulfill the requirements of marriage are either unwilling or unable to accept its claims, changes, and challenges. Some potential marriage partners are unable to form secure relationships or covenants of trust with others. Many of them have been manipulated by some trusted authority figure into abusive sexual activities. Several counseling sessions may be required prior to marriage in order to prepare survivors of family abuse for committed marriage relationships.[23] Much suffering among married couples, their offspring, and their families of origin might be prevented by effective marital preparation.

Ministers frequently hear laments from parents who have failed to prepare their children for adult family commitments. A mother whose teenage son had eloped with his high-school sweetheart confessed to her minister: "John grew up before we realized it. His father and I haven't talked with him about these things like we should have." A couple whose only daughter had been severely restricted in social relations and selection of her friends were shocked when she married a divorced man nearly twice her age. "That marriage will never work out," the father said bitterly. "He is too old for Jane. Besides, he has no regular employment and is a heavy drinker." His prediction eventually came true, but not before they had all experienced much suffering and remorse. While repentance for omissions may assuage the grief of shaken parents, their postponements and permissiveness may permanently cripple their children's chances for a successful marriage. Adult family members must *bless* the young and give them "the gift of power" in preparing them for marriage. Such blessing involves collective accountability from generation to generation.[24]

What are some reasons for premarital conferences or group sessions with couples planning marriage? What needs should the pastor perceive and prepare to face with the couple? *First,* many young people are immature. They are often guided by erotic fantasies rather than wise choices when they agree to marry. People need a Christian interpretation of sexuality and of God's intentions for durable couple commitments.[25] There should be an intent on the part of the couple to relate their marriage to God so that, in so far as their abilities permit, they make their family relationships an expression of their commitment to God.

Second, some individuals are not well-suited for each other because of radical differences in age, values, cross-cultural background, ethnic origin, money management, and religious orientation. The more disparate they are in these basic areas of identity and life goals, the more susceptible their marriage will be to conflict and deterioration. Reliable spiritual guidance will enable some couples to discuss such differences, to defer their plans, or to work through maladjustments prior to marriage.[26] Others bring deep intrapsychic conflicts from dysfunctional family systems to the wedding celebration. Still others do not believe that a marriage should be forever.

Third, divorced persons with a previous history of marital failure need to face their loss of confidence, grief, self-doubt, and feelings of guilt, suspicion, and hostility before sealing marriage vows again. And "trial" marriages often fail to thrive. Many such persons will never seek marriage and must make the most of what life brings.

Fourth, the Christian pastor and marital parties need to agree upon the ceremony to be used, the place for the service, rehearsal plans, and specific wedding procedures. As may be seen in the case that follows, religious ideals have great significance in the choice of a place for marriage and the kind of vows that shall be taken by a couple.

Finally, there are special problems—such as premarital pregnancy, previous abortions, extended educational plans, genetic "time bombs," family objections, and serious illness or handicap—that must be considered prior to marriage. The pastor's attitudes, public statements, and model of commitment as a single or family person will greatly affect one's ministry and functions of marriage rituals.

A specific occasion for pastoral consultation is indicated when persons of different faiths contemplate marriage. Such an experience involving a Jewish man, Gary, and a Presbyterian woman, Sue, offers us some helpful lessons. Both Gary and Sue were warmly identified with their respective religious groups. They began to realize that, if they married, some important adjustments would have to be made. They elected to talk to Rev. George Blackham, Sue's minister, because he had developed a reputation as a reliable counselor in the community. Sketches from the case follow.

> Neither of them had really thought through the importance of religion and its relationship to marriage and family living. . . . Gary told Reverend Blackham that both he and Sue enjoyed their own groups and certainly "a house divided would not bring unity within a family." Several possibilities were discussed but no final conclusions were reached. . . . Sue was concerned not only with the place for the wedding and membership in different religious groups but also with the religious training of their future children. . . . Another problem they talked over with [the minister] was "What are the important spiritual values in living?" They were somewhat surprised to find as they talked with the minister individually and with each other that they wanted basically the same things. Through their discussions they detected real spiritual resources which they said should give them a firm foundation for marriage. Various possibilities were pursued, but no conclusions were reached. . . . During the last interview Gary and Sue met together with Reverend Blackham, who made a few suggestions regarding reading materials, summarized some of their personal resources, problems, and potentialities, helped them understand better what marriage involves, and gave them a cordial invitation to return at any time. He also suggested that before final decisions were made they discuss their concerns with Gary's rabbi.[27]

We may note several things from this summary of a series of premarital interviews. In the first place, the couple's conversations with the pastor focused their divergent backgrounds. Clearly, however, he respected their profound affection for each other and desire for marriage. The pastor did not ask them to deny their basic decision for marriage and family tasks. Rather, he helped them to see that they had been avoiding the issue of their diverse religious orientations—a potential problem area in marriage.

Again, Rev. Blackham listened to the couple's concerns rather than list-
ing his concerns for them. As Gary and Sue explored their positive feelings
and honest differences, they discovered what they really loved and desired
about one another. Their love was so complex! They found that every
choice involves not only action, not only desire and reasons for desire, but
love and the reasons they loved each other. Third, the couple assumed ultimate responsibility for a suitable course of action. The minister did not
force them into a superficial, conforming, or premature decision. As things
stood, they may have broken their love affair, deciding to form relationships
with more compatible mates. Although the grief of a broken engagement is
bitter, it need not be permanent. On the other hand, Gary and Sue may
have chosen marriage, conscious of their differences and need for deep
commitments in the future.

Because preventive pastoral work can open the way to healthier family
life, *most Protestant ministers ask couples considering marriage to meet with
them for one or a series of premarital interviews.* They become better
acquainted with those anticipating marriage in the church and plan for the
ceremony together.[28]

Persons anticipating marriage can explore imaginatively tasks like bud-
geting, decision making, household jobs, power issues, parenting, and
investing in one's significant communities at work, at church, and in recreation. While parents have taught their children to walk, then to "walk away"
in marriage, the minister can point the couple to God, who planted the
family in their essential natures.

Some ministers find that common interest groups help couples to experience their inner strengths and share the needs of others planning marriage. Personal "shipwrecks" and blind spots prevent many parents from
loving their children wisely and preparing them well for marriage. Shared
experiences encourage participants to name and forgive their parents' failures and to support each other for future family tasks. When couples get in
touch with their true feelings, attitudes, and motives during courtship they
are able to face the demands of marriage more honestly.[29] Preconceived
notions about love and sex are exposed, and some fears may be dispelled.

Following a Christian wedding ceremony, the church's ministry should
be continued through pastoral aftercare. Many adjustments are required of
newly married couples—economic, physical, religious, and relational.
What shall be their relationship to their parents and other relatives? Shall
both of them continue in school or in their previous vocations? What plans
shall they make for the coming of children into their lives? Such questions
have Christian answers and may be approached in a spirit of wise facilita-

tion. The couple should be visited by a church representative and included in congregational life. There is no greater ministry for new families than helping their homes to be Christian.

Beyond counseling and calling, there are additional ways in which churches may prepare persons for marriage and strengthen Christian family life. Family tasks should be interpreted in a continuing process of education. Providing literature on family themes for engaged and newly married couples strengthens the possibility of success in marriage. A number of books provide a blueprint of husband-wife relationships and obligations. An informed couple may avoid many pitfalls and work through crises in relationships when they arise.[30]

Ministers should preach intentionally on practical aspects of family life. Biographical texts on marriage, child rearing, and family themes abound in the Scriptures.[31] Some churches observe a Christian Family Week each year with videos, films discussion groups, and worship devoted to family themes. Resource persons from varied professions may be enlisted for conference sessions with different age groups. Such periods of special emphasis enable families to face problems, to gain insight into solutions for areas of tension, and to seek improved relationships in the future.

The Christian pastor is in a unique position to guard the entrance into marriage, preside at wedding rituals, and undergird family life. We are not to perform "cookie-cutter" ceremonies and burble sentimental lines for a fee. Rather, we are principled persons of God, sensitive to the sacredness and uniqueness of the marital relationship. As representatives of both the religious and civic communities, we will preside over the commitments of life with kindness, conviction, and courage.

V. The Reality of Death

Thus far, we have considered the church's ministry in four major rituals of the human life span: physical birth, religious conversion, vocational selection, and marriage. We have seen how people turn to religious communities in these life-cycle events and have suggested how pastors may celebrate each of these "rites of passage" with their congregations.[32] The scope of this discussion prevents consideration of responsibilities during the spiritual and psychological changes of midlife and the sources of meaning in later life. Ideally, life's middle years take the form of an "inner journey," along with career and family tasks, and later life is a time for simplification of status and functions, whatever one's culture.[33] At the close of the human pilgrimage lies the experience of death and the life beyond. Death is life's last frontier. We each will discover it for ourselves; no one escapes it. The ancients taught us to "number our days" in order to achieve a sense of continuity with the past, worth and status in the present, and wisdom for the life to come (Ps. 90:12).

The fact of one's own death is not discovered all at once. Scientists have demonstrated that we are always dying. The dying process is reflected in the gradual decline of all essential bodily functions and deterioration of vital organs. While instantaneous death is often hidden from view, people do die suddenly in a variety of ways—gunshot, drug overdose, fire, auto and airplane accidents, explosions, heart attacks, wounds of battle, and suicide. Others die gradually through infection, as with AIDS; heart disease; epidemics, like cholera; and cancer—in a hundred ways and more. Death may strike in infancy, youth, the prime of life, or old age. There is never a time when its trauma should surprise us, and yet never a 'right' time for dying.

Physicians encourage creative rethinking in order to clear up illusions about life's termination. They would have us "worry well" about dying. Medical research reveals there is little perceptible pain in death, for the process provides its own anesthesia. I once heard psychiatrist Elisabeth Kübler-Ross recite the litany of "stages" of dying discovered in her research—from shock and denial, to anger and acceptance. Her *On Death and Dying* has been a standard source of wisdom for a generation.[34] Practitioners of both the medical and pastoral arts have helped people "come to terms" with dying with greater serenity because of her pioneering work. We know that medications reduce the pain of terminally ill patients, nursing care becomes more specialized and intense, critical care units in hospitals monitor vital signs, and technological advances ease distress on vital organs. We are told that, in hospitals, dying is peaceful at the last. There are no violent throes or convulsions, agony or resistance except in our imagination.

There is a time when the will to live and the fact of one's demise merge in human experience—the moment of dying. I recall the last words spoken by a dying youth who had been injured critically in an automobile accident. He whispered a prayer before losing consciousness: "Don't cheat me, God. I want to live." Ultimately, each of us will face the final reality of death in the cold sweat of some field of battle, on one's own deathbed, or in the stark terror before a fatal crash or pull of a trigger.

Humankind has known through the centuries that there is a time "to be born, and a time to die" (Eccles. 3:2; Heb. 9:27). The fact of one's death is written into one's creatureliness. We are of the natural order; yet, we are threatened by death. Modern culture has devised many ways of extending life, of prolonging vitality, of maintaining the illusion of earthly immortality. Yet the fact of a person's exodus from the world's stage remains life's ultimate certainty. The time awaits us all when we shall be called "the deceased," when our earthly estate will be settled in our absence, and we shall leave existence as we know it for the life everlasting.

In an earlier generation, we learned that persons live in the conscious or unconscious anxiety of having to die. "Non-being is present in every moment of . . . being. Suffering, accidents, disease, loss of relations to nature and man, loneliness, insecurity, weakness, and error are always with [us]. Finally, the threat of having to die will become the reality of death."[35] What lies behind this natural antipathy to dying? Biblical theology suggests that "the sting of death is sin" (1 Cor. 15:56). The pain of human mortality is estrangement from God, not merely fear of the unknown. Those persons who die "in the Lord" may resist their "image of dust," even though they are convinced of eternal life. The Christian person believes that God "has put all his enemies," including death, "under his feet." Through Christ's resurrection, God has "abolished death" and brought "life and immortality to light through the gospel" (1 Cor. 15:20–58; 2 Tim. 1:10). While we dread death, the Christian faith affirms that "whether we live or die, we belong to the Lord" (Rom. 14:7–9). Accordingly, the church's primary concern is not how long a person lives but how well one lives with the years granted in God's kindly providence. The Christian faith thus prepares persons, not merely to die, but to *live*. In this way, the prospect of dying becomes, as a soldier wrote before going into battle, "a blessing in disguise."

Contemplation of a *time* beyond this time, a *place* beyond this place permits us to use the "past as prologue" to whatever lies ahead. Lillian Hellman described this experience in a paradigm from art:

> Old paint on canvas, as it ages, sometimes becomes transparent. When that happens it is possible, in some pictures, to see the original lines: a tree will show through a woman's dress, a child makes way for a dog, a large boat is no longer on an open sea. That is called pentimento because the painter "repented," changed his mind. Perhaps it would be as well to say that the old conception, replaced by a later choice, is a way of seeing and then seeing again. . . . The paint has aged now and I wanted to see what was there for me once, what is there for me now.[36]

The human self is designed, upon reflection, to use the past as a resource for creating meaning in present situations. Original impressions of oneself, acquired over the lifespan, blend into a larger consciousness. The self continues into old age—being toward death—yet, beyond present structures, into a larger scheme of cosmic consciousness.

Ideally, a person's preparation for this last great "rite of passage" begins long before the experience of departure. However, the process of dying is almost imperceptible as retrogressive changes in the organism lead to old age. One doesn't die merely of disease or accident; one dies of his or her whole way of life. Sermons, group discussions, literature, musical compositions, personal conversations dealing with questions and mysteries—all are resources for facing the reality of death. And when release approaches, the pastor can stand with the dying individual, hear his or her confession, offer prayer for a peaceful journey into God's blessed presence, and comfort grieving persons left behind. The family gives up its mortal member, but the dying person gives up much more—everything on earth.

I once shared a physician's ministry with a terminally ill cancer patient in her mid-thirties. Exploratory surgery had failed to reach a rapidly spreading tumor. A second major operation merely confirmed the certainty of her early death. The physician "leveled" with the young mother and her husband because he felt they could face reality better than uncertainty and anxiety. Billie was told that she had approximately six months to live. Cancer had decreed the death sentence. "But why?" she protested. "I have so much to live for." She enumerated her reasons for life and hope: her husband, her son, her church, her friends, desire to travel, unachieved goals, her love of life. As they talked quietly, the doctor reasoned, "You are thirty-three, married; you've had one child, own a home, have traveled some. You've lived wisely and fully. Actually, Billie, every other experience from now on will be simply a repetition of the past. You have had a good life. You should be able to die with no regrets." His words were reasonable and compassionate, but they did not reassure her.

In time, the drama of Billie's activities, interests, and contacts narrowed to her bedroom, her family and a few close friends, and her constant pain. Her husband was a courageous sentinel, guarding his home against their bitter enemy—death. Yet the enemy approached as Billie grew weaker during passing weeks. Brief periods marked by concern for other persons and things were interspersed with long, depressed periods of self-concern. Like liquid poured into a funnel, her glowing life narrowed to a trickle of interest in life around her.

As Billie was transferred to a hospital during her last days, sensations of other persons diminished slowly. She suffered intense pain. She was irritable and depressed, restless, unresponsive to her husband's soft words and the nurses' kind hands. The night she died, her pastor was with the family in the hospital. Billie seemed to experience a vision in which the incoming waves of "that immortal sea" lapped first at her feet and then at her waist, finally overwhelming her in its surging power. She slipped quietly from safe moorings with her family and close friends and joined her Lord on the distant shore. As sense perception failed, circulation ceased, and breathing stopped, it seemed that Billie had gone to sleep. Physicians tell us that, clinically, dying is like falling asleep. For her, there was peace at the last, and for her family there was the knowledge that she would suffer no more.

Members of the health team do not agree on the matter of whether or not to tell a person that death is imminent. Some physicians feel that the patient gives up if he or she thinks death is near. Frequently, a dying person senses a subtle change in the family's solicitude or in the words of the professional strangers who combat life's vicissitudes. One facing the body's demise, if conscious, may not mention death to a minister or to the family for fear of upsetting them. Ernest Becker's research helps us here. He held that one's self-awareness of creatureliness points beyond itself to God, in Kierkegaard's terms, "faith that one's very creatureliness has some meaning to a Creator."[37]

Billie talked with her pastor about death on several occasions. While they disagreed on some of her efforts to stay alive longer, including attending a healing service of "signs and wonders," they remained friends. Like Christ with his disciples, the pastor and his spouse did not abandon Billie. "Having loved her, they loved her to the end," including the ritual of a deeply meaningful memorial service when she died (John 13:1).

The pastor's ministry to the dying person and to his or her family is mirrored in the following excerpt from a conversation with a woman whose husband was critically ill. The man had suffered a stroke and was in the intensive care unit of a hospital when the pastor called. Mrs. S. had been at the hospital many hours; she was very tired and began to cry when she saw the minister.

MRS. S.: If I did not have God, I could not face this hour. I can't imagine what it would be like to go through this experience without him.

PASTOR: In times like this, God becomes very real to us. We can feel his presence with us.

MRS. S.: I can't imagine what life without Ralph [her husband] would be like. He's been sick before, and I have never given up. I just won't give up for him to die now. I just have to believe that he won't leave me. [Silence followed as she wept.]

PASTOR: [The pastor did not know what to say—he tried to reassure her with a reminder of the past]: Now is the time to thank God for those thirty-seven years he gave you together. Remember telling me about those years—how wonderful they were?

MRS. S.: Yes, I do remember. I know that I couldn't ask for anything more than God has given me. I suppose I must be concerned that his going be as peaceable as possible, since I know that he can never completely recover.

PASTOR: Giving up a loved one is hard to do. But we know that Christ has a place for all of us who trust him. . . . Now, we don't know what is going to happen, but we do know that God will do what is right.

They read Psalm 23 and prayed together, standing near the helpless man's side. The pastor asked God's help for the man, for those who ministered to him, and his care for Mrs. S. As he left the room with its mood of death, the woman said: "God is with us. We're fine. God will do what is right." The grieving process had begun. The pastor's struggling faith had sparked her own. Evidently, "After the suffering of her soul," she experienced "the light of life and [was] satisfied" (Isa. 53:11). Even in the sorrowful pangs of death, her faith in God was secure. Thus pastors support those who are trapped in the drag of creatureliness, comfort downcast spirits, and preside at memorial ritual events.[38]

Summary

In the final chapter, we shall pay attention to how people of faith learn and grow in difficult circumstances, including the work of grief. Here we have viewed pastoral attention to people in key events through the life span. Along with one's congregation, the Christian pastor shares one's fellow pilgrims' experiences of a fully human existence. One who shares the epochs of life, from birth to death, is subject to the peril of faithlessness. By God's grace and power, the minister serves as a providential reminder of eternal life. Living in the cities of humankind, the faithful pastor helps people envision the "city which is to come."

Notes

1. Bridget Clare McKeever, "Social Systems in Pastoral Care," in *Handbook for Basic Types of Pastoral Care & Counseling,* edited by Howard W. Stone and William M. Clements (Nashville: Abingdon Press, 1991), 74.
2. Darius Salter, *What Really Matters in Ministry* (Grand Rapids: Baker Book House, 1990), 82–91.
3. Sharon Parks, *The Critical Years: The Young Adult Search for a Faith to Live By* (San Francisco: Harper & Row, 1986), 198.

4. See H. Stephen Glenn, *Raising Self-Reliant Children in a Self-Indulgent World* (Rocklin, CA: Prime Pub. and Communications, 1988); also, Jane Nelsen, *Positive Discipline*, 3d ed. (New York: Ballantine Books Div. of Random House, 1987).

5. Psychologist Charles E. Schaefer helps parents frankly discuss sensitive topics, from birth of a child to death of a loved one, in *How to Talk to Children about Really Important Things* (San Francisco: Harper & Row, 1984). Also, see Dolores Curran, *Traits of a Healthy Family* (San Francisco: Harper & Row, 1983). Video also available.

6. The late British Baptist Ernest A. Payne wrote, "We are not born Christians, nor can we be made Christians by others, not even by the church. God has given us freedom, and salvation is by personal faith." See *The Free Church Tradition in the Life of England* (London: S.C.M. Press, 1951), 174. Also, cf. D. M. Baillie, *The Theology of the Sacraments* (New York: Charles Scribner's Sons, 1957), 72–90.

7. See, for example, Anne Amos, ed., *The Scandal of Family Violence* (Melbourne, Australia: Uniting Church Press, 1990); Andre Brooks, *Children of Fast-Track Parents* (New York: Viking Press, 1989); Archibald D. Hart, *Children and Divorce: What to Expect, How to Help* (Dallas: Word Books, 1989); Philip H. Kilbride, *Changing Family Life in East Africa: Women and Children* (University Park, PA: Pennsylvania State University Press, 1990); Andrew D. Lester, *Pastoral Care with Children in Crisis* (Philadelphia: Westminster Press, 1985); Cathy Ann Matthews, *Breaking Through: No Longer a Victim of Child Abuse*, rev. ed. (Claremont, CA: Albatross Books, 1990); and Judith and Michael Murray, *When the Dream is Shattered: Coping with Child-Bearing Difficulties* (Adelaide, Australia: Lutheran Publ. House, 1988).

8. Dorothy C. Briggs, *Your Child's Self-Esteem* (Garden City, NY: Doubleday Dolphin Books, 1975); Lynn Clark, *SOS! Help for Parents: A Practical Guide for Handling Common Everyday Behavior Problems* (Bowling Green, KY: Parents Press, 1985); Polly B. Berends, *Whole Child/Whole Parent*, rev. ed. (San Francisco: Harper & Row, 1983); Michael Popkin, *Active Parenting: Teaching Cooperation, Courage, and Responsibility* (San Francisco: Harper & Row, 1987); David Elkind, *The Hurried Child: Growing Up Too Fast Too Soon* (Reading, MA: Addison-Wesley, 1981).

9. Daniel O. Aleshire, *Faithcare: Ministering to All God's People through the Ages of Life* (Philadelphia: Westminster Press, 1988). Also, see, Cos. H. Davis, Jr., *Children and the Christian Faith*, rev. ed. (Nashville: Broadman Press, 1990).

10. Erik H. Erikson, *Identity and the Life-Cycle* (New York: International Universities Press, 1959), 50–100; also, his *Toys and Reasons: Stages in the Ritualization of Experience* (New York: W. W. Norton, 1977), 116.

11. See Robert Coles, M.D., *The Moral Life of Children* (Boston: Atlantic Monthly Press, 1986).

12. Gordon Allport noted that the individual's religious sentiment is not fully developed until adolescence. See *Becoming: Basic Considerations for a Psychology of Personality* (New Haven: Yale University Press, 1955), 93–97.

13. Earl A. Loomis, Jr., "Religion and Childhood," in *Religion in the Developing Personality* (New York: New York University Press, 1960), 32.

14. See, for example, Glenn A. Smith and Henry Webb, *Planning and Conducting New Church Member Training* (Nashville: Convention Press, 1989); and Ernest E. Mosley, *Basics for New Baptists* (Nashville: Convention Press, 1989). Each denomination provides appropriate discipleship resource materials.

15. Richard S. Hanson, *Worshiping with the Child* (Nashville: Abingdon Press, 1988), 96.

16. Otto Weber, *Karl Barth's Church Dogmatics*, translated by Arthur C. Cochrane (Philadelphia: Westminster Press, 1953), 248.

17. Frederick Buechner, *Wishful Thinking: A Theological ABC* (New York: Harper & Row, 1973), 95; cited by Sharon Parks, *The Critical Years: The Young Adult Search for a Faith to Live By* (San Francisco: Harper & Row, 1986), 199–200.

18. See Richard A. Hunt, John E. Hinkle, Jr., and H. Newton Malony, eds., *Clergy Assessment and Career Development* (Nashville: Abingdon Press, 1990). Also, see Robert Schnase, *Testing and Reclaiming Your Call to Ministry* (Nashville: Abingdon Press, 1991).

19. David A. Norris has explored forgiveness—human and divine—in *Forgiving from the Heart: A Biblical and Psychotherapeutic Exploration* (Ph.D. diss., Union Seminary, 1983). His process view of forgiveness—beginning with the "intention to forgive" and continuing to "reintegration . . . of those parts of the self that had been isolated by earlier experiences of injury"—is detailed in John Patton, *Is Human Forgiveness Possible?* (Nashville: Abingdon Press, 1985), 159–65. While Patton wishes to avoid moralism in the matter of intentionality, he is deeply indebted to Norris and NT scholarship.

20. James Archer, Jr. *Counseling College Students* (New York: Crossroad/Continuum, 1991).

21. Lewis B. Smedes, *Caring and Commitment: Learning to Live the Love We Promise* (San Francisco: Harper & Row, 1988), 101–31. Also, see *Leader's Notebook and Couple's Guide, Covenant Marriage* (Nashville: BSSB Family Ministry Dept., 1987), "Marriage as Promise."

22. Margaret A. Farley, *Personal Commitments: Beginning, Keeping, Changing* (San Francisco: Harper & Row, 1986), 25.

23. James Poling models the process of ethical choices for counselors in cases of child sexual abuse in "Ethics in Pastoral Care and Counseling," in Stone and Clements, *Handbook for Basic Types of Pastoral Care and Counseling*, 56–69; also, see James Leehan, *Pastoral Care for Survivors of Family Abuse* (Louisville: Westminster/John Knox Press, 1989). The personal stories of men and women in recovery from childhood sexual abuse are told by

Connie Brewer, *Escaping the Shadows, Seeking the Light* (San Francisco: HarperCollins, 1991).

24. See Myron Madden, *Blessing: Giving the Gift of Power* (Nashville: Broadman Press, 1988). Also, see Edwin H. Friedman, *Generation to Generation: Family Process in Church and Synagogue* (New York: The Guilford Press, 1985), 67–99.

25. See Susan Muto and Adrian van Kaam, *Commitment: Key to Christian Maturity* (Mahwah, NJ: Paulist Press, 1989); also, Robert E. Money, *Christian Marriage: Grace and Work* (Nashville: Broadman Press, 1991).

26. See Theodore K. Pitt, *Premarital Counseling Handbook for Ministers* (Valley Forge, PA: Judson Press, 1985). Cf. Denise L. and John T. Carmody, *Ways to the Center: An Introduction to World Religions*, 3d ed. (Belmont, CA: Wadsworth, 1989).

27. Rex A. Skidmore, Hulda Garrett, and C. Jay Skidmore, *Marriage Consulting: An Introduction to Marriage Counseling* (New York: Harper & Row, 1956), 71–73.

28. See the couple's guide by Joan and Richard Hunt, *Preparing for Christian Marriage* (Nashville: Abingdon Press, 1982); and Pastor's Manual by Antoinette and Leon Smith, *Preparing for Christian Marriage* (Nashville: Abingdon Press, 1982); also, see Jim Henry, *The Pastor's Wedding Manual* (Nashville: Broadman Press, 1985).

   Marriage ceremonies appear in service manuals of the major denominations as well as in books of etiquette for brides. *Ethical note:* Ministers serve as representatives of both the church and the state in marriage, and usually must have filed their ordination papers at the local county seat or at the state capital prior to performing a wedding ceremony. The minister should become familiar with such legal obligations upon arrival in a new community.

29. See Harville Hendrix, *Getting the Love You Want: A Guide for Couples* (New York: Harper & Row, 1990). Also, Alan E. Craddock, *Enabling Marriages: Counseling with Prepare-Enrich* (Zillmere, Queensland, Australia: Prepare-Enrich Australia, 1986).

30. Such books include Clifford and Joyce Penner, *The Gift of Sex: A Christian Guide to Sexual Fulfillment* (Waco, TX: Word Books, 1981); Diane and David Garland, *Marriage: For Better or for Worse?* (Nashville: Broadman Press, 1988); Charles R. Swindoll, *Sanctity of Life: The Inescapable Issue* (Dallas: Word Books, 1990); and Truman Esau, *Making Marriage Work: Developing Intimacy with the One You Love* (Wheaton, IL: Victor Books, 1990).

31. Illustrations of such sermons may be found in Elizabeth Achtemeier, *The Committed Marriage* (Philadelphia: Westminster Press, 1976) and *Preaching about Family Relationships* (Philadelphia: Westminster Press, 1987); and David H. C. Read, *Preaching about the Needs of Real People* (Philadelphia: Westminster Press, 1988).

32. See Elaine Ramshaw, *Ritual and Pastoral Care* (Philadelphia: Fortress Press, 1987) for suggestions of rituals in public worship and private settings.

33. See Robert and Carol Ann Faucett, *Intimacy and Midlife: Understanding Your Journey with Yourself, Others, and God* (New York: Crossroads/Continuum, 1991); and Sharon R. Kaufman, *The Ageless Self: Sources of Meaning in Late Life* (Madison: The University of Wisconsin Press, 1986).

34. Elisabeth Kübler-Ross, *On Death and Dying* (New York: Macmillan, 1959).

35. Paul Tillich, "The Theology of Pastoral Care," *Pastoral Psychology* 10 (October 1959): 23.

36. Lillian Hellman, *Pentimento,* cited in Kaufman, *The Ageless Self,* 164.

37. Ernest Becker, *The Denial of Death* (New York: Free Press, 1973), 90.

38. Al Cadenhead, Jr., *The Minister's Manual for Funerals* (Nashville: Broadman Press, 1988).

Suggested Reading

Balswick, Jack O. and Judith K. Balswick. *The Family: A Christian Perspective on the Contemporary Home.* Grand Rapids: Baker Book House, 1989. Colleagues at Fuller Theological Seminary collaborate on biblical and social science issues vital to Christian family life. They suggest ways in which community and social structures should help create a healthier family environment.

Koons, Carolyn A. and Anthony, Michael J. *Single Adult Passages: Uncharted Territories.* Grand Rapids: Baker Book House, 1991. Deals with what it means to be a Christian single adult.

Lester, Andrew D., ed. *When Children Suffer: A Sourcebook for Ministry with Children in Crisis.* Philadelphia: Westminster Press, 1987. Pastoral care specialists and religious educators challenge caregivers to spare children some ills of grown-ups, share their sufferings when they hurt, and show them the pathway to God's Kingdom of love.

Schorr, Lisbeth B., with Daniel Schorr. *Within Our Reach: Breaking the Cycle of Disadvantage.* New York: Doubleday Anchor Press, 1988. Offers a vision of hope and life-transforming possibilities for millions of America's marginal citizens. A guide for public policymakers as well as pastoral caregivers.

Thornton, Edward E. *The Christian Adventure.* Nashville: Broadman Press, 1991. A wise student of the human heart examines our spiritual journey and the dynamics of religious experience.

Weenolsen, Patricia. *Transcendence of Loss Over the Life Span.* New York: Hemisphere, 1988. A remarkable inspection "tour" into lifespan psychology, with particular attention to losses in relationships and ordinary circumstances as well as in the finality of death.

Wynn, J. C. *Family Therapy in Pastoral Ministry,* rev. ed. San Francisco: Harper San Francisco, 1991. A veteran family specialist considers what family therapists are doing that general ministry practitioners may adapt in pastoral caregiving.

CHAPTER NINE

SUPPORTING PERSONS
IN LIFE'S CRISES

In chapter 8's overview of the life span, I designated birth, religious conversion, vocational choices, committed relationships, and recognition of finitude as "primary moments" in human experience. Life thrusts these *acts of being* upon humankind, requires major decisions in each epoch, and issues in some form of character growth or failure. Each of these experiences is crucial in that it involves appropriate spiritual response, that is, responsible behavior, at the right time *(kairos)* in the course of the human pilgrimage *(chronos)*. Such eras of change and growth may be regarded as creative crises when they prompt a person to place life "in God's hands" (Ps. 31:15). Conversely, one who clutches life in narcissistic self-sufficiency misses both creative human relationships and true joy in God's Kingdom (Luke 9:24–25).

Disruptive crises, on the other hand, may arise at any stage of development, turning an ordinary experience into an unbearable situation. There are disasters, emergencies, and malevolent dysfunctions during which a person may be hard pressed to endure. Such situations are multiplied *ad infinitum* in human experience and pastoral practice. At such times, a person or family turns to a support community for rescue, reassurance, companionship, even survival itself. A congregation may be plunged into disbelieving grief over a pastor's illicit sexual liaisons, a treasurer's mismanagement of finances, or multiple deaths of its key leaders in some disaster. A coalition of nations, enforcing United Nations' sanctions against a common enemy, may be plunged into horrors of war and human dislocations and losses in war's aftermath.

The word "crisis," from the Greek *krisis* or *krinein*, "to separate," implies a turning point or decisive moment in experience. A crisis, viewed medically, is that change in a person's health experience leading either to recovery or death. A crucial event or epoch in a nation's life may become a watershed, a shaping influence in its destiny. We are told that one Chinese dialect uses two characters, meaning "dangerous opportunity," to express this idea. Crisis experiences thus embody a dualism of possibility and danger. They denote a perilous turning of life's tide. Precarious situations become either decisively constructive or regressive experiences for persons, families, institutions, and nations. Crises are thus characterized by decisiveness, urgency, and a sense of ultimate concern.

Karl Jaspers calls experiences when we are exposed to danger and become vulnerable to life or death "limit-situations" or "boundary-situations." They also may be viewed as revelatory moments; for in the New Testament, a *krisis* implies God's presence and participation in the human situation. No crucial situation is adequately lived through by our parishioners that does not take into consideration the dynamic of their God-relationship. The fact of divine providence pervades every developmental crisis and failure in life's pilgrimage. The church's task, therefore, is to enable persons to hear God's voice in human tragedy. Viewed in light of this God-relation, crises not only test our spiritual stability, they challenge our growth and maturity as well.

The purpose of this chapter is to distinguish the Christian helper's therapeutic ministry in three disruptive crises—guilt, illness, and grief. They may serve as paradigms of a whole spectrum of hazardous situations that hold life at bay: child, spouse, and elder abuse; addictions and codependency; issues surrounding the right to life and abortion; the changing roles of women in society, and pressures on men to change as women change; divorce, blended families, and adoption; and aging as an important epoch in human development. Our knowledge of such matters is partial, for human feelings and social changes are incredibly complex. From the sufferer's point of view, a crisis may be a foe from which he or she seeks help or protection. From faith's perspective, human extremities may become divine opportunities for health or salvation. Trouble destroys some persons even as it turns others to God and Christian community. It is hoped that, by means of people who care, God himself may break through to kindle a person's faith and offer life beyond tragedy. In this way the church becomes a shaping environment to help individuals interpret religious meaning in life's crucial situations.

I. The Crisis of Shame and Guilt

The burden of shame and guilt has had a powerful effect on the development of human personality from the beginning of recorded time. The

Bible says that Adam and Eve disobeyed God, then "hid themselves from the presence of the Lord" because they were ashamed (Gen. 3:8). Shame and guilt must be distinguished for us to understand properly their effects on the human psyche. Erik Erikson characterized *shame* as a feeling of humiliation in others' eyes, of failing to measure up to others' expectations, with consequent self-consciousness and fear of being exposed.[1] It is like being caught "with one's pants down" or one's hand in the cookie jar. Shame-based persons work overtime to "cover all the bases" because they feel vulnerable. This cover-up operation requires them to expend enormous emotional energy in an attempt to avoid the appearance of weakness or flawedness, and an almost pathological need for approval.

Guilt, on the other hand, may be illustrated in the experience of Cain, who thought he was rid of his brother Abel after he had killed him. The accusing finger of a culpable conscience marred his hollow victory. God found Cain blameworthy and exposed him. Undone by his blood-guilt, Cain was exiled as "a fugitive and a wanderer on the earth." Guilt thus provoked a crisis for him as its burden became unbearable. Cain found no place to hide in the "land of Wandering" and no promise of hope as he "went out from the Lord's presence and lived . . . east of Eden" (Gen. 4:8–16). In today's parlance, he had committed a capital crime.

1. The Complexity of Guilt

Human beings alone of all God's creation experience feelings of moral failure, painful reproaches of conscience, dread of eternal punishment, and hope through the gospel of Jesus Christ. Fashioned for fellowship with God, "a little lower than the angels," humanity rejected the divinely intended grandeur and became what Pascal called a "deposed king." In the individuation process, this good-evil polarity precludes easy access to life goals of self-realization or self-actualization. It complicates the caregiving process. Protestant theologians are generally agreed that, as sinner, one retains the capacity to perceive life with intelligence and sensitivity, while sharing the guilt of a sinful world. Pastoral counselors are constantly challenged to diagnose the relationship of constructive and destructive forces in people and to find ways to nurture the constructive ones.[2] A major developmental task is making sense of this "in-between" polarity of the human predicament.

Personality is so constituted that some persons suffer an overpowering sense of shame about matters that others view lightly or overlook entirely. This complicates the matter of confession and resolution of guilt. While a person may be guilty of sinning against God or another individual (forensic guilt), he or she may or may not "feel" guilty about it. On the other hand, a person with an overburdened conscience may not be guilty of sin or moral error yet feel driven in life. The person with an intrapunitive conscience may be experiencing what psychologists call "neurotic guilt" and what some theologians call "anxious dread." Christian confessors, therefore, cannot assume that sin against God, others, or oneself always lies behind a person's guilt feelings in linear fashion. Nor is confession of sin the equivalent of "realized forgiveness" in human experience. While God forgives freely, some persons cannot forgive themselves for past misdeeds. Accordingly, those who would help others to live with purity of heart need to appreciate the complexity of shame, guilt, and forgiveness in an imperfect world.

2. Perspectives on Guilt and Forgiveness

The impasse of persons bound by conscience is laid bare in biblical character sketches, in literary works, in technological advances, in psychoanalytic theory, and in pastoral practice. Since guilt feelings may be handled in various ways, some of which are destructive, those who seek resolution of guilt should view it from every angle of possible help. Varied sources of wisdom have sounded a strangely similar note to people who care: "You are not what you think you are." Both theology and psychology, for example, hold that human beings have a far greater capacity for good *and* evil than we think. Fortunately, the Christian caregiver sees this ambiguous grandeur and misery silhouetted against the brilliant backdrop of the Christian faith (John 1:5).

From the biblical perspective, guilt refers not only to a human *feeling* about disobedience, or a ruptured relationship with God or others; it is also a forensic term. It implies one's status of *being* guilty, of having one's guilt established under the divine law. Two terms translated "guilt" are used in the New Testament: (1) *hupodikos*, meaning "under judgment" or "liable to punishment"; and (2) *enochos*, meaning "guilty of anything, bound, under obligation, subject to" or responsible for something.[3] Both terms imply a human being's guilty status and condition as sinner before God (cf. Rom. 3:19; 1 Cor. 11:27; James 2:10).

The experience of King David is a classic case of a person's confinement in the bonds of guilt, sickness of shame-filled secrets, and joy in confession and pardon. Nathan the prophet, who knew of David's sin against Uriah and Bathsheba, became his brother's keeper by relating a parable to the king. Portraying an economic evil—a rich man taking a poor man's one ewe lamb—he aroused the king's sense of justice. "As the Lord lives," vowed

David, "the man who had done this deserves to die." When confronted with reality: "You are the man!" David's stricken conscience prompted his admission: "I have sinned against the Lord" (2 Sam. 12:1-15). His confessional prayers, in Psalms 32 and 51, reveal anxious longing for divine cleansing and renewal. As long as his moral fault remained unconfessed David experienced great distress. "When I kept silent, my bones wasted away . . . for day and night your hand was heavy upon me" (Ps. 32:3-4). Yet when he implored: "Create in me a pure heart, O God, and renew a steadfast spirit within me," David experienced forgiveness and release from bondage in guilt.

Shakespeare's characters frequently mirror human guilt and desire for pardon. Lady Macbeth's poignant cry, "Out, damned spot!" is a dramatic paradigm of all human longing for freedom from the stain of guilt. In Manuel Komroff's story "The Death of Judas," Lazarus encounters Judas following the crucifixion. Lazarus, feeling implicated in the crime against Christ, accuses Judas: "Your face has become loathsome." Judas replies, "The face of every murderer is loathsome. This is God's imprint, the hot iron brand, so that all mankind may know what guilt looks like." But note what happened. Lazarus admitted that he, too, had failed Jesus Christ by accusing Judas. He took his own guilt out on the betrayer, a mechanism of defense called *projection* in psychology. The biblical account of the betrayal, meanwhile, reports that Judas Iscariot was so remorseful about his sin that he returned the blood money, then hanged himself (Matt. 27:3-5). Unresolved guilt, unfreely revealed, led Judas from self-accusation to self-destruction.

Modern technology obscures accountability, erases complicity, covers ineptitude, and appears to make a game out of otherwise risky or hideous experiences. In wartime, television treats us to a front-row view of battle. We fly with the pilot at mach-speeds, fix the crosshairs in the jet's bomb scope, zero in over the enemy, and make the aerial run with anti-aircraft missiles bursting around us.[4] It's like a giant video game — except that there is a real person in that cockpit facing one of two grisly options: kill or be killed.

In medicine, we see the patient's compliant body slipped into a giant CAT-scan cylinder for a brain or body scan. "That tumor has to come out!" is the diagnosis. Major surgeries on brains, eyes, hearts, livers, and kidneys appear miraculous — even if they must sometimes advance the cause of science when a patient dies. "Come, let us play god" is an ancient invitation to take God's place. Whether for good in surgeries or ill in wartime, technology obscures humanity. Life blurs conscience; we become refugees from our own scientific achievements.

The psychoanalyst Sigmund Freud observed a "normal conscious sense of guilt (conscience)" in some analysands of his clinical practice, but others masked destructive guilt feelings at unconscious levels of existence. Repressed guilt found "atonement in illness," said Freud, so that some of his patients refused to "give up the penalty of suffering." This resistance to analysis put "the most powerful obstacles in the way of recovery."[5] While he thought that a great deal of guilt remained inaccessible, Freud recognized improvement in patients who experienced catharsis and gained *ego* control (of destructive *id* impulses) through therapy.

Carl Jung, Freud's contemporary, moved beyond his former colleague's biological formulations of psychoanalysis and took human beings' cultural environment into systematic consideration. For example, Freud thought that guilt neuroses developed from the superego's function as a vindictive vehicle—"a punitive inner agency of 'blind' morality."[6] He conceived no norms, no objective moral standards, for human behavior. He was concerned not with objective (factual) guilt but with a patient's neurotic guilt feelings. Jung, on the other hand, advanced a theory of cultural archetypes by which society provides models of morality and encourages the development of conscience—an inner sense of obligation. When an individual violated his or her internalized moral standards, Jung held that any consequent guilt feelings should be confessed. Otherwise, a person might experience psychic conflict to the point of physical or mental illness. "To cherish secrets and to restrain emotions," wrote Jung, "are psychic misdemeanors for which nature finally visits us with sickness."[7] He felt that psychic concealment alienated one from oneself, one's family, and a helping community. The self, thus damaged, might be restored on the path of individuation—a search like a medieval quest for the Holy Grail.

Psychiatrist Karl Menninger and I visited in Texas shortly after the publication of his Stone Lectures at Princeton Theological Seminary, *Whatever Became of Sin?*[8] We talked about social sins, which were his concerns: the mistreatment of Native Americans, the "crime of punishment" in our criminal justice system, family abuse, environmental evils, inexcusable slaughters in wartime, and white-collar crime. Whether in government, education, business, or industry—stealing, bribing, and cheating infect human communities. With well-publicized exceptions, white-collar crime has been winked at or largely overlooked, despite outcries for professional ethics. With reference to his "sin" book, Menninger wished to encourage Christian ministers to take their work of biblical preaching, teaching, and leading congregations more seriously. Above all, he was displeased with the glossing of *real* sin against the one true God by ministers who had "sold out" to psychotherapy. Much has been done in recent years to close the "morality gap" among pastoral care specialists which Menninger exposed.[9]

Christian pastors, meanwhile, are compelled to forego the luxury of theoretical tilting because of their practical efforts to make divine forgiveness effective in human experience. The skilled minister knows that the human heart is a rebel against God. Because human evil wears clever masks, ministers out on the "firing line" see sin in terms of (1) bondage to addictions one cannot master; (2) inability to sustain durable marriage relationships; (3) character-disordered manipulation of "the good," through narcissism; (4) violation of the laws of God and the human community; and (5) depression, often masked as chemical, substance, or sexual abuse. For resolution of guilt, the pastor turns from such unacceptable remedies as (a) classical psychoanalysis; (b) magical uses of the sacrament of penance; and (c) "integrity therapy" to biblical realities of ownership, confession, grace, repentance, faith, forgiveness, and responsibility before God.[10]

3. The Resolution of Guilt

Guilt does not always prompt a crisis in human experience. The responsible person handles his or her guilt constructively by facing its sources, confessing it to God, appropriating forgiveness, then learning from the experience. Thus what Calvin called "inward integrity of heart" is renewed before God and the human community. Admittedly, some persons do not feel a sense of responsibility toward the community nor sin toward God. Such sociopathic personalities shrug off moral defections with a "So what!" attitude because of an insulated or devitalized conscience.

From a phenomenological perspective, sin against God, others, or oneself causes deep suffering and sabotages fulfillment of the human promise. Heinz Kohut suggested in *The Restoration of the Self* that the self, so damaged, must be restored in a process something like reparenting.[11] Researcher Ali Beg found wisdom in the Sufi tradition. Beg sought to strengthen the guilt-scarred self beyond the biblical admonition, "Repent; go and sin no more," through practicing positive virtues. He held that "courage, honesty, patience, humility, charity, prudence, and love are all skills" we must develop, not primarily moral qualities we possess.[12] Such virtues are actional resources with which to combat the self-destructiveness and damage to others caused by sinful behaviors. Such inner strengths may then be used, not merely to repair or stabilize oneself, but to connect with others in true community.

Such phenomenological research leads us to the natural question, how may a Protestant congregation function as a fellowship of confession and reconciliation for persons suffering guilt? To those bowed beneath the weight of sin, shame, and guilt, the church offers the opportunity of corporate confession through public worship and private confession through prayer. Ideally, each member of the community of faith is to be an agent of reconciliation. At times, as in the following instance, a congregant confesses to God through a minister.

Margie White, a public school teacher and single adult member of a village congregation, made an appointment with her minister. Before their meeting, the pastor knew that Miss White (1) lived with her widowed mother, since he had visited them; (2) had secured a temporary leave from her teaching position because of ill health; and (3) was seeing a psychiatrist, who had advised her to forego church attendance temporarily.

Margie White asked for an evening appointment in order that adequate time might be given to her story. She requested that her mother and the minister's wife be present during the interview. This was arranged. Their conversation in the pastor's home revealed misgivings about violation of her value system and grief over an unfulfilled life.

The counselee described compulsive symptoms that had kept her away from church in recent months and revealed much insight into their cause. She experienced a strong psychosexual attraction to a certain businessman in the community. She wanted to talk with the man each time she saw him and controlled this urge with great difficulty. Moreover, Miss White felt compelled to confess her past misdeeds publicly to the entire congregation each time she attended worship services. Her absence from church was explained as an effort to cope with this compulsion to repeat a confessional act. She indicated that neither prayer to God nor sessions with her psychiatrist had relieved her overpowering sense of guilt.

Margie White quoted a familiar Bible passage: "I know that God forgives us, for he has said, 'If we confess our sins, he is faithful and just, and will forgive us our sins and cleanse us from all unrighteousness' (1 John 1:9). But, Pastor, I have confessed again and again and still feel unworthy. I know God hears my prayers; he will forgive, but I don't *feel* forgiven." She felt that her past behavior was unforgivable.

Margie related that years before she had engaged in an illicit love affair with a man whom she had planned to wed. Their marriage plans failed, however. Since that clandestine affair she had self-pleasured sexually for many years, yet suffered much guilt in the process. Her repressed sexuality aggravated feelings of grief over a forfeited marriage and deep human hunger for intimacy—unfulfilled through physical activity alone.

A depressive reaction had set in and she had turned to a psychiatrist for help. She had "cleared" with him about talking with her minister.

The pastor indicated that he knew something of how hard it was to carry one's past into the present and future. They talked of God's acceptance and of the discovery of forgiveness, since "from everlasting to everlasting the Lord's love is with those who fear Him" (Ps. 103:17). In the past, Margie White had mishandled her guilt and loneliness by suffering psychic illness and withdrawing from potential sources of help, save one, until she called the pastor.

She needed strength to love in order to turn from her incredible loneliness and sexual inversion to constructive social relations. This conversation represented a real breakthrough in socialization. She also needed to accept God's acceptance of her and to forgive herself. A pastoral prayer focused the counselee's feelings of self-blame, desire for forgiveness, and hope to "move into the world again." They agreed to meet periodically, since Margie White needed companionship and guidance in redirecting the course of her life.

Several clues to counseling persons searching for forgiveness may be noted from this experience. (1) The stated problem is rarely the true source of a person's predicament. Miss White apologized first for her absence from worship services; she felt badly about that. But that was not all! In time, she revealed shame for past misdeeds and confusion over uncontrollable urges. (2) The burden of guilt is both isolating and depressing. Therefore the minister suggested that Miss White remain in her doctor's care until he dismissed her. (3) The confessional group pledged themselves to confidentiality, for the counselee dreaded betrayal to the community. Fear of betrayal to those who may not understand is involved in all confessional situations. (4) Confession may be a meaningless, compulsive act until a person achieves power over the sources of his or her temptation.

In time, Margie White *saw* reality in a larger way: She had left her "first love" of God in attempts to meet her own needs. Need-love had outrun Gift-love, in C. S. Lewis's words. The cure was not only to *feel loved* but to learn to *practice love* in a reintegration of the self. Fear of discovery lost its terror when she experienced acceptance and sought, in turn, to embrace her own sexuality.[13] (5) To count one's sin as "unpardonable," instead of placing its burden in God's hands, may be a subtle form of pride. "Hardness of heart" is a component in some pseudo-confessions, particularly when a person gains some gratification through his or her behavior. A depressed person may cling to her or his symptoms in order to manipulate others or to gain sympathy.

Margie White's psychiatrist had advised therapeutic activities, such as needlework and gardening, to help her regain self-esteem. (6) While therapeutic activity may enhance feelings of self-esteem, crafts cannot substitute for companionship. People need people. (7) As Christians confess their faults "one to another" and forgive each other to the degree that Christ forgives them, loving community becomes more real to them. (8) The ultimate criterion of release from guilt is not merely confession but restoration of community. Human effort by itself is futile. Forgiveness is discovered through God's grace and love. Experiencing community—human and divine—affirms one's bond in God's Kingdom and provides the strength to love oneself and others in return.

II. The Crisis of Illness

Accidents, hospitalized illnesses, and surgical procedures disrupt life's serenity and threaten the security of individuals and their families. Hospitalization creates a crisis as the ill or injured person experiences finitude, suffers pain, and copes with alien forces and people. A person leaves the familiar security of work, home, and leisure for the unfamiliar surroundings, sterile procedures, complex equipment, and uncertain future of a medical setting. Illness is a depersonalizing crisis, disrupting relationships and draining physical and financial resources. A businessman who develops a heart ailment, for example, temporarily loses his vocational identity and status in a modern hospital setting. His life-situation becomes disconnected; a strong ego sags into dependence on powerful healthcare providers. Life's normal stress is intensified as he becomes a shut-in and the world outside functions without him.

That a parishioner has become a patient does not alter the fact that she or he still needs understanding, affection, and support. Organic dysfunction, whether its source be accident, disease, aging, distress, or infection, is accompanied by emotional distress. The pastor's hospital ministry has been enriched by the research of psychiatrists Thomas Holmes and Richard Rahe of the University of Washington Medical School. Their "Social Readjustment Rating Scale" places numerical stressor-weighted equivalents alongside forty-three life events.[14] Potentially stressful situations were rated on a scale from 11 to 100, with "death of one's spouse" highest. For a person who scored over 300 stress points on their scale, Holmes and Rahe noted a high risk potential for developing major illness within the following two-year period. Stress did not cause the illness, Holmes emphasized—"It takes a germ"—but heavy stressors seemed to promote the disease process.

The first requisite of church representatives who visit hospitalized members, therefore, is that they be wise and sensitive persons of faith. The

Christian caller represents God's healing power to patients through positive virtues of trust, steadfast love, and undiscouraged hope. One cares wisely by joining the medical community in providing appropriate conditions for God's healing forces to work in a patient's life. The shepherd of the sick will also be alert to each patient's private world. Rarely will we find people so stripped of psychological and social defenses. Illness humbles individuals and prompts "teachable moments" in life. "When I was down," confessed a man who had broken his back, "there was no way to look but up." Through caring conversation, creative suggestion, and realistic prayer, God's servant becomes a healing agent in the crisis of illness.

1. Visiting the Hospitalized Patient

Since the appearance of Cabot and Dicks's *The Art of Ministering to the Sick* in 1936, numerous resources have appeared in this specialized area of pastoral care.[15] Although I am presupposing the reader's acquaintance with such literature, some practical suggestions are germane to this discussion.

When moving to a new locality, a minister should become acquainted with the medical facilities and personnel of that city or region, including physicians, hospital administrators, and chaplains. As to the question of whom to visit, the pastor will call upon hospitalized church members, persons he or she is requested to visit, and anyone for whom there is special spiritual concern. Some hospital residents have no church affiliation, yet they need a minister. Others are from out of town with no pastor available unless the hospital employs a chaplain. As a general rule, we should visit members of another church only at the request of a fellow pastor or family member.

In seeking to personalize visits with congregants, the minister should inquire at the nursing station about the patient's general condition. The church caller knows that each patient's welfare is the hospital's first concern. Any Christian visitor should remember that, while he or she represents God and life's central values in the sickroom, *that visit is not indispensable to the patient's recovery.* In protecting the patient's welfare, hospital visitors will be guided by the following principles:

1. Regard signs on the door, such as: Isolation, X-ray, No Visitors, and the call light. Knock before entering. Introduce yourself when being received into the sickroom.
2. Call back later when a patient's meal is being served, when his or her physician appears, or when several visitors are present in the room.

3. Be sensitive to God's presence and identify with the patient's situation. It is easy for a caller unconsciously to assume a patronizing air of "looking down" on the person in bed.

4. Address others in the room to be pleasantly sociable; yet focus as much as possible on a face-to-face ministry to the patient. Stand or sit in the patient's line of vision. Avoid leaning on the bed or jarring equipment like an infusion flask or catheter. If the patient is unconscious, asleep, or too ill to talk, visit briefly with family members.

5. Conduct the call in a spirit of confident prayer (Matt. 18:20). It is best not to talk loudly or laugh boisterously, since a spirit of serenity promotes healing in the sickroom. When a Scripture selection and verbal prayer are employed, the patient should feel that his or her own concerns are being expressed to God. Spontaneous use of these resources is more effective than canned phrases offered as a pious gesture.[16]

6. Visitors should acquaint themselves in advance with a brief glossary of medical terms to avoid embarrassment or ignorance about standard hospital abbreviations and communications.

7. In some religious traditions, it is customary to serve private communion as assurance of God's presence and care. Such rituals are an exception in my own Free Church tradition.

8. It is impossible to say how long a visit should last. Its duration will vary according to the level of relationship—social, supportive, confessional, or guidance—achieved with the patient. The presence of others in the room, interruptions, and the patient's condition and responsiveness also influence a visit's length.

2. Entering the Patient's Private World

A pastoral visit, like a sermon, proceeds from an introduction through the body of the call to a conclusion. Each patient is unique; the same technique will not work in every case. Factors such as the person's age, gender, physical condition, cultural linguistic origin, religious heritage, emotional state, and relationship patterns condition the call. *Why* the person is there provides a clue to the person's felt anxiety. Has he or she been hospitalized for an examination, an injury, emotional disorder, chemical abuse, acute infection, surgical procedure, chronic infirmity, or catastrophic illness? An individual may be experiencing a whole cluster of feelings: anxiety, disconnection from familiar support systems, fear of the unknown, pain, anger, depression, guilt, fear of death, or anxious longing for health.

Primarily by *listening*, the caller enters the patient's private world in order to determine what the real concerns are. Then one attends empathically to the patient and family members who may be present. Prefabricated responses are a poor substitute for genuine encounter. The following conversation illustrates how a minister entered a patient's world by listening and responding to the patient's perceptions of reality. This was the first meeting between Mr. Coleman, a newly admitted patient, and a general hospital chaplain.

CHAPLAIN: [introductions had been exchanged]: Mr. Coleman, you've just come into the hospital?

COLEMAN: Yes, I came in yesterday afternoon. The doctor is giving me some tests [very soft voice].

CHAPLAIN: You say that you are in for some tests?

COLEMAN: Yes, the doctor thinks that I may have a brain tumor or something. Dr. Young wants me to get a CAT scan and have a spinal tap. They'll probably get a brain-wave test, too.

CHAPLAIN: He thinks it may be a tumor?

COLEMAN: Uh-huh. See, I've been having these blackout spells. I've had three of 'em. Sometime I just get rigid—like this—[demonstrated] and I can't even talk. The doctor thinks it may be a pressure on my brain. [Pause.] When they tap my spine, that may take off some of the pressure. I sure hope so.

CHAPLAIN: I'm sure you do. You've probably been pretty concerned about yourself.

COLEMAN: I'll say! Why, the other day—about three weeks ago now—I just fell on my face on a concrete floor. [He rubbed his face.] I cut it up here, and here, and here. It's a wonder I hadn't broken it up.

CHAPLAIN: That must have been a frightening experience! [The patient related other blackout experiences. Once, while driving, he froze at the wheel and ran into a parked car. Also, he said that his nerves interfered with little things around the house where a fellow needed steady hands.]

CHAPLAIN: So your family has noticed this, too.

COLEMAN: I guess you'd say they have. [Pause.] See, my wife and I have been separated for six months now. I love my wife and my two boys, but we don't live together any more. [Real grief and depression were apparent—he told of his wife's sexual infidelity.] Man, this experience has been the hardest thing I ever ran into in my life. I love her and the boys. I just couldn't believe it at first.

CHAPLAIN: This must have come as a terrible shock.

COLEMAN: It has nearly killed me. [He explained how he learned of her infidelity and had talked to her "boyfriend."] He didn't deny it. In fact, he just made one request—that I shouldn't tell his wife. And I haven't. My home has been wrecked. I don't see any reason for seeing theirs busted, too.

CHAPLAIN: So you've been under this pressure for about six months?

COLEMAN: I'd never been sick a day in my life till this happened.

CHAPLAIN: You'd never been sick before . . . never been a patient in a hospital like this?

COLEMAN: Not 'til about three months ago, when I started having these blackouts spells. The doctor said that it could be my nerves. He said I'd been through enough to make 'em bad and I guess I have. I'm real shaky.

CHAPLAIN: You feel then that there may be some connection between your broken home and your blackout spells?

COLEMAN: Yes . . . I guess I do.

CHAPLAIN: While the doctors check every possibility with you, Mr. Coleman, to see if there is some physical cause behind the blackouts, I want to be your pastor here in the hospital. Spiritual and medical skill can work together to improve your health, and perhaps to save your home as well.

COLEMAN: I sure hope so. [A nurse entered and gave Mr. Coleman a tablet.]

CHAPLAIN: Your doctor can give you a tablet to ease the pain in your head. Your minister represents the living God who can ease the pain in your heart. [Pause.] Mr. Coleman, I shall see you again after the tests.

We may observe *first* that the chaplain attended to the patient's predicament and tried to understand his plight. Obviously, Mr. Coleman felt (1) betrayed in the loss of his wife's love, and anger—even suppressed rage—because of her infidelity. He carried (2) an unresolved grudge against the man who had shattered the serenity of his home. Perhaps Mr. Coleman had unconsciously turned this destructive hostility in upon himself through somatic symptoms. (3) The blackouts compounded his suffering but had prompted little sympathy (secondary gain) from others. The patient was experiencing real depression. He felt cut off "from the land of the living." At one point he admitted, "It has nearly killed me." (4) Mr. Coleman had discovered the desert places of loneliness. He was experiencing isolation symptoms, yet he spoke hopefully of one medical procedure: "That may take off some of the pressure. I sure hope so." (5) His ontological status as a person was threatened. While denying it, he may have preferred death to suffering continual defeat as a man, husband, and father.

Second, not all hospitalized patients experience such stress and anxiety. The casualness of an ordinary call, however, would have been inappropriate in Mr. Coleman's case.

Third, note that the chaplain refrained from reassuring the patient prematurely. All the facts were not in hand. He might have a brain tumor. The advantage of a thorough diagnostic work-up on such a patient lies in checking every possible source of difficulty. The minister has no right to tell such a patient that everything will be fine or that his trouble is only emotional. While religious factors impact illness, the chaplain in this instance did not blame Coleman's trouble on sin. Assessing blame is often an "out," not a solution in a family crisis.

Fourth, both Mr. Coleman and the chaplain were realistic about what they expected to accomplish in one interview. They did *not* see his wife as a destructive individual, even though marital separation had caused undue stress and grief. Rather, they opened themselves to the healing presence of God. The hospital pastor pledged continued concern during the tests and promised a return visit. He realized that Mr. Coleman's eyes were open to several possible causes of illness and that he had taken a small step to reweave religious faith into life. Coleman was trusting God and the medical community for healing, and there was room to grow.

3. Pastoral Responsibility in Illness

The Christian caregiver supports individuals and their families in many kinds of physical and psychic illness. The family system as the unit of illness may require more time and skill than does the patient. Families of critical accident victims or heart attack patients, for example, do some anticipatory grief work prior to the event of death. In cases of major surgery, psychiatric hospitalization, stroke, AIDS, attempted suicide, or cancer, the pastor or a church representative stands with a family that is experiencing dependency, grief, and anxiety.

After being with her hospitalized husband many days, a parishioner confessed to her minister, "I think I'm coming apart at the seams. I asked the doctor for a prescription for myself—something for my nerves. I've taken some of the capsules in order to rest at night. I just have to be here with Jim during the day." A religious ministry to a patient and the family is essential during the crisis of illness.

Because of the magnitude of this task, a pastor should enlist and train capable laypersons for a shared ministry to the sick and their families.[17] In smaller congregations, a key member's illness may constitute a crisis for the entire congregation. Parishioners may share such caring responsibilities as child care; financial support; providing companionship, food, or transportation; visitation, and prayer support. A person may require nursing care, housekeeping assistance, or specialized rehabilitation services during convalescence. The church's ministry of receiving former psychiatric patients, chemical substance or alcohol abusers, and ex-prisoners into its fellowship is also significant, though often ambivalent. Just as God hides a person's past "behind his back," church members should help former patients and prisoners to put the past behind and face the future with confident faith.

III. The Crisis of Grief

Studies by health care and lifespan specialists remind us that we are called on to transcend diverse losses — both at individual and community levels — throughout our lives. As the hero in Bernard Malamud's *The Natural* expressed it to his girlfriend, after an extended, mysterious absence during his baseball career: "Things just didn't work out the way I thought they would." They seldom do. Life histories are filled with recurring themes of actual or threatened loss, major and minor struggles, chosen separations (like divorce), imposed alienations (as in wartime and job terminations), surgical loss of part of oneself (amputation or mastectomy), and crushing disappointment of a couple's infertility.

Whatever the shape of such diverse losses, they are a metaphorical reminder of our life-and-death struggle. When would-be comforters standing alongside grievers are speechless, "the Spirit himself intercedes for us with groans that words cannot express" (Rom. 8:26). There will be occasions of loss — suicide, deaths in wartime, and tragic family alienations — when no explanation suffices for the bereft. When hearts are broken persons do not need explanations. They need the healing presence of God, who in all things "works for the good of those who love him, who have been called according to his purpose" (Rom. 8:28).

Guidance, old and new, is available for carers who faithfully represent the "God of all comfort" in the crisis of grief (2 Cor. 1:3). Christ's ministry with acutely bereaved persons, as with Mary and Martha of Bethany, reminds us that God still enters into experiences of loss (John 11:1–44). God himself is the bereaved person's true burden-bearer, not those of us who minister for his sake (Heb. 4:14–15).

A vast amount of literature on grief has appeared from pastoral care specialists and psychologists in recent decades. Laypersons for example, turned to Harold Kushner's *When Bad Things Happen to Good People* because they identified immediately with his own predicament over loss. Pastors have turned to many other sources.[18] Such studies offer wisdom for care providers who would help grieving persons experience what Granger Westberg appropriately termed "good grief."

While ministers deal primarily with acutely bereaved persons, psychiatrists see exaggerations of behavior in delayed, unresolved, and distorted grief reactions. Pathological grief behaviors of survivors who have lost loved ones in accidents, in divorce, suicide, or wartime have been the subject of extensive scientific investigations. Two of the earliest reports of research in pathological grief behavior were Freud's "Mourning and Melancholia," and Erich Lindemann's studies of grief following the Coconut Grove nightclub fire in Boston. Other, recent studies are also available.[19] Certain observations regarding pathological grief processes offer valuable wisdom to those who minister in normal bereavement situations. We know, for example, that grief work involves a whole spectrum of emotions and reactions that "deserve respect and reverence." Though we speak of bereavement "as an experience," noted psychiatrist Clemens E. Benda, "we understand that human beings will react [to that process] in many different ways."[20] Accordingly, no one method of comfort will work in all cases of loss, for each grief experience is clothed in its own unique circumstances.

1. Grief Situations in Life

There are grief situations in life that are often more disruptive and painful than the loss imposed by death. (1) The birth of a physically deformed or mentally defective child is a bewildering experience for most parents. Prior planning is shattered with feelings of self-doubt, anger, guilt, and questions about the future. (2) Some persons, including church leaders, are misunderstood in public life and suffer grievous psychic injury through unjust criticism and rejection. The likelihood of such misunderstanding is much greater in a small town than in a city, where people may live anonymously most of their lives. For example, a woman who had been falsely accused of infidelity almost lost her sanity before her husband agreed to move from their rural home to a nearby city. She found acceptance in the new situation and an opportunity to start life over again.

The family (3) whose only child marries against parental advice or becomes an unwed parent may suffer deeply. While parents may forgive a drug-abusing or disobedient child, whatever the nature of his or her dysfunction, the scars may never disappear. (4) The social stigma often attached to the family of an ex-prisoner or former psychiatric patient compounds their grief and guilt. The pastor's role as interpreter of trauma to the community is a necessary aspect of one's healing ministry with persons and families. (5) Betrayal of covenant trust may prompt any of a whole gamut of grief reactions — from depression, to substance abuse, to violence, to suicide. A shattered courtship, a disloyal marriage partner, a dishonest business associate, or any broken covenant may precipitate a serious crisis. (6) Events such as the loss of home and friends by moving from a community, failure in school, forced retirement, or an undesired job assignment may isolate an individual and stab life with grief.

In discussing the anxiety of grief, Wayne Oates once wrote: "Grief by death cuts with a sharp edge like unto a razor; grief [in life] cuts with the jaggedness of a saw."[21] Grief situations in life are frequently unrecognized and unresolved. There has been no death to call a faith community to the sufferer's side. Persons grieved in life often have "tears for food day and night" because they are left, without rituals or community support, to bear their burdens alone (Ps. 42:3). What shall be said of supporting persons bereaved by death applies generally to those suffering losses in life as well.

2. Considerations in Grief Work

A person's earliest grief experiences occur through the losses of childhood. A small girl's doll is mutilated by a mischievous brother. A treasured pet is killed by a passing car in the street. The family moves and a child loses his or her best playmate or a favorite teacher. Grief prompted by a close relative's death may require parents to serve their children as ministers of comfort and instruction. Yet some parents feel ill-equipped to face life's losses with their children. It is not atypical to hear a mother say, "I never want my child to attend a funeral." Such unrealism, while avoiding morbid circumstances temporarily, does not prepare the young for future grief work. Experience indicates that children generally accept and adjust to life's losses more easily than do adults.[22] Early grief experiences become a training ground for more severe losses in the future. When life's events warrant tears, parents should not be ashamed to weep openly in front of their children. When a relative or friend dies, grownups should not distort the truth to children. A mother might say, for example, "Grandmother is dead. She has gone to be with God and we shall miss her very much." Children's questions about death should be answered honestly in terms that they understand.

Another consideration is a person's reaction to loss *in the normal process of grief work*. Reactions to an accident, fateful medical diagnosis, amputation, divorce, or death are remarkably similar. The process of grief work was evidenced by a man whose foot had been crushed in an industrial accident. He faced a forced decision after being hospitalized several weeks. His surgeon advised amputation of his foot and installation of a prosthesis. When the word about amputation came, it plunged the man into shocked grief and depression. The day he received the report he confessed tearfully to a friend: "I have prayed so long and suffered so much that, sometimes, all I do is say God's name. I know that God will not place more on me than I am able to bear, but I never thought one person could suffer so much." In ensuing days, his grief proceeded with decreasing intensity from (1) shock and physical distress symptoms, such as vomiting; to (2) acts of mourning for the anticipated loss by tears, talking, and restlessness; (3) mild depression and expectant dread; and (4) adaptation to the limb's removal and new prosthesis by participation in hospital rehabilitation rituals, concern for his family's welfare, and plans for future employment.

We overlook the fact that grief often crushes an entire community when a major industry or military base closes and thousands of workers lose jobs, or when a natural disaster strikes. The wound of grief has been called "the illness that heals itself," but not automatically. Bereavement properly becomes *grief work* when a person, family system, or entire community: (a) internalizes the loss and often deep suffering that goes with it, (b) cherishes memories of the past, (c) reshapes future plans in the light of the reality of the person's death, and (d) assumes responsibilities for life's new demands. Comforters during the grief process should encourage families to grieve openly and successfully over their common loss. Normal expressions of grief—shock, resignation or anger, tears, rote behavior, numbed dependence, and impulsive talking about the deceased—permit healthy therapeutic work.

Some ministers mistakenly imply that true Christians should "prove their faith" by remaining dry-eyed and composed during a funeral service. Their repressive statements and reassuring actions may prompt guilt feelings in a person or family that displays strong emotional reactions to loss. Thus some people conduct the business of funeral arrangements and attend the memorial service with a masked composure that hides their true state of mind. "Good grief" encourages the bereft family to share in plans for the funeral, which is a worship service of the church. During the public funeral ritual, grieving family members may reveal their faith in God and their true feelings, according to their cultural, racial, and religious background. Different cultures care for the mortal remains of the deceased and mourn in uniquely appropriate ways.

If we ourselves are ministering to a family when a loved one has died, the first call on a family supports their faith and accepts their natural grieving responses. My own approach is to schedule a second meeting with family members to plan the memorial service proper. Give the survivors a chance for input. Sometimes their ideas are well ordered, with suggestions for Bible readings and hymn texts. The service may contain a eulogy, "to speak well" of the deceased, but is more than *that*. The memorial service honors God and magnifies the risen Lord Christ, even as it honors the memory of the deceased person (or persons).

The Christian pastor should rely upon several resources in helping family and faith community members to work through grief.

1. *The Christian funeral* undergirds the bereft family with its strengthening fellowship of friends, hymns of consolation, inspiration from God's Word, and hope of the resurrection. There is a growing conviction that the church itself, rather than a commercial funeral chapel, is the most appropriate setting for a Christian funeral service. That, however, is a matter of taste, theological conviction, personal preference, convenience, and economics, and will involve a joint clergy-family-funeral director decision. Some persons designate that their remains be used for organ transplants and medical research, or that they be cremated. The memorial service (with or without mortal remains present) provides a community of understanding and occasion for the expression of grief and affirmation of the Christian hope.

2. Prior to and following the funeral, *the church fellowship incarnates God's comforting grace* to persons pained by bereavement. Local customs and traditions in a community will influence the congregation's services of meal preparation, child care, financial aid, and provision of companionship temporarily for the survivors.

3. *The congregation's work does not end with the funeral.* Through followup calls, aftercare, and friendship, the pastor and the community of faith help family members to undertake life's responsibilities again. Our traditional resources of comfort—prayer, Bible readings, funeral rituals, visits, and reassurance—may be supplemented with a support group, correspondence, phone calls, and devotional literature. Along with relatives and friends, the pastor serves as a spiritual guide, assisting bereaved persons to resume life's tasks and relationships. Sometimes, it is an entire congregation or city, not one family system alone, that needs "the God of all comfort."

4. Finally, Christian comforters remain alert to *unresolved and abnormal manifestations of grief.* Rather than effecting a smooth transition through

stages of mourning to new life patterns, a person may fixate or regress to an earlier emotional state. A person who is relatively insecure, guilty, or hostile, for example, may go all to pieces following a loss. He or she may "act out" a neurotic grief pattern through flight from reality, alcohol or substance abuse, reactive depression, or by aggressive talk or bizarre behavior. Of course, guilt may be present in so-called normal grief as well, manifested by excessive funeral expense, excessive crying over the corpse, and the like.

One such distorted grief manifestation is the *deification of the deceased relative.* The survivor, in an unconscious act of idolatry, elevates the dead person to a state of saintly perfection. The survivor may adopt the deceased's phrases, gestures, church affiliation, or life philosophy; or assume his or her business tasks and obligations. Or the dead person's room may remain undisturbed. Things have to stay the way the child or relative left them "for the last time." One family whose son had been killed in a motorbike accident erected a statue of the youth on their lawn. A garden spot was developed around the statue, which became a shrine for their continual mourning over the loss of their deceased son.

Distortions of conduct or relationships that appear immediately or even years after a loved one's death are often abnormal grief reactions. A man once cried at his wife's open grave: "I can't let her go down there alone. I can't let her go! I'm going to get down there with her." His shocked minister asked the funeral director, "What shall we do?" "Let him get down in there if he wants to," came the calm reply. Later the minister learned that the man had been unfaithful to his wife. The funeral director and several persons in the community knew about his infidelity. It was not grief but guilt that drove him to such extreme behavior.

An elderly man once related to me how he had kept his deceased mother's clothing through the years. Occasionally, he said, it helped him to dress in her clothing and to sit in the old rocking chair that she had used across the years. Such transvestism requires more than acceptance—it takes wisdom and "the courage to confront." "The desire to dress or appear as a member of the opposite sex" is found in a minority of homosexuals and heterosexuals, notes Theodore Jennings, "but the great majority of transvestites are heterosexual."[23] The man in this instance worked as a chaplain in a state mental hospital but did not understand his own sexual orientation. His grief work was compounded by confused sexual identity.

A person may develop a *deep depression* and feel that he or she cannot continue life without the deceased. A clue may appear when the depressed person seeks to drown trouble with alcohol or over-medicates with prescription drugs. A woman whose mother had died of cancer at the age of forty-nine *developed the same symptoms* her mother had manifested in her last illness. The symptoms were purely psychosomatic, according to physicians, yet she had cancer as far as she was concerned. When a person manifests abnormal or bizarre behavior following a grief situation, the minister should consult with both the person's family and a physician. Temporary hospitalization may be indicated in such a crisis. A medical moratorium from intrapsychic strife may help the person to regain inner serenity and regroup resources for life's tasks again.

Summary

In this final chapter, we have considered the pastoral action of the church during three disruptive crises—guilt, illness, and grief. Beyond human skill and understanding, those who serve in such crises must "pray at all times in the Spirit," seeking to be "strong in the Lord and in the strength of his might." The results of their labors are in God's hands for time and eternity. Paul's admonition to the Ephesian Christians provides an appropriate epilogue to this treatise concerning "pastoral care in the church." "As slaves of Christ, [do] the will of God from the heart. Render service with enthusiasm, as to the Lord and not to men and women, knowing that whatever good we do, we will receive the same again from the Lord" (Eph. 6:6–8 NRSV).

Notes

1. Erik H. Erikson, *Identity: Youth and Crisis* (New York: W. W. Norton, 1968), 110. Also, see Gershen Kaufman, *Shame: The Power of Caring* (Cambridge, MA: Shenkman, 1980); and Merle A. Fossum and Marilyn J. Mason, *Facing Shame: Families in Recovery* (New York: W. W. Norton, 1986).
2. See John B. Cobb, Jr., "Pastoral Counseling and Theology," in *Handbook for Basic Types of Pastoral Care and Counseling*, 21–23; also, see Daniel J. Levinson, *et al.*, *The Seasons of a Man's Life* (New York: Alfred A. Knopf, 1978), 195–98.
3. J. H. Thayer, *A Greek-English Lexicon of the New Testament*, rev. ed. (New York: American Book Co., 1886), 217, 643.
4. "War: Tragedy or Adventure?" in *The Second Page* (Lubbock, TX: Second Baptist Church, February 22, 1991), 4.
5. John Richman, ed., *A General Selection from the Works of Sigmund Freud* (Garden City, NY: Doubleday & Co., 1957), 228–30 *et passim*.
6. See Erik H. Erikson, *Identity and the Life Cycle* (New York: International Universities Press, 1959), 148.

7. Carl G. Jung, *Modern Man in Search of a Soul*, translated by W. S. Dell and C. F. Baynes (London: Paul, Trench, Trubner & Co., 1933), 39.

8. Karl Menninger, M.D., *Whatever Became of Sin?* (New York: Hawthorn Books, Inc., 1973), 223–30.

9. See Don S. Browning, *The Moral Context of Pastoral Care* (Philadelphia: Westminster Press, 1976); Donald Capps, *Life Cycle Theory and Pastoral Care* (Philadelphia: Fortress Press, 1983), 33–54; Gaylord Noyce, *The Minister as Moral Counselor* (Nashville: Abingdon Press, 1989); and Wayne E. Oates, *Temptation: A Biblical and Psychological Approach* (Louisville: Westminster/John Knox Press, 1991).

10. Walter C. Jackson in *Codependence and the Christian Faith* (Nashville: Broadman Press, 1990) shows the creative impact biblical faith provides in lives of persons trapped in counterproductive patterns of behavior.

11. Heinz Kohut, *The Restoration of the Self* (New York: International Universities Press, 1977).

12. Cited by Hunter Beaumont, *Shame: Phenomenology, Theory, Treatment* (Perth, Australia: Gestalt Therapy Institute of Perth, 1985); also, his "Encountering Sin in Pastoral Counseling," in *Handbook for Basic Types of Pastoral Care and Counseling*, 41–55.

13. Psychiatrist Truman Esau wrote that "sex was never intended to be satisfying as a merely physical activity. It may be physically gratifying, but by itself it cannot fill the deep human hunger for intimacy." See *Making Marriage Work* (Wheaton, IL: Victor Books, 1990), 138.

14. See T. H. Holmes and R. H. Rahe, "The Social Rating Scale," *Journal of Psychosomatic Research* 11: 213–18, 1967. Modified for persons in cross-cultural assignments by C. W. Brister in *Caring for the Caregivers: How to Help Ministers and Missionaries* (Nashville: Broadman Press, 1985), 98–107.

15. See Richard Dayringer, ed. *Pastor and Patient: A Handbook for Clergy Who Visit the Sick* (Northvale, NJ: Jason Aronson, 1981); Lawrence D. Reimer and James T. Wagner, *The Hospital Handbook: A Practical Guide to Hospital Visitation* (Wilton, CT: Morehouse-Barlow, 1984); Aarne Siirala, *The Voice of Illness*, a study in the community nature of illness, (Philadelphia: Fortress Press, 1964); "Carenotes," One Caring Place (Abbey Press, St. Meinrad, IN 47577); available with floor display unit of thirty individual title-compartments; counter display or wall mountings are also available.

16. See Wayne E. Oates, *The Bible in Pastoral Care* (Philadelphia: Westminster Press, 1953); also, Howard W. Stone, *The Word of God and Pastoral Care* (Nashville: Abingdon Press, 1988).

17. See Katie Maxwell, *Bedside Manners: A Practical Guide to Visiting the Ill* (Grand Rapids: Baker Book House, 1991).

18. Kenneth R. Mitchell and Herbert Anderson, *All Our Losses, All Our Griefs: Resources for Pastoral Care* (Philadelphia: Westminster Press, 1983); and Wayne E. Oates, *Your Particular Grief* (Philadelphia: Westminster Press,

1981). Special topics were investigated in such reports as: Robert W. Buckingham, *The Complete Hospice Guide* (San Francisco: Harper & Row, 1983); Donna and Rodger Ewy, *Death of a Dream: Miscarriage, Stillbirth and Newborn Loss* (New York: E. P. Dutton, 1984); R. Scott Sullender, *Losses in Later Life* (Paulist Press, 1989); and Joanne Feldmeth and Midge Finely, *We Weep for Ourselves and Our Children: A Christian Guide for Survivors of Childhood Sexual Abuse* (San Francisco: Harper & Row, 1990).

19. See Sigmund Freud, "Mourning and Melancholia," *Collected Papers*, vol. 4 (London: Hogarth Press, 1949), 152–70; and Erich Lindermann, "Symptomatology and Management of Acute Grief," *American Journal of Psychiatry* 101 (September 1944): 141–48. (Reprinted in *Journal of Pastoral Care* 5 [Fall, 1951]: 19–31.) Also, see Vamik D. Volkan, "The Recognition and Prevention of Pathological Grief," *The Virginia Medical Monthly* 99 (May 1972): 537; and David K. Switzer, *Pastoral Care Emergencies* (Mahwah, NJ: Paulist Press, 1989), 109–28; and his "Unresolved Grief," in *Handbook for Basic Types of Pastoral Care and Counseling*, 231–55.

20. Clemens E. Benda, "Bereavement and Grief Work," *Journal of Pastoral Care* (Spring, 1962): 2.

21. Wayne E. Oates, *Anxiety in Christian Experience* (Philadelphia: Westminster Press, 1955): 49.

22. See Robert V. Dodd, *When Someone You Love Dies: An Explanation of Death for Children* (Nashville: Abingdon Press, 1986).

23. T. W. Jennings, "Homosexuality," in Rodney J. Hunter, gen. ed., *Dictionary of Pastoral Care and Counseling* (Nashville: Abingdon Press, 1990), 529–32.

Suggested Reading

Aden, LeRoy and J. Harold Ellens, eds. *The Church and Pastoral Care.* Grand Rapids: Baker Book House, 1988. Each contributor appreciates the priority of rooting pastoral care in the dynamic insights of biblical theology. Affirms pastoral care as an essential function of Christian ministry.

Friedman, Edwin H. *Generation to Generation: Family Process in Church and Synagogue.* New York: The Guilford Press, 1985. A rabbi and practicing therapist applies the concepts of systemic family therapy to the lives of congregations and their leaders. Addresses common crises and traumas of life.

Knight, James A., M.D. *Conscience and Guilt.* New York: Appleton-Century-Crofts, 1969. A psychiatrist writes from the wisdom of both clinical practice and careful research about the development, violation, and modification of conscience. He explores the many faces of guilt and suggests a stable morality.

McGoldrick, Monica, Carol M. Anderson, and Froma Walsh, eds. *Women in Families: A Framework for Family Therapy.* New York: W. W. Norton, 1989. A major study of women in families and in family therapy.

Oates, Wayne E. *Temptation: A Biblical and Psychological Approach.* Louisville: Westminster/John Knox Press, 1991. Shows how temptation functions in the formation of human character. Offers suggestions for overcoming temptation.

Patton, John. *Is Human Forgiveness Possible?* Nashville: Abingdon Press, 1985. Should be read in dialogue with Lewis B. Smedes, *Forgive and Forget.* San Francisco: Harper & Row, 1984. Patton holds that forgiveness is not something we do; it is, rather, a relationship we *discover* along the journey of faith.

Reimer, Lawrence D. and James T. Wagner. *The Hospital Handbook.* Wilton, CT: Morehouse-Barlow Co., 1984. A practical guide to hospital visitation. Suggestions for training lay caregivers. Excellent resources and guidelines for ministering in special situations.

Switzer, David K. *Pastoral Care Emergencies: Ministering to People in Crisis.* Mahwah, NJ: Paulist Press, 1989. Sets forth a wise, theologically based approach to pastoral care in every conceivable kind of crucial human situation.

INDEX OF NAMES

INDEX OF SUBJECTS

INDEX OF SCRIPTURE REFERENCES